# The A to Z of Norway

Jan Sjåvik

*The A to Z Guide Series, No. 234*

The Scarecrow Press, Inc.
Lanham • Toronto • Plymouth, UK
2010

Published by Scarecrow Press, Inc.
A wholly owned subsidiary of
The Rowman & Littlefield Publishing Group, Inc.
4501 Forbes Boulevard, Suite 200, Lanham, Maryland 20706
http://www.scarecrowpress.com

Estover Road, Plymouth PL6 7PY, United Kingdom

British Library Cataloguing in Publication Information Available

**Library of Congress Cataloging-in-Publication Data**

The hardback version of this book was cataloged by the Library of Congress
as follows:

Sjåvik, Jan.
  Historical dictionary of Norway / Jan Sjåvik.
    p. cm. — (Historical dictionaries of Europe ; no. 62)
  Includes bibliographical references.
  1. Norway–History–Dictionaries. I. Woronoff, Jon. II. Title.
DL443.S63  2008
948.1003–dc22                                        2007045120

ISBN 978-0-8108-7213-4 (pbk. : alk. paper)

⊗™  The paper used in this publication meets the minimum requirements of
American National Standard for Information Sciences—Permanence of Paper
for Printed Library Materials, ANSI/NISO Z39.48-1992.
Printed in the United States of America

# Contents

# Editor's Foreword

Few countries have changed as much over the centuries as Norway. Once inhabited by fierce Vikings who attacked much of the nearby coast, neighboring England, and further afield, it was long subjected to Danish or Swedish rule and actually only became independent again in 1905. Once rather poor, its people living off a soil that yielded few crops (but fortunately also fishing in the surrounding seas) and without many natural resources, it suddenly became rich with vast finds of oil and natural gas. Unlike most other lucky countries, it is managing this wealth wisely, putting much of it aside for later, but enough is generated so that income levels are comparatively high. At one time remarkably uniform in religion, culture, and society, it has become increasingly diverse. Yet in other ways, Norway has remained unusually true to itself. Always relatively egalitarian and with an independent streak, it is still one of the few places that looks after those who are less well off, provides an excellent education for all, and has gone furthest in creating genuine equality for women. Although thoroughly European and surrounded by members of the European Union, it has twice refused to join and clings to its sovereignty.

These features may seem paradoxical at first sight, but they are much easier to understand when placed in the broader context provided by *The A to Z of Norway*. The importance of its history emerges as soon as one scans the chronology, listing the long succession of foreign rulers before finally starting with Norway's own kings and then tracing the route from absolute monarchy to one of the most democratic systems around. This transformation is explained more amply in the introduction, which looks into not only the political but also the economic, social, and cultural manifestations. The essential details are contained in the dictionary section, with numerous entries on significant persons, not only politicians, but writers, composers, academics, and some adventurers as well. Of course, the more noteworthy kings of whatever provenance are included. And there is also information on the larger cities, the major economic sectors, and more memorable events, alas many of these wars in which Norway was not always on the winning side. This book does more than just scratch the surface but will not be enough for some, who should then consult the bibliography. Unfortunately, not that much is written on Norway in English, so the listing is rounded out with titles drawn from the more abundant Norwegian literature.

It was difficult to find a suitable author, someone who is sufficiently familiar with the country and can write about it in English. The problem was finally resolved when this elusive combination was found in the person of Jan Sjåvik. An American citizen of Norwegian birth and upbringing, he knows a considerable amount about Norway, not only from written sources but also frequent visits. He has also taught about it for some three decades as a professor of Scandinavian studies at the University of Washington in Seattle. This has given him a broader view, including not only of Norway but its neighbors, and helped him to understand the regional dynamics. Yet, his main interest is not history or politics—which he handles very well in this volume—but literature and theater. Indeed, he is the author of the *Historical Dictionary of Scandinavian Literature and Theater*, among other books and numerous articles. The result is an impressively broad and insightful picture of a very special country, one that will intrigue and inform foreigners and certainly teach Norwegians a thing or two as well.

Jon Woronoff
Series Editor

# Acknowledgments

I thank my colleagues at the Department of Scandinavian Studies, University of Washington, for their interest in and support of this project. Special thanks to Benjamin Sjåvik for producing the maps.

# Reader's Note

The entries in the dictionary appear alphabetically according to the order of the 26 letters used in English and not as it is done in Norwegian. Consequently, *æ* and *å* are treated as if they were *a*, and *ø* is treated the same as *o*.

When a term has an entry of its own in the dictionary, the term appears in **boldface** the first time it is mentioned in an entry other than its own.

In entries in the dictionary section of the book, Norwegian-language titles are followed by parentheses that contain the year of publication as well as the title in English translation. The notation *tr.* before the title in English signifies that the book has been published in English translation with that title. Otherwise, the translations of titles are my own.

# Acronyms and Abbreviations

| | |
|---|---|
| AIK | *Demokratiske Sosialister* (Democratic Socialists) |
| AKP | *Arbeidernes kommunistparti* (Workers' Communist Party) |
| AUF | *Arbeidernes Ungdomsfylking* (youth division of the Labor Party) |
| Comintern | Communist International |
| DnA | *Det norske Arbeiderparti* (Norwegian Labor Party) |
| EC | European Community |
| ECSC | European Coal and Steel Community |
| EEA | European Economic Area |
| EEC | European Economic Community |
| EFP | Electric Furnace Products Company |
| EFTA | European Free Trade Association |
| ESA | EFTA Surveillance Agency |
| FAO | Food and Agriculture Organization |
| FrP | *Fremskrittspartiet* (Progress Party) |
| GATT | General Agreement on Tariffs and Trade |
| GNP | gross national product |
| ISAF | International Security Assistance Force |
| ISS | International Summer School |
| ITO | International Trade Organization |
| IWC | International Whaling Commission |
| IWW | International Workers of the World |
| KP | *Kystpartiet* (Coastal Party) |
| KrF | *Kristelig Folkeparti* (Christian Democratic Party) |
| LO | *Den faglige Landsorganisasjon* (The National Trade Union Association) |
| MRA | Mutual Recognition Agreement |
| MF | *Menighetsfakultetet* (Norwegian School of Theology) |
| NATO | North Atlantic Treaty Organization |

| | |
|---|---|
| NKF | *Norsk Kvindesagsforening* (Norwegian Women's Rights Association) |
| NKP | *Norges Kommunistiske Parti* (Norway's Communist Party) |
| NORAD | *Direktoratet for utviklingssamarbeid* (Norwegian Agency for Development Cooperation) |
| NRK | *Norsk rikskringkasting* (Norwegian Broadcasting Corporation) |
| NS | *Nasjonal Samling* (Norwegian National Socialist Party) |
| NSA | *Norges Socialdemokratiske Arbeiderparti* (Norway's Social-Democratic Labor Party) |
| NTNU | *Norges Teknisk-Naturvitenskapelige Universitet* (Norwegian Technical and Scientific University) |
| NUPI | *Norsk Utenrikspolitisk Institutt* (Norwegian Foreign Policy Institute) |
| OD | *Oljedirektoratet* (Oil Directorate) |
| OECD | Organization for Economic Cooperation and Development |
| OEEC | Organization for European Economic Cooperation |
| PLO | Palestine Liberation Organization |
| RU | *Rød Ungdom* (Red Youth) |
| RV | *Rød Valgallianse* (Red Electoral Alliance) |
| SF | *Sosialistisk Folkeparti* (Socialist People's Party) |
| Sp | *Senterpartiet* (Center Party) |
| SUF | *Sosialistisk Ungdomsforbund* (Socialist Youth Federation) |
| SUF (m-l) | *Sosialistisk Ungdomsforbund (Marxist-leninistene)* (Socialist Youth Federation [Marxist-Leninist]) |
| SV | *Sosialistisk Venstreparti* (Socialist Left Party) |
| UN | United Nations |
| UNEF I | United Nations Emergency Force I |
| UNIFIL | United Nations Interim Force in Lebanon |
| WCED | World Commission on Environment and Development |
| WHO | World Health Organization |
| WTO | World Trade Organization |

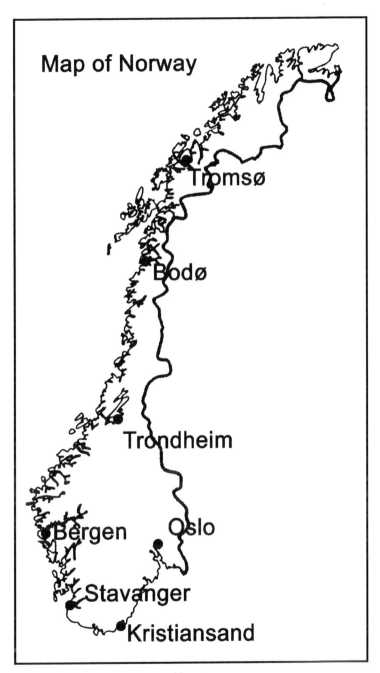

## Map of Norway

Tromsø

Bodø

Trondheim

Bergen        Oslo

Stavanger

Kristiansand

*Norway*

# Map of
# Scandinavia

*Denmark, Norway, Sweden, and Finland*

# Chronology

## PREHISTORY (BEFORE 1030 CE)

**c. 10,000 BCE**   The first hunters arrive in Norway.

**c. 4000 BCE**   Early agriculture begins.

**c. 2000 BCE**   The earliest farms are established.

**c. 500 BCE**   Iron is becoming known and mined.

**c. 100 BCE**   There is contact between Norway and the Roman Empire.

**c. 400–600 CE**   The Migration period and the use of the older runes.

**793**   The attack on the monastery at Lindisfarne marks the beginning of the Viking Period.

**832**   The date assigned to the burial of the Oseberg ship.

**c. 872**   The Battle at Hafrsfjord, won by King Harald Fairhair, marks the beginning of the unification of Norway.

**c. 931–33**   The reign of King Eirik Bloodaxe.

**933–c. 960**   The reign of King Haakon the Good.

**995–99**   The reign of King Olaf Tryggvason.

**997**   The town of Nidaros (later known as Trondheim) is established.

**1015–28**   The reign of King Olaf Haraldsson, later known as Saint Olaf.

## FROM SAINT OLAF TO THE KALMAR UNION (1030–1397)

**1030 29 July:**   King Olaf Haraldsson killed at the Battle of Stiklestad.

**c. 1050**   The town of Oslo is established.

**1066**   King Harald Hardrada is defeated by Harold Godwinsson in the battle at Stamford Bridge in England.

**1070**   The town of Bergen is founded.

**c. 1125**   The town of Stavanger is founded.

**1134**   The Norwegian civil wars begin.

**1152–53**   Norway gets its own archbishop, located in Trondheim.

**1177**   Sverre Sigurdsson is accepted as king by the *birkebeiner* (birch-leg) opposition.

**1178**   The birth of the Icelandic historian Snorri Sturluson.

**1184–1202**   The reign of King Sverre Sigurdsson.

**1196**   King Sverre is crowned in Bergen.

**1227**   The civil wars end.

**1260**   Hereditary kingship established.

**1261**   The wedding of Magnus Haakonsson and Ingebjørg, the daughter of the Danish king Erik Plogpenning, is held at the recently completed Haakon's Hall in Bergen.

**1263–80**   The reign of King Magnus IV Haakonsson Lagabøte.

**1274**   King Magnus IV Haakonsson Lagabøte establishes his national code of law.

**1276**   King Magnus IV Haakonsson Lagabøte establishes his national code of law for cities.

**1299–1319**   The reign of King Haakon V Magnusson.

**1349**   The Black Death arrives in Bergen.

**c. 1360**   A Hanseatic trading post is established in Bergen.

## THE KALMAR UNION (1397–1536)

**1397**   The beginning of the Kalmar Union. While Erik of Pomerania is crowned king of Denmark, Norway, and Sweden, the effective ruler is Queen Margareta.

**1503 12 August:** The future King Christian III is born at Gottorp.

**1513–24** The reign of King Christian II.

**1520** The Stockholm Bloodbath, at which King Cristian II has numerous Swedish noblemen killed, effectively marks the end of Sweden's participation in the Kalmar Union, although the formal end is in 1523.

**1523** Olav Engelbrektsson is chosen archbishop over Norway.

**1524** The New Testament is translated into Danish.

**1535** Olav Engelberktsson has Vincents Lunge killed.

## FROM THE REFORMATION TO THE END
## OF THE UNION WITH DENMARK (1536–1814)

**1536 29 July:** King Christian III takes control of Copenhagen, ending opposition to him in Denmark. **12 August:** Three Roman Catholic bishops who are members of the council of the realm are arrested, which marks the beginning of the Protestant Reformation in Denmark and Norway. The Norwegian council of the realm is abolished, and Norwegian territory becomes part of Denmark.

**1537** Olav Engelbrektsson is forced to flee Norway.

**1563–70** The Seven Years War.

**1588–1648** The reign of King Christian IV.

**1611–13** The Kalmar War.

**1618** The Thirty Years War begins.

**1623** The Kongsberg silver mine is opened.

**1624** Oslo is destroyed by fire, then moved and rebuilt under the name Chistiania.

**1641** The town of Christiansand is established.

**1643–45** The Hannibal Affair, a war against Sweden.

**1645 8 February:** By signing the peace treaty at Brömsebro, Christian IV cedes Jemtland and Herjedalen to Sweden.

**1648–70** The reign of King Frederik III.

**1657–60**   The Three Years War.

**1660**   Norway loses Båhuslen to Sweden at the signing of a peace treaty in Copenhagen. A coup d'état by King Frederik III establishes the absolute monarchy.

**1663–66**   The first census of Norwegian males is taken.

**1665 14 November:**   The Royal Law (*Kongeloven*) is signed, codifying the absolute monarchy.

**1670–99**   The reign of King Christian V.

**1675–79**   The Gyldenløve Affair, a war against Sweden.

**1699–1730**   The reign of King Frederik IV.

**1701**   A census of all Norwegian males is taken.

**1711–20**   The Great Northern War.

**1730–46**   The reign of King Christian VI.

**1736**   Confirmation is introduced, eventually leading to a system of public education.

**1739**   First decree relating to the public education of children.

**1741**   Second decree relating to the public education of children.

**1746–66**   The reign of King Frederik V.

**1766–1808**   The reign of King Christian VII.

**1786–88**   The uprising led by Kristian Lofthus.

**1794**   The town of Tromsø is established.

**1797**   Hans Nilsen Hauge begins his lay ministry.

**1801**   First Norwegian population census in which people are listed by name, age, occupation, and place of residence.

**1807**   The British destroy the Danish fleet at Copenhagen, and Denmark joins the war on Napoleon's side.

**1808**   War against Sweden.

**1808–14**   The reign of King Frederik VI.

**1811**   The decision is made to establish a Norwegian university.

**1813**   Crown Prince Christian Frederik comes to Norway as viceroy.

## THE UNION WITH SWEDEN (1814–1905)

**1814 14 January:**   The Treaty of Kiel transfers Norway from Denmark to Sweden. **16 February:** A meeting of 21 important citizens is held at Eidsvoll. **19 February:** Summons issued for a constitutional assembly. **24 March:** Carsten Anker arrives in London in order to advocate for Norway's independence. **10 April:** The constitutional assembly meets for the first time at a church service. **17 May:** The Norwegian constitution is signed at Eidsvoll, and Christian Frederik is named King of Norway. **26 July:** Crown Prince Karl Johan, the head of the Swedish armed forces, orders attack on Norway. **14 August:** An armistice is signed at Moss, preserving Norway's constitution. **7 October:** The *Storting* (Parliament) meets. **20 October:** The *Storting* votes to enter into a union with Sweden. **4 November:** The changes to the constitution necessitated by the union with Sweden are finalized, and the *Storting* formally accepts Christian Frederik's abdication. Karl XIII of Sweden is elected king of Norway.

**1818–44**   The reign of King Karl III Johan.

**1827**   *Mellomriksloven*, the law that governs trade relations between Norway and Sweden, goes into effect.

**1837**   Local government is introduced.

**1844–59**   The reign of King Oscar I.

**1848–51**   Marcus Thrane's trade union movement.

**1854**   The railroad from Christiania to Eidsvoll is opened. Camilla Collett publishes the first part of *Amtmandens Døttre*, Norway's first novel to deal with women's issues.

**1859–72**   The reign of King Karl IV.

**1861 17 December:**   The government headed by Fredrik Stang Sr. is established.

**1869**   Annual sessions of the *Storting* are begun.

**1872–1905**   The reign of King Oscar II.

**1873**   The position of vice regent (*stattholder*) is abolished in favor of a prime minister as the head of the Norwegian government.

**1880 9 June:**   The *Storting* declares that its vote in favor of a separate Norwegian consular service has the force of law in spite of the king's refusal to sign it. **11 October:** Christian August Selmer's government is formed.

**1884 3 April:**   Christian Homann Schweigaard's government is formed. The government is impeached and convicted for violating the constitution, effectively giving Norway the beginnings of parliamentarism. The Liberal Party and the Conservative Party are organized. **26 June:** Johan Sverdrup's government is formed.

**1887**   The Norwegian Labor Party is formed.

**1888**   The Moderate Liberal Party is formed.

**1889 13 July:**   Emil Stang's first government is formed. Seven years of compulsory education for all children is established.

**1891 6 March:**   Johannes Steen's first government is formed. The Liberal Party proposes that Norway should have a separate minister of foreign affairs.

**1892 22 June:**   The law establishing a separate Norwegian consular service is presented to King Oscar II, who refuses to sign it, after which the Norwegian government resigns and the *Storting* stops meeting. **26 July:** The *Storting* meets and asks the government to withdraw its resignation.

**1893 2 May:**   Emil Stang's second government is formed.

**1895 11 May:**   The Swedish parliament rescinds the law regulating trade between Sweden and Norway (*Mellomriksloven*). **17 May:** The Swedish parliament allots additional money for the Swedish armed forces, showing that a war with Norway is expected. **7 June:** The *Stort-*

*ing* proclaims its willingness to negotiate with Sweden about the consular service issue.

**1898 17 February:** Johannes Steen's second government is formed. Universal suffrage for men is established.

**1902 21 April:** Otto Albert Blehr's first government is formed.

**1903** The United Party is established. **22 October:** Francis Hagerup's government is formed.

**1905 1 March:** The government headed by Francis Hagerup resigns, paving the way for Christian Michelsen's government. **11 March:** Christian Michelsen's government is formed. **15 March:** Michelsen tells the *Storting* that his task is both to give Norway its own constitutionally authorized consular service and to show that Norway is a sovereign and independent nation. **5 April:** Sweden offers to negotiate with Norway. **27 May:** The consular service bill is presented to King Oscar II, who refuses to sign it, after which the Norwegian government resigns. **7 June:** The *Storting* declares that because the king has not arranged for a new government to be formed, he has stopped functioning as the king of Norway, and the union with Sweden is therefore dissolved. **21 June:** The Swedish parliament meets to consider Norway's actions. **23 July:** Sweden states its willingness to accept the dissolution of the union subject to a Norwegian referendum and negotiations about the details of the settlement between the two countries. **13 August:** The Norwegian people vote overwhelmingly in favor of dissolution. **31 August:** Negotiations begin in Karlstad. **23 September:** The agreement concerning the details of the dissolution is signed. **18 November:** After a referendum, Prince Carl of Denmark is elected king of Norway by the *Storting*.

## FROM INDEPENDENCE TO THE
## END OF WORLD WAR II (1905–45)

**1905–57** The reign of King Haakon VII.

**1907 23 October:** Jørgen Løvland's government is formed. Great Britain, France, Germany, and Russia sign an agreement guaranteeing the integrity of Norway's national borders.

**1908 19 March:**  Gunnar Knudsen's first government is formed.

**1909**  The Liberal Left Party is formed. Laws concerning the licensing of rights to exploit Norwegian national resources are passed.

**1910 2 February:**  Wollert Konow's government is formed.

**1912 20 February:**  Jens Bratlie's government is formed.

**1913 31 January:**  Gunnar Knudsen's second government is formed. Universal suffrage for women is established.

**1916**  The sale of liquor is prohibited.

**1917**  The sale of strong wine is prohibited.

**1918**  The Norwegian Labor Party declares its commitment to revolution as a means of social change.

**1920 21 June:**  Otto Bahr Halvorsen's first government is formed. The Agrarian Party is formed. The Norwegian Labor Party joins the Communist International (Comintern). Norway joins the League of Nations.

**1921 22 June:**  Otto Albert Blehr's second government is formed. Norway's Social-Democratic Labor Party is formed.

**1923 6 March:**  Otto Bahr Halvorsen's second government is formed. **30 May:** Abraham Berge's government is formed. The Norwegian Communist Party is formed. The prohibition against the sale of strong wine is rescinded.

**1924 25 July:**  Johan Ludwig Mowinckel's first government is formed. Norwegian sovereignty over Spitzbergen is established.

**1926 5 March:**  Ivar Lykke's government is formed. The prohibition against the sale of liquor is rescinded.

**1928 28 January:**  Christopher Hornsrud's government is formed. **15 February:** Johan Ludwig Mowinckel's second government is formed.

**1931 12 May:**  Peder L. Kolstad's government is formed.

**1932 14 March:**  Jens Hundseid's government is formed.

**1933 3 March:** Johan Ludwig Mowinckel's third government is formed. The Christian Democratic Party is formed. The National Socialist Party is established under Vidkun Quisling.

**1935 20 March:** Johan Nygaardsvold's government is established. The crisis agreement between the Agrarian Party and the Labor Party is made.

**1940 8 April:** The Norwegian government is notified that the Allies have laid mines in Norwegian territorial waters. **9 April:** Germany attacks Norway. **9–15 April:** Vidkun Quisling declares that he is Norway's new prime minister and establishes his first government. **April 10:** King Haakon refuses to appoint Quisling prime minister. **17 April:** An administrative council is established in Oslo. **5 May:** Norwegian resistance in southern Norway ceases. **7 June:** King Haakon and the government leave Tromsø for England. **25 September:** Josef Terboven establishes a provisional government with Quisling as the head. All political parties except the Nazi Party are dissolved.

**1941 10 September:** Terboven declares martial law in Oslo.

**1942 1 February:** Quisling establishes his second government.

**1945 8 May:** The German forces in Norway capitulate. **7 June:** King Haakon returns after five years in exile. **24 October:** Vidkun Quisling is executed.

## THE POSTWAR ERA (1945–2007)

**1945 25 June:** Einar Gerhardsen's first government is formed. **5 November:** Einar Gerhardsen's second government is formed.

**1945–52** Quotas and rationing are in force.

**1946** The University of Bergen is established.

**1947** Norway joins the General Agreement on Tariffs and Trade (GATT).

**1948** Norway joins the Organization for European Economic Cooperation (OEEC).

**1949**  Norway joins the North Atlantic Treaty Organization (NATO).

**1951 19 November:**  Oscar Torp's government is formed.

**1952**  The leftist political weekly paper *Orientering* (Orientation) is started.

**1953**  The Nordic Council is established.

**1955 22 January:**  Einar Gerhardsen's third government is formed.

**1957**  The Treaty of Rome establishes the European Economic Community (EEC).

**1957–91**  The reign of King Olav V.

**1960**  Norway joins the European Free Trade Association (EFTA). Private automobiles are no longer rationed. Television broadcasts begin.

**1961**  The Socialist People's Party is formed.

**1962**  Norway considers joining the EEC. The Kings Bay mine disaster occurs.

**1963 28 August:**  John Lyng's government is formed. **25 September:** Einar Gerhardsen's fourth government is formed.

**1965 12 October:**  Per Borten's government is formed.

**1967**  Norway considers joining the EEC.

**1968**  The Norwegian Technological and Scientific University is established in Trondheim. The University of Tromsø is founded.

**1969**  The Socialist Youth Federation breaks away from its mother party, the Socialist People's Party. Nine years of schooling becomes mandatory nationwide.

**1970**  Norway applies for membership in the European Community (EC).

**1972 25 September:**  In a referendum, Norway votes not to join the EC. The New Left People's Party is formed.

**1973 16 October:**  Trygve Bratteli's second government is formed. Anders Lange's Party is formed. The Workers' Communist Party is formed.

**1975**  The Socialist Left Party is formed.

**1976 15 January:**  Odvar Nordli's government is formed.

**1977** The Reform Party is renamed the Progress Party.

**1981 4 February:** Gro Harlem Brundtland's first government is formed. **14 October:** Kåre Willoch's first government is formed.

**1983 8 June:** Kåre Willoch's second government is formed.

**1986 9 May:** Gro Harlem Brundtland's second government is formed.

**1989 16 October:** Jan P. Syse's government is formed.

**1990 3 November:** Gro Harlem Brundtland's third government is formed.

**1991** The reign of King Harald V begins.

**1992 22 November:** Norway applies for membership in the European Union (EU).

**1994 12–27 February:** The Winter Olympics take place in Lillehammer. **28 November:** A referendum rejects Norwegian membership in the EU.

**1996 25 October:** Thorbjørn Jagland's government is formed.

**1997 17 October:** Kjell Magne Bondevik's first government is formed.

**1999** The Coastal Party is formed.

**2000 17 March:** Jens Stoltenberg's first government is formed.

**2001 19 October:** Kjell Magne Bondevik's second government is formed.

**2004 22 August:** Two of Edvard Munch's most famous paintings, *Scream* and *Madonna*, are stolen from the Munch Museum in Oslo by armed robbers.

**2005 1 January:** The University of Stavanger is founded. **17 October:** Jens Stoltenberg's second government is formed.

**2006 9 November:** The United Nations (UN) ranks Norway the world's most livable country for the sixth year in a row.

**2007** The left-wing party Red is formed by an alliance between the former Workers' Communist Party (AKP) and the Red Electoral Alliance (RV).

# Introduction

One of the smallest countries in Europe, Norway has created for itself a position in the world community that is completely out of proportion to the size of its population. Originally the home of subarctic hunters and gatherers, then of ferocious Vikings, it lost perhaps half of its population to the Black Death in 1349, ended up in a union with Denmark that lasted until 1814, and then became united with Sweden, gaining complete independence as recently as 1905. Over the centuries, the Norwegians eked out a meager living from stony fields and treacherous seas while suffering through hunger, darkness, and cold, but in the summertime, they enjoyed the perpetual light and sunshine of some of the world's most beautiful natural surroundings. At times they were also blessed with the abundance provided by the sea, their ever-present companion, as migrating schools of herring and other fish provided the food on their tables and commodities that could be exchanged for precious grain.

The contrasts between light and darkness, calm and storm, plenty and poverty that characterize traditional life in Norway are also reflected in the historical development of its culture, society, and economy. While struggling toward a level of social and economic justice exemplified hardly anywhere else at the time, Norway produced writers and artists who created some of the most magnificent art and literature ever read and viewed. Works by Henrik Ibsen, Knut Hamsun, Edvard Munch, and Gustav Vigeland are known and loved all over the world. After grasping the opportunity to frame one of history's most liberal constitutions in 1814, the people of Norway worked hard to combat poverty and ignorance as the freedoms enshrined in the constitution blossomed into a genuinely egalitarian democracy where caring for the weaker members of society seemed as natural as trying to rescue a fellow fisherman from the hull of a capsized boat. Some of the milestones along the road to

Norway's version of the good life are the introduction of parliamentarism in 1884, productive use of such natural resources as hydroelectric power, the creation of a genuine social-democratic alternative to the brutality of unfettered market forces, and the successful defense against the inhuman totalitarian conception of social relations visited upon peace-loving Norwegians during World War II.

It is perhaps the personal experience of struggle and hardship that has motivated the people of Norway to seek solutions to common problems and resolve conflicts through diplomatic activity and international cooperation. Since achieving complete independence in 1905, Norway has participated in and provided leadership to the League of Nations and the United Nations (UN), as well as defense pacts and trade organizations. While not a member of the European Union (EU), Norway makes a sizable contribution to the budget of the EU through its membership in the European Economic Area (EEA), thus showing that they are truly Europeans at heart.

To some observers, it has seemed paradoxical that Norway, with its record of involvement in the international community, would show reluctance to joining the EU. Some have explained its lack of enthusiasm for membership with reference to the tremendous wealth of oil and natural gas that Norway has obtained from its traditional fishing grounds along the coast since the 1970s, which has allowed the country to create a gigantic pension fund. There may be some truth to this idea. Bitter experience has taught Norwegians the value of caution, however, and it may well be that their slow approach to European integration is motivated primarily by the value they find in their egalitarian and democratic society rather than the oil that has transformed their economy and made them some of the richest people in the world.

## LAND AND PEOPLE

Norway is located on the north end and the west side of the Scandinavian Peninsula, bordering on Russia, Finland, and Sweden. It covers 385,155 square kilometers and had a population of 4,681,000 as of 1 January 2007, which gave it a population density of 12.15 individuals per square kilometer. On average, Norwegian women live until they are 82.5 years old, while the average Norwegian male lives to the age of

77.7. Norwegians are highly productive and in 2006 had a gross domestic product (GDP) of $46,300 per capita (in comparison, the *CIA World Factbook* estimates the U.S. GDP per capita for 2006 as $44,000). Norway is also a very long country, which has historically made it difficult to travel easily from north to south and vice versa. The distance from the capital, Oslo, to Norway's northernmost point is roughly equivalent to the distance from Oslo to Milan, Italy. Travel has historically been even more challenging because the country is broken up by numerous fjords and interior valleys separated by tall mountains. There is a good reason the name *Norway* refers to the ancient way north that was followed by ships, which, owing to Norway's many islands, could travel inside a protected passage along most of the coast.

The land's broken-up surface has also had consequences for such features of Norwegian life as settlement patterns and regional and local dialects. Only 3 percent of Norway's surface is arable land, and only three regions—eastern Norway, the district of Jæren to the south of the city of Stavanger, and the area around Trondheim—have significant extents of reasonably level farmland. Elsewhere, most farmland is steep or broken up into small fields by numerous outcroppings of bedrock.

The language, too, has historically been broken up into a large number of dialects, as phonology, grammar, and lexicon changed over time in small and isolated communities. A detailed map of Norwegian dialects reveals that often there will be an isogloss—a boundary line between places that differ in a particular linguistic feature—that runs right through a community with only a few hundred inhabitants. While all Norwegian dialects are mutually intelligible, some differ more from each other than do the national languages, Norwegian and Swedish.

The great distance from north to south and the differences between coastal and inland climates account for great variations. Almost half of Norway, in terms of its length, lies north of the Arctic Circle. In the 1990s the average annual temperature in Oslo was 6.4 degrees Celsius, while it was only 2.5 in Tromsø. There is generally more snow in the inland than on the coast and more snow farther north than farther south. It can be much colder in the interior valleys of southern Norway than on the coast of northern Norway, however, as a branch of the Gulf Stream has a significant moderating effect on the coastal climate.

Many people think of the midnight sun when they think of Norway. At the Arctic Circle there will be approximately three months during the summer when there is no darkness at night, and there will be roughly four hours of daylight at the time of the winter solstice. The extremes are greater the farther north one goes. Some people also wonder how it is possible to get a good night's sleep when it is light outside. Natives seem to have no problems getting enough sleep, although it is not necessarily had during the time that most people are habituated to thinking of as the night, and one can always have a nap when it is raining.

Historically, there have been two broad population groups in Norway, the Sámi and the ethnic Norwegians. The Sámi are known as nomadic reindeer herders in the interior of northern Scandinavia, but many Sámi people have traditionally lived as fishermen, hunters, and small farmers along the fjords of northern Norway. The Sámi have been gradually displaced by ethnic Norwegians over the past several hundred years. Norway is also inhabited by a small minority of ethnic Finns; since 1970, it has become the home of more than 300,000 immigrants, many of them from Africa and Asia. The recent immigration has changed Norway's religious composition significantly. While 96 percent of the population belonged to the Evangelical-Lutheran State Church in the 1950s, the number has declined to 87 percent as of 2006.

## HISTORICAL SURVEY

### Ancient Norway

The first known Norwegians lived along the coast as far back as 10,000 BCE, when the last ice age was drawing to a close. It is probable that they came from the North Sea continent, the land mass that connected present-day England with Denmark and southern Sweden, and that they reached Norway by crossing the frozen sea between the now-submerged continent and the Norwegian coast. They were hunters in pursuit of reindeer but also lived on seals, whales, and fish. As the inland ice in Norway retreated, some of them followed the reindeer flocks into the interior plateau, while others spread out along the coast. They were most likely dressed in skins of various kinds and used tools made from bone, flint, quartz, and quartzite. They lived in caves and tents, and some of them built turf huts. A seafaring people, they had boats made from skins and later from hollowed-out logs. Few in numbers, they most likely traveled in groups consisting of just a few families but probably had frequent contact with other small bands, with whom they intermarried. Their average life expectancy was probably less than 30 years. People buried their dead, and the rock carvings attest to religious beliefs that were closely connected with their need for success in hunting and fishing.

As the climate grew warmer, the conditions of life gradually changed, but hunting, fishing, and gathering remained the people's source of food for the next 6,000 years. As agriculture arrived in Norway in approximately 4000 BCE, growing barley and keeping sheep and cattle functioned as supplements to hunting and gathering. The ground was not properly cultivated, as the early hunter-farmers simply burned off the vegetation in well-drained spots and sowed directly in the ashes, moving frequently as the fertility of the fields was quickly exhausted. Two thousand years later, the first primitive farms emerged, as people learned to clear the fields of stones and roots, loosen the soil, and use animal manure as fertilizer. While hunting, fishing, and gathering were still important, they now became supplements to farming and animal husbandry. Changes in social organization accompanied the economic developments, as the population was more firmly tied to their home ground, lived in reasonably stable communities that were larger than those of the earlier hunters, and gradually developed the concept of ownership of land. This agricultural revolution is probably the greatest social and economic change experienced by people living in Norway.

The early farmers still used tools made primarily of stone, bone, and wood, while some objects were made of bronze. Iron became known in Norway in approximately 500 BCE, and its source was primarily bogs. A few hundred years later, people learned how to harden it and fashion such iron tools as axes and scythes, the Celts being their teachers. When the Celts were subjugated by the Romans at approximately 100 BCE, contact was established between Norway and the Roman Empire, and the first written sources of information appeared about life among the Germanic tribes. Norwegian life continued much as before, but the archeological material attests to increased social stratification, with rich and powerful chieftains occupying strategic places along the coast. While religious beliefs and practices appear to be similar to the fertility cults of the past, there is now also evidence of human sacrifice.

During the first centuries CE, there is proof of significant population growth, as many new farms were established in the outskirts of the older ones, and the fields of the early farms were divided into smaller holdings so that local communities arose. This is also most likely the time of the first local assemblies held for the purpose of administering justice and carrying out public worship. Between 400 and 600 CE, however, there was also much warfare, as whole tribes migrated, and the existing population groups had to band together to defend themselves. As the Migration period waned and the Viking age dawned, the number of both archeological and documentary sources increased. While the former must be interpreted with caution and the latter may be suspected of bias because they were written mostly by medieval Christians, to whom the ancient Norwegians were people with barbaric beliefs, they nevertheless attest to a complicated religion in which sacrifices to both male and female fertility deities played a central role. Human sacrifice was also practiced, as shown by some tapestries found with the Oseberg ship and dating to the decades before the year 832.

By the time the Oseberg burial took place, however, the Viking Period had already begun, and Norwegians fanned out across northern Europe, killing and plundering. The earliest recorded attack, on a monastery located on the island of Lindisfarne on the coast of Northumberland in Great Britain, took place in the year 793 and led to much consternation among medieval monks and priests. Large-scale expeditions as well as isolated raids followed, particularly in Ireland, but there were also voyages that had trade and colonization as their aims. Norwegian Vikings went not only to such islands of the North Atlantic as the Orkneys, Shetland, and the Faeroes but also to Iceland, Greenland, and North America. Their ships were long and had shallow draft, which made them ideal for invasion, as they could operate in shallow coastal waters and estuaries. The end of the Viking Period is generally set at 1066, when King Harald Hardrada was killed at the battle of Stamford Bridge in England.

## Christianity Arrives

At the time of Harald Hardrada's death, however, Christianity had arrived in Norway and was well on its way to being generally accepted. The first Norwegian king who is known to have subscribed to the new religion was Haakon the Good, the youngest son of Harald Fairhair. According to the sagas, Harald had fathered Haakon when he was almost 70 years old, and the mother was a young woman named Tora Mosterstong. King Harald saw to it that the boy stayed with his mother while he was little, and mother and son moved around with Harald as he traveled from place to place, living on his royal farms and exacting hospitality from the local people. Later King Harald sent Haakon to be fostered by King Athelstan of England, who taught him the Christian religion. When Haakon later returned to Norway, people were drawn to him and helped him drive off his hated older brother, Eirik Bloodaxe, who fled first to the Orkneys and later settled in York in England. King Haakon was friendly and brought good luck to the people and kept his Christian mindset, even though he swore off his faith for political reasons. One of the genuine heroes of the sagas, he is portrayed as a remarkable person who would have liked to introduce Christianity to Norway but who was prevented from doing so by the political realities of his time.

The sagas give an equally heroic portrait of Olaf Tryggvason, the grandson of King Harald Fairhair, who, according to tradition, was hidden away as a baby because Gunhild, the wife of Eirik Bloodaxe, wanted to have him killed. Sold into slavery, Olaf and his mother were freed and ended up in Russia, where Olaf grew up. After various adventures and marriage to an Irish princess who died early, the widowed Olaf went to Norway to claim the kingdom for himself. Earl Haakon of Lade, near present-day Trondheim, who had at first shared the control of Norway with the Danish king, Harald Bluetooth, had tried to conquer all of Norway from his base in Trøndelag before he was murdered by a slave. Olaf realized the wisdom of having his headquarters as far from Denmark as was practical and settled down in Nidaros (later known as Trondheim), which he founded near Earl Haakon's farm. From this power base, he tried to both conquer and Christianize Norway. Although the local people were very staunch in their pagan beliefs, Olaf used ruthless methods and got many people to accept the new religion. His enemies combined against him and waylaid him at a place called Svolder, where he died in the year 1000. While the account of Olaf's life given in the sagas is perhaps not always strictly accurate, archeological evidence shows that there was a strong Christian presence both in eastern and western Norway during his lifetime.

The Christianization of Norway was completed by King Olaf II Haraldsson, the son of Harald Grenske and the man later known as Saint Olaf, Norway's eternal king and patron saint. Olaf had grown up in eastern Norway and spent his youth on Viking raids, making it all the way to Jerusalem according to the saga writer Snorri Sturluson. A dream showed him that he was to return to Norway to claim his kingdom, after which Olaf accepted Christianity while in Normandy. Having fought Danish Vikings while in the service of the English king, he returned to Norway in 1015. For the past three generations, the Danish kings had controlled the area around the Oslo fjord and other parts of eastern Norway, while the kings and earls based in Trøndelag had governed northern Norway and the west coast. Through his father, Olaf felt that he had a claim on some of the Danish-controlled territory. In 1016, he beat Earl Svein, whose power was based in Trøndelag and who had the support of the most powerful chieftains in northern and western Norway, at the Battle of Nesjar. After the victory, he gained the support of many of his former enemies, using them as his administrators around the country, as he built up his power according to a pattern he may have observed while abroad. One of his major purposes was to secure the influence of the church among the people, which he did with both political acumen and at times ruthless exercise of power. Sunday was legally made a day of rest, other ecclesiastical feast days were established, fasting was mandated, and the Roman Catholic prohibition against marriage to close relatives was introduced. The people were made responsible for building and maintaining churches and were obligated to support the priests.

Olaf's administration was politically astute and effective, but there were many local chieftains who did not appreciate his efforts to get rid of the old religion and to extend his own personal power. Some of them supported the Danish king, Knut the Great, who also ruled England and used English silver to buy support for himself in Norway. Olaf was driven from the country in 1028, and when he returned two years later, he was mortally wounded at a battle at Stiklestad in Trøndelag. Miracles were associated with his remains, however, and he was soon considered a saint. His death in 1030 marks the victory of Christianity in Norway.

## From Christianity to the Kalmar Union

Saint Olaf's death had a unifying effect on the various factions in Norway. As Christianity consolidated its position in the country, there was an amalgamation of earlier religious ideas and the new Christian ones. The pagan god Odin became attached to the Christian Satan, the enemy of all righteousness, and some of the beliefs associated with the goddess Freya were transferred to the Virgin Mary. Five years after Olaf's death, the men who had killed him fetched his son Magnus home from Russia, making him Norway's king. It was the beginning of a century of peace at home.

Through a great victory in the battle at Lyrskog Heath in 1043, Magnus Olafsson, at the age of 18, proved himself both a great warrior and a man who had the protection of his sainted father. As the Viking Period was drawing to a close, a Norwegian king was also the king of Denmark and had a legitimate claim on England. When Magnus died in 1047, his half-uncle, Harald Sigurdsson Hardrada, was poised to collect on that claim and died in 1066 in the battle at Stamford Bridge in England while trying to do so. His grandson, Magnus Olafsson, expanded his dominion to the Hebrides and the Isle of Man but was killed at a battle in Ulster on 24 August 1103. Sigurd, the second son of Magnus, left on a crusade in 1108, visiting the city of Jerusalem and bathing in the River Jordan in 1110. After conquering the city of Sidon and sparing the lives of its population, he and his men went on to Byzantium. Sigurd's grandfather, Olaf Haraldsson Kyrre (1066–93), had been a good Christian as well, but he learned Latin and was bookish and peaceful rather than a crusader. During his time, it became common to write the vernacular language with the Latin alphabet. Sigurd's brother, Øystein, inherited his propensity for good government.

Things turned bad shortly after the death of Sigurd Jorsalfare—the Crusader—in 1130, however. He had a daughter but no legitimate male heir, and a number of pretenders to the throne were fighting each other. As of 1134, Norway was engaged in a protracted civil war. In order to bring about peace, the church supported Sigurd's grandson Magnus Erlingsson, who was crowned a boy king in 1163 or 1164, while the real ruler was his father, Erling Skakke. Erling's most serious challenger was Sverre Sigurdsson, who believed that he was the natural son of King Sigurd Munn (1136–55) and that he therefore had a legitimate claim to the throne. On 19 June 1177, Sverre won a decisive victory in the battle of Kalvskinnet in Trondheim, in which Erling Skakke and many other leading men were killed. In 1184, Magnus Erlingsson was killed in battle at Fimreite. Sverre was crowned on 29 June 1194, but the Norwegian archbishop, Eirik Ivarsson, refused to acknowledge

Sverre's claim to authority over the church and had him excommunicated. Those opposing Sverre rallied around the leaders of the church, and this party, called *baglere*, supported a series of pretenders until Sverre's death in 1202.

Sverre's lineage was victorious in the war against their opponents, however, as his grandson, Haakon IV Haakonsson, managed to organize the country's secular leaders into a royal *hird*, a group that supported the king and brought the civil wars to an end. Haakon's coronation on 29 July 1247 marks a high point in Norwegian medieval history, and he was succeeded by his son Magnus VI Lagabøte, a great law giver. Magnus' son, Haakon V Magnusson, was a capable and responsible administrator, but when he died on 8 May 1319, the ancient Norwegian royal family came to an end.

## The Kalmar Union: Norway Becomes a Part of Denmark

The work of Queen Margareta (1353–1412) of Norway, the Kalmar Union was a series of personal unions that brought Denmark, Norway, and Sweden together under one head of state. The first of these kings, Magnus VII Eriksson (1316–75), was the grandson of Haakon V Magnusson through Haakon's daughter Ingeborg, who was married to Duke Erik Magnusson (c. 1282–1318). He was the king of both Norway and Sweden. In 1343, however, he agreed that his younger son Haakon would become king of Norway, while Haakon's older brother would inherit the crown of Sweden. Haakon VI Magnusson (c. 1340–80) was married to Margareta, the daughter of King Valdemar IV Atterdag (c. 1320–75) of Denmark, in 1363 and was for a time co-king of Sweden with his father. In 1370, he and Margareta had a son named Olav, who was in line to succeed his maternal grandfather as Denmark's king. When Albert III of Mecklenburg (c. 1338–1412) and the Swedish nobles deposed Magnus VII Eriksson in 1364, Haakon lost his claim to Sweden, but his wife claimed the title of queen of Sweden as long as she lived.

A political genius, Margareta was at first able to have her son Olav named king of Norway, later also king of Denmark, while she ruled both countries as his guardian. When Olav IV Haakonsson died in 1387, she was elected regent of Denmark, and the following year, she also became regent in Norway. After adopting her sister's grandson, Erik of Pomerania (1382–1459), she succeeded in making him king of Norway in 1389, with herself as his guardian. Aided by a faction among the Swedish nobility that controlled part of the country, she went to war against its ruler, Albrecht III, who had deposed her father-in-law (as well as her husband) in 1364 and in turn was deposed in 1389. Erik III of Pomerania then became king of both Denmark and Sweden in 1396. This arrangement was formalized by the Treaty of Kalmar on 17 June 1397. Erik III and his descendents were to rule the three Scandinavian countries forever, but each country was to be governed separately by its own councils and according to its own laws.

Things went reasonably well as long as Margareta was alive, but the eventual result of the union was a series of wars between Denmark and Sweden until Sweden finally broke out of the union in 1523, after Christian II had killed a large number of Swedish nobles in the Stockholm Bloodbath in 1520. In 1536, at the time when the Reformation was being pushed through in Denmark and Norway, King Christian III (1503–59) and the Danish council of the realm declared Norway henceforth to be simply a part of Denmark, which marks the formal end of the Kalmar Union. It also marks the end of Norway's independence and existence as a separate state, as Olav Engelbrektsson, who was the head of Norway's council of the realm and the archbishop of Norway, had to flee into exile after an attempt to defend both the Roman Catholic Church and his country against Christian III's designs.

The next king of Denmark and Norway, Frederik II, attempted to regain control of Sweden during the Seven Years War (1563–70) but failed. His successor, Christian IV, was a capable and energetic man but had no more luck fighting the Swedes and paid for it by having to cede two Norwegian provinces, Jemtland and Herjedalen, in 1645. He also established the Kongsberg silver mine and the town of Christiansand in Norway and moved Oslo, renaming it Christiania.

Christian IV's successor, Frederik III, became first in the line of succession to the Danish throne when his older brother, Christian, died in 1647. Not well regarded by the Danish nobles, however, he was forced to allow his rights as king to be significantly diminished as a condition of being elected to the throne. He also had to fight the Swedes, whose King Karl X attacked Denmark in early 1658 by marching his forces across from Sweden on the frozen sea. The attack came as a surprise, and it was only through the intervention of English and French government representatives that the Danish monarchy survived. When Karl X attacked two years later and laid siege against

Copenhagen, Frederik III and Copenhagen's mayor organized such a valiant defense that the Swedes had to give up when a Dutch fleet came to the aid of the Danes. However, Frederik III had to cede another Norwegian province, Båhuslen.

As a result of his valiance during the siege, Frederik III became very popular among the citizenry and determined to strike at the Danish nobility through a coup d'état. Denmark became an absolute monarchy in 1660, and its constitution, *Kongeloven* (the Royal Law), was signed by King Frederik III on 14 November 1665. The only written constitution of a European absolute monarchy, it specified that the only significant limitations to the power of the king were that he could not depart from Lutheranism and that he could not divide his kingdom or diminish his own power. He was subject only to God, his judgments could be appealed only to God, and he had total legislative power. He could declare war, sign peace treaties, and join confederations, as well as compel his subjects to pay any tax or duty. He was also the supreme head of the church and the clergy.

His successors, Christian V and Frederik IV, also fought Sweden, particularly during the Great Northern War (1711–20). The reign of the latter was a time of significant intellectual flourishing, particularly through the work of the Norwegian-born comedian and historian Ludvig Holberg. Both Frederik IV and his successor, Christian VI, had an interest in religion, and Christian VI was a strict pietist who introduced both confirmation and the beginnings of a system of public education.

Like his father, Frederik V managed to keep Denmark and Norway strictly neutral, but his personal life was tragically affected by alcoholism. His son, Christian VII, lived a life of debauchery and was plagued by mental illness, making it necessary for others to govern in his stead. Christian VII's son, Frederik VI, on the other hand, instituted a number of liberal reforms but, after losing the Danish fleet in an attack upon Copenhagen by England in 1807, made the fatal mistake of supporting Napoleon in the war against his enemies, including Sweden, Denmark's arch nemesis.

## Norway's Constitution and the Union with Sweden

Frederik IVs decision drove a wedge between Norway and Denmark. First, Norway's true interests have traditionally been tied to those of England, which has largely controlled the high seas on which Norwegian trade and shipping have been dependent, and second, Norway became subjected to a merciless British blockade. In 1810, one of Napoleon's most controversial marshals, Jean Baptiste Bernadotte, was elected as Sweden's heir apparent, adopted by Karl XIII under the name Karl Johan, and given command of the Swedish armed forces. A brilliant strategist, Karl Johan sided with England and Russia against his former emperor and made a treaty with the Russian czar that promised him Norway in exchange for his support of the war against Napoleon. Great Britain also agreed that Sweden should be given Norway once it had been taken away from Denmark. A surprise military move by Karl Johan against Denmark brought about the Treaty of Kiel, in which Norway was ceded to Sweden by Denmark. Frederik VI immediately informed his son, Crown Prince Christian Frederik, who was staying in Christiania (now Oslo) as viceroy, and the news reached him on 24 January 1814.

Christian Frederik offered to step in as king of a wholly independent Norway and issued a call for a constitutional convention. He was quickly brought to understand, however, that to the Norwegians, the Treaty of Kiel meant that Norwegian sovereignty had been transferred to the people of Norway and that it did not rest with him. Christian Fredrik also sent his close friend Carsten Anker to London, there to persuade the British government to support Norway's bid for independence.

As of 10 April 1814, 112 representatives from various part of the country were gathered for the constitutional convention at Eidsvoll, a short distance north of Oslo. There were two factions, one of which believed that Norway might indeed succeed in winning its independence, while the other side was more realistic and acknowledged the reality of the politics of the European Great Powers. The constitution was officially accepted and signed on 17 May 1814. Christian Frederik was also elected to the throne.

Not without reason, the Great Powers suspected that Christian Frederik's activities in Norway were taking place at the instigation of his father, who would someday yield the Danish throne to Norway's new king, thus restoring the union between the two countries. It was soon understood, however, that the constitution was the outgrowth of a genuinely popular movement. Because the Great Powers wanted to avoid a war in Scandinavia, Christian Frederik had to sacrifice his personal ambitions in favor of negotiating the best possible terms for Norway within a union with Sweden. When Karl Johan went to war against Norway anyway, he met more resistance than he had probably expected, so he chose to negotiate, which pleased the Great Powers. An agreement was signed in Moss, Norway, on 14 August 1814, and the *Storting* made revisions to the constitution made necessary by the union and elected the Swedish king to Norway's throne. In 1815, the procedures governing the relationship between Norway and Sweden were enshrined in the Union Law, which regulated the joint affairs of the two countries for the next 90 years.

The relationship between the two union partners was at times rocky, but peace prevailed through negotiations. Karl Johan enjoyed great popularity in Norway, and the Norwegians were pleased once again to be enjoying their status as a separate country with its own parliament and government. Great strides were made both economically and culturally during the first several decades of the union. Norwegian literature and art flourished with such writers as Henrik Arnold Wergeland, Johan Sebastian Welhaven, and Henrik Ibsen, and Norwegian history, language, and folk-life were studied. A system of local government was introduced in 1837, there was a nascent trade union movement in the late 1840s, and the farm population increasingly asserted itself in national politics, claiming some of the power and influence traditionally had by the *embedsmann* (public official) class. The Swedish vice regent in Norway was replaced by a Norwegian prime minister who stood at the head of the Norwegian government. The beginnings of industrialization manifested themselves in the 1840s, roads were improved, and a railroad line opened in 1854.

One of the burning issues of the 1870s and 1880s was the question of whether the members of the king's cabinet should be answerable for their decisions and actions to the *Storting*. As long as they were not, the executive power did not have to be exercised in a manner acceptable to the people and according to democratic principles. The king and the conservative public officials, who benefited from the status quo, resisted any call to compel the cabinet members to appear before the *Storting*. As long as a parliamentary majority felt the same way, there was no way to change the system. As the liberal influence in the *Storting* increased, however, steps were taken by the leader of the liberals, Johan Sverdrup, to force a confrontation with the government. After the parliamentary elections of 1882, his majority was sufficiently large that he could impeach the government for not following the constitution. The special court that tried the government ministers rendered its decision in 1884, and they were all found guilty and stripped of their appointments. When King Oscar II realized that he would be unable to have any impeachment-proof government formed unless he went along with the wishes of the majority in the *Storting*, parliamentarism became the rule in Norwegian politics. A government would henceforth have to act in such a way as to not forfeit the confidence of the *Storting* if it wished to remain in power.

An important development associated with the events of 1884 was that a system of political parties developed. The Liberal Party was formed first, closely followed by the Conservative Party, both in 1884. The Norwegian Labor Party was organized in 1887. Over the next few decades the Liberal Party was split and recombined in different ways and at different times, giving Norway a multiparty system. The franchise was also gradually extended to more and more people, until it became universal for males in 1898 and for women in 1913.

After 1884, there was also increasing tension in the relationship between Norway and Sweden. Before the system of parliamentarism got its start in 1884, a liberal *Storting* could not as easily bring its wishes to the attention of the king and his Swedish advisers as afterward, when members of a liberal government would sit in council with him. The consular service issue was the biggest Norwegian thorn in Sweden's side, for the constitution specified that they were to have the same minister of foreign affairs, a common diplomatic corps, and a common consular service. The significance of shipping and trade to Norway's economy made this arrangement problematic, for Norwegian economic interests needed effective representation in foreign ports. The *Storting* repeatedly voted to establish a separate Norwegian consular service, but the king refused to sign the bill into law. In 1895, Sweden was preparing to go to war against Norway concerning the matter, but the Norwegian government backed down, preserving the peace.

The issue came to the fore again shortly before 1905, when Norway also demanded to have its own minister of foreign affairs. The matter had become of such great national importance that there was a strong feeling in Norway that it was worth going to war over. Under the leadership of Christian Michelsen, the Norwegian government maneuvered

King Oscar II into a position where the *Storting* could claim that he was not performing his functions as Norway's king, and the union, which Norway insisted was a personal union—the two countries were separate but had the king in common—was therefore dissolved. Not surprisingly, the Swedish parliament did not share this view, but in the heated debate that ensued, cooler heads prevailed, and the union was dissolved without any blood being spilled. Swedish sentiments were understandably bitter, however, and Oscar II felt personally mistreated. He therefore rejected Norway's offer that the throne be given to a member of the Swedish royal house, and Norway elected to instead offer it to the Danish Prince Carl, who became the first king of Norway in modern times under the name of Haakon VII.

## From Independence to the Present

A fully independent country for the first time in more than 500 years, Norway experienced both ups and downs during the first several decades of the 20th century. Norwegian industry was growing rapidly, and the loss of population experienced through immigration to America was coming to an end. Norwegian hydroelectric development was progressing rapidly, and the merchant marine was being modernized. World War I was a very difficult experience, however, for Norwegian seamen were being mercilessly torpedoed by the Germans in spite of Norway's neutrality. The Russian Revolution of 1917 led to the radicalization of the Labor Party, which for a time associated with the Communist International (Comintern). In the early 1920s, the rampant conspicuous consumption during the war years gave way to unemployment and economic crisis, as prices were cut almost in half, costs fell less rapidly than prices, traditional export markets for fish and forest products were lost, and businesses closed. The deflationary pressure on Norway's economy led to significant problems, and a major concern during the decade was to reduce public debt by cutting expenditures.

When the country was hit by the Great Depression of the late 1920s and 1930s, it became necessary to leave behind the liberalist economic principles espoused by both the Conservative Party and the Liberals. Some of the ideas of the British economist John Maynard Keynes were put into practice, allowing for a more successful management of the economy starting in the mid-1930s. Both organized labor and the Norwegian Labor Party made great strides forward at this time, as basic principles of collective bargaining became increasingly accepted in all segments of society, and the Labor Party's share of the seats in the *Storting* increased dramatically, especially after it had left the Comintern and become a completely social-democratic party. A watershed in Norwegian political life was reached when Labor entered into an agreement with the Agrarian Party that made a stable Labor Party government a reality in 1935.

One of the consequences of the emphasis on budgetary savings during the 1920s and 1930s was that Norway was severely lacking in military preparedness. Germany's attack on Norway on 9 April 1940 came as a complete surprise and led to five extremely difficult years. The royal family and the government barely escaped Oslo ahead of the invaders, owing to the fortuitous sinking of the German warship *Blücher* and the quick and decisive action of the president of the *Storting*, Carl Joachim Hambro. Later, the government and the king were forced to flee to London but not before the *Storting* had transferred to the government the authority that made it legitimate while in exile for the next five years. During the war, Norwegian society underwent a radical alteration, as there were as many as 400,000 enemy troops in the country, Norwegian institutions were recreated in the Nazi image, and Norwegians were arrested, tortured, and killed, sometimes as reprisals for acts of resistance with which they had no connection. The top German official in Norway, the commissar Josef Terboven, carried out a campaign of terror, at one time threatening to imprison all Norwegian men of military age. Food was scarce, liberty was nonexistent, and neighbors could not always be trusted not to turn people in to the Nazis. When the dark years finally came to an end, the Norwegian infrastructure was worn out, a large number of collaborators had to be brought to justice, and the political and social institutions had to be rebuilt. After a few years of rationing and quotas, most of the work of rebuilding the country was accomplished, however, and the general quality of life could become the primary object of attention.

While it was led by a long-serving Labor Party government that operated under the direction of Einar Gerhardsen, Norway created something close to an economic miracle during the 1950s and the 1960s. As a founding participant in the United Nations, Norway became a valued and respected member of the international community. Membership in the North Atlantic Treaty Organization provided for its security needs. Norway also joined such other international organizations as the Organization for Economic Cooperation and Development, the General Agreement on Tariffs and Trade, and the European Free Trade Association. The educational system was developed, eventually creating an opportunity for 12 years of schooling for all, as well as a network of universities and regional university colleges. The transportation system was modernized, with standard and short-runway airports dotting the country. The work week was drastically shortened, the amount of paid vacation for all workers increased, and the social safety net substantially strengthened to the point that the effective retirement age has dropped below 60. Roads and bridges were built, tunnels drilled, and high-speed ferries and catamarans placed in service.

When the off-shore oil industry took off during the 1970s and 1980s, government policy prevented the lion's share of the profits from ending up in the coffers of foreign and multinational concerns. Instead, the very substantial profits from the oil industry were carefully husbanded and invested according to high ethical principles. In order not to negatively affect the Norwegian economy, all such investments were to be made abroad. The result is that Norway now has a gigantic pension fund that could, if it wanted to, buy all the real estate in Manhattan, and then some.

There has, of course, been disagreement concerning these and other policies, but while particularly one political party—the Progress Party—would like to see more of these funds used for immediate consumption in order to reduce taxes, there is wide agreement that the funds provided by the oil industry should be held in trust for future generations. Contemporary Norwegians need to pay their own way as much as possible and to solve their economic and social problems through the resources created by the application of Norway's traditional work ethic. With their high level of education and careful investments in such long-standing economic sectors as fishing, farming, forestry, and energy-intensive industry, as well as with an emphasis on such knowledge-based industries as telecommunications and data processing, today's Norwegians enjoy a very high quality of life.

The most divisive political issue in recent decades is undoubtedly the question of whether Norway should seek to become more fully integrated into the European economic and political order that has been developing since the Treaty of Rome was signed in 1957. The Norwegian government has made a formal application for membership on several occasions, and twice a referendum has been held in order to determine if the result of negotiations with what has become known as the European Union (EU) were acceptable to the people of Norway. The first referendum was held 25 September 1972 and resulted in a rejection of the agreement that had been worked out. Some of the major concerns of those who voted against the agreement were the loss of Norwegian sovereignty and the consequences of membership for Norwegian farmers and fishermen. When the Norwegian Labor Party government led by Gro Harlem Brundtland decided to hold another referendum on the issue 28 November 1994, Norway had already successfully integrated itself into the European Economic Area, which seemed but a small step away from full EU membership. The voters again said no, however, and their concerns were similar to those felt in 1972.

Although Norway's recently found oil wealth may have made it economically feasible to remain less than completely tied to a more fully integrated Europe, Norwegians have a sense of tradition and independence that most likely also plays a role in their desire to be a bit different from the norm. Strong environmental policies in support of the country's relatively unspoiled nature, an egalitarian society, and a widely felt sense of social cohesion augur well for Norway's future. There are, of course, some social maladies. The misuse of alcohol has a long history in Norway, and the government's alcohol policy has not yet managed to solve this problem. Illegal drugs have been a significant public health issue since the late 1960s. While Norway has become a magnet not only for tourists but also for immigrants from Asia and Africa, many of these recently arrived Norwegians have not yet been successfully integrated into their new society.

# The Dictionary

## – A –

**AASEN, IVAR (1813–96).** Norwegian writer and scholar. The son of a smallholder on the coast of western Norway, Aasen became a self-taught linguist and dialectologist who devoted his life to studying the lexicon and grammar of Norwegian dialects, with special attention to their relationship with the **language** of **Viking**-age **Scandinavia**, publishing a grammar in 1848 and a dictionary in 1850. Steeped in the ideology of **national romanticism**, he was nevertheless no dreamer but a diligent promoter of the idea that Norway's written language, which after 400 years of political union with **Denmark** was strongly colored by Danish, ought to be replaced by a written norm that was founded on Norway's many different popular dialects. To this end, Aasen single-handedly created a written form of Norwegian called *Landsmaal* (country language) that he then employed as a medium for both poetry and prose. Perhaps predictably, his poetry is heavily colored by the conventions of Old Norse poetry and shows his fondness for both ancient-sounding vocabulary and grammatical features that had become extinct in most forms of Norwegian, even in Aasen's own day. His best-known literary works are the play *Ervingen* (1855; The Heir) and a poetry collection titled *Symra* (1863; The Anemone). Both of these works are considered classics in Norwegian **literature** written in *nynorsk* (New Norwegian), a less old-fashioned norm that has succeeded Aasen's own *Landsmaal* as an alternative to standard written Norwegian.

**ABSOLUTE MONARCHY.** The idea of absolute monarchy entails the notions that the monarch has absolute sovereignty, that no sovereignty resides with the people, and that society should be governed by the absolute, centralized power that flows from the idea of absolute sovereignty. To some proponents of absolute monarchy, the sovereign is responsible only to God. At a meeting of representatives for the **Danish** estates in the fall of 1660, the prior system of electing the king—the system was formally one of election, although it was customary to elect the oldest son of the previous king as the next king—was replaced by an inherited monarchy. *Kongeloven* (the Royal Law), signed by King Frederik III on 14 November 1665, which was kept secret until 1709 when it was first printed in a limited edition, specified the rules of succession and was in effect in Norway until 1814 (in Denmark until 1849). The only written **constitution** of a European absolute monarchy, it specified that the only significant limitations to the power of the king were that he could not depart from Lutheranism as expressed in the Augsburg confession, he could not divide his kingdom, and he could not diminish his own power. Some of his rights were that he was the foremost head on earth, subject only to God; he was the highest judge in both secular and ecclesiastical matters, whose judgments could be appealed only to God; he had total legislative power in that he could promulgate and rescind any law with the exception of rescinding *Kongeloven*; he could appoint and fire any public official (this was a major reason the Norwegian constitution of 1814 offered very strong protection for the *embedsmann* class); he could declare war, sign peace treaties, and join confederations; he could compel his subjects to pay any tax or duty; and he was the supreme head of the church and the clergy.

While the rule of the king was in practice not quite as draconian as *Kongeloven* seems to indicate, the king could control every aspect of life among his subjects through his extensive bureaucracy in both the civil and the ecclesiastical administration. During the Enlightenment period, the idea of enlightened absolutism arose; in Denmark and Norway, Johann Friedrich Struensee tried to put into effect numerous reforms that were in the Enlightenment spirit. The idea of popular sovereignty gradually replaced the idea of the absolute sovereignty of the king.

**AGRARIAN PARTY.** *See* CENTER PARTY.

**AGRICULTURE.** Only 3 percent of Norway's surface is arable land, and much of that land is steep and divided into small parcels by numerous outcroppings of bedrock, especially in the north and west. Large contiguous fields can be found mainly in the eastern part, the district of Jæren south of the city of **Stavanger**, and the area around **Trondheim** in the middle of the country.

As long as agriculture was based on cultivating relatively small plots by hand, there was a basis for some kind of agriculture in the entire country. Wheat can be grown in eastern Norway, where it is hot enough for it to ripen successfully, and other cereal grains as far north as the Arctic Circle. However, grains have not been grown that far north in modern times, except during wartime, for northern farmers can expect to receive only about three times the amount of the seed when the harvest comes, and the grain will fail completely some years. Throughout history, Norway has therefore been dependent on imported cereal grains.

Norway's rough terrain is well suited to animal husbandry, however. Sheep and goats make efficient use of grass and browse, and cattle, while requiring large quantities of hay, ensilage, and grain, are efficient producers of milk and meat. Swine and poultry have also been common. The horse was ever present on Norwegian farms until the post–**World War II** era, when even the smaller farms converted to tractors.

It is arguable that the biggest change to Norwegian farm life came with the introduction of the potato shortly before 1800. Well adapted to brief and cool summers and suitable to nonmechanized cultivation, it can be grown all over the country and quickly became a staple in the Norwegian diet.

Norway is, however, fundamentally unable to feed its population without imports. As Norwegian agriculture was mechanized during the second half of the 20th century, many small farms fell into disuse, and the need for imported food continues to grow. *See also* ECONOMY; TRADE.

**AMUNDSEN, ROALD ENGELBREGT GRAVNING (1872–1928).** Norwegian polar explorer. Amundsen was born in Borge, Østfold County, on 16 July 1872 to Jens Amundsen, a shipowner who died when the boy was 14 years old. By his mother's wishes, Amundsen began studying medicine but left his studies at the age of 21 and joined the crew of a seal-catching ship. He got his mate's license in 1895 and his skipper's license 10 years later. His first expedition was as mate onboard the *Belgica*, which wintered in Antarctica in 1898. From 1903 to 1906, he led the first expedition that traveled through the Northwest Passage to Nome, Alaska. His ship was the shallow-drafted *Gjøa*. During this voyage, Amundsen studied the clothing and use of sled dogs of the Inuit.

From 1910 to 1912, Amundsen used **Fridtjof Nansen**'s ship *Fram* during an expedition to Antarctica for the purpose of being the first person to reach the South Pole. After carefully establishing and marking depots of food and equipment along the route from their base camp to the pole, Amundsen and four of his men traveled to the pole and back in 99 days, using skis and sled dogs. They reached the South Pole on 14 December 1911.

After an expedition through the Northeast Passage from 1918 to 1920, in which Amundsen used his own ship *Maud*, he set about reaching the North Pole by air. During a visit to the **United States**, he had become fascinated with air travel and was the first civilian in Norway to receive a pilot's license. In 1925, Amundsen and five others tried to reach the North Pole by flying two hydroplanes from Spitzbergen. After landing on the ice at 87 degrees, 44 minutes northern latitude, they found it difficult to take off again but eventually managed to fly one of the planes back.

The following year, Amundsen and a crew of 15 others flew a dirigible, the airship *Norge* (Norway), from Spitzbergen across the North Pole on 12 May 1926 and on to Teller, Alaska. While three other expeditions have claimed to have reached the pole earlier, these claims are considered controversial by some scholars.

Amundsen returned to the Arctic again in 1928, when his former partner, Umberto Nobile, had been lost there during an expedition with the dirigible *Italia*. Amundsen was on board the hydroplane *Latham*, which left **Tromsø** on 18 June 1928 and disappeared in bad weather somewhere in the vicinity of Bear Island. Some of the wreckage was found and positively identified, but the remains of those onboard were never recovered.

**ANKER, CARSTEN TANK (1747–1824).** Norwegian diplomat and official. Born to Erik Anker on 17 November 1747 in Fredrikshald, Østfold County, Anker spent a significant time traveling in his youth. He also held several responsible government posts. While living in Copenhagen, he became a close friend of **Christian Frederik**, the son of Frederik, the heir presumptive to the **Danish** throne. While Christian Frederik stayed as viceroy in Norway from 1813 to 1814, Anker was one of his closest advisers. Anker lived at Eidsvoll, an iron works north of **Oslo** that he purchased in 1811, which was the location of the **constitutional** convention that resulted in the signing of Norway's constitution on 17 May 1814.

*ARBEIDERDEMOKRATENE. See* WORKER-DEMOCRATS.

*ARBEIDERNES KOMMUNISTPARTI. See* WORKERS' COMMUNIST PARTY.

*ARBEIDERPARTIET. See* LABOR PARTY.

**ARCHITECTURE.** The earliest Norwegians lived in caves, under rock overhangs, and in primitive shelters made with wattle-and-daub. At the time of the Migration period, c. 400–600 CE, there is evidence that at least the better-situated members of society lived in large longhouses with thick walls of sod and stone and roofs that were held up by vertical posts and covered with birch bark and sod. There were several fire pits in the middle of the floor in each house, and the smoke drifted out through holes in the roof. In some places, there were clusters of such houses, which apparently gave shelter to several families each. This kind of structure was also built during the **Viking** period, and they are referred to in the Icelandic sagas as well. The pagan temples, where people worshiped the gods Odin, Tor, and Frey, were most likely wooden structures and may have been adorned with dragon heads.

The coming of Christianity led to a significant change in sacred architecture, in that many churches, starting around the year 1000, were built with stone. Approximately 160 of the approximately 300 stone churches that were built have been preserved in whole or in part.

Other churches were built of wood. Norway's famous stave churches are wooden structures, built with vertical staves rather than horizontal logs or planks. Some of the stave churches that have been preserved were ornamented with dragon heads as well as crosses. These old churches were small and dark and had no pews, as the people stood during the masses. The stone churches were bigger and had windows in Romanesque or Gothic style. The preferred building material was soapstone, especially around windows and doors; however, sandstone, limestone, and granite were also used for the walls. Starting around 1250, bricks came into use. The largest and most famous of the medieval stone churches is the Nidaros Cathedral in **Trondheim**, which had a reputation for being the most impressive cathedral in northern Europe. Other well-known medieval churches are the **Stavanger** Cathedral and the Mary Church in **Bergen**.

Some secular buildings were also built with stone, for example, Håkon's Hall in Bergen, which was completed by 1261, when the wedding feast of King Magnus Lagabøte was held there. **Olav Engelbrektsson**'s fortress at Steinvikholmen in the Trondheim fjord, built in 1525, was built of stone, as was Akershus Fortress, started in the late 1200s. As a rule, only royalty or powerful church leaders were able to build with stone. An early example is *Erkebispegården* (the Archbishop's Residence) in Trondheim, on which construction may have started around 1161.

Norway's rural population mostly lived in *årestuer*, small windowless log structures, the origin of which goes back to pre-Christian times, with earthen floors that had a fireplace in the middle and a *ljore* (smoke hole) in the roof, which usually was covered with birch bark and sod as insulation. The hole could be covered when it rained by moving a rod tied to a cover. The threshold was high in order to protect against drafts, and there were dirt-filled benches—the dry dirt was also a protection against drafts—around the walls. Some of these houses had masonry fireplaces without chimneys. Around 1700, the open fireplace was replaced by a masonry fireplace with a chimney, usually placed in a corner of the room. The masonry stored heat that was radiated back into the room when there was no fire. Because it was possible to install a damper in the chimney, the house was also much less drafty than the old *årestue* and its close cousin, the house with the chimneyless fireplace.

Cast iron stoves are known from written sources as far back as the 1600s but were used to a significant degree as late as the 1700s. They were expensive, and only city-dwellers, members of the *embedsmann* (public official) class, and rich farmers could afford them. As the stoves became less expensive, they were used by more people, but because they gave no light, the masonry fireplaces were still in use well into the 1900s, especially in the rural areas. When modern petroleum lamps replaced candles and the old fish and whale oil lamps, however, the open fireplace was no longer needed, and building practices were adjusted to fit the new illumination technology. Houses also became larger as it became possible to heat individual rooms.

In the 1900s, rural log houses were replaced by framed structures with or without insulation in the walls and set on foundations made with concrete blocks or reinforced concrete. The development of better insulation techniques and the use of electricity made possible the modern well-insulated and centrally heated home that has become the norm in Norway.

Throughout the modern period, larger buildings, especially in the cities, were increasingly made with bricks and stone rather than wood. Stone or brick exteriors were sometimes required in the cities in order to reduce fire danger. These building materials are of less significance now, as reinforced concrete, combined with steel framing, has replaced most other materials in large construction projects.

**ART.** The beginning of Norwegian art can be found in rock carvings dating back to the Paleolithic era, for example, the "Rødøy Man" from Nordland County, a stylized image of a skier that is approximately 4,000 years old. Rock art is always stylized and often nonfigurative, so it is difficult to assess its precise meaning, but solar motifs and images related to hunting are prevalent. A spectacular example of the latter is a bear hunt depicted as part of a collection of as many as 2,000 carvings in Alta, Finnmark County. Most rock art is found on smooth, sloping outcroppings of bedrock and is known from all parts of Norway. Other examples of prehistoric art are found on utilitarian objects left behind by hunters living in eastern Finnmark during the same period as those who made the "Rødøy Man." Various bronze objects with ornamentation have also been found, as well as gold bracteates and other miniature thin gold plates that depict a sacred couple, possibly the fertility god Frey and his consort. These objects are associated with the Migration period and the early **Viking** age.

Animal ornamentation was also common during the Viking period, when the so-called gripping beast style was popular. One of its classic examples is the bow on the Oseberg ship, which was built shortly after 800 and found in a grave mound near Tønsberg, but smaller objects decorated in the same style have also been found. The gripping beast style persisted into the Christian medieval period and can be observed on the north portal of the Urnes stave church, built around 1150.

Norway is also known for its folk art, especially wood carving and *rosemaling* (decorative flower painting). The wood carving traditions can be seen as early as the Viking period and lasted throughout the centuries, particularly in connection with church **architecture** and as adornments on altar pieces, pulpits, and baptismal fonts but also in the homes of the farmers. Starting in the 1700s, the acanthus vine became a particularly important motif. *Rosemaling* dates to approximately 1750 and originated in eastern Norway, but regional styles developed as it spread. Both smaller objects, such as spoons and bowls, and articles of furniture, such as chests and cupboards, were decorated with flower painting.

Little is known about **religious** painting in Norway during the pre-**Reformation** period, and during the 1600s and 1700s, the relative austerity of the Lutheran church buildings did not promote the development of a specifically Norwegian tradition of religious art. Altar pieces were often painted by foreign artisans who specialized in this craft, and most of the Norwegian paintings known from this period are of mainly historical interest. With the rebirth of the Norwegian state in 1814, however, the nationalistic movement known as **national romanticism** manifested itself in pictorial art as well as in other areas of culture. Improved **economic** conditions made it increasingly feasible for talented artists to receive quality instruction, usually abroad. Such painters as **Johan Christian Dahl**, **Adolph Tidemand**, and **Hans Gude** used motifs taken from rural life and Norwegian nature. *Brudefærden i Hardanger* (the Bridal Journey in Hardanger), painted in 1849, on which Gude collaborated with his colleague Tidemand, is Norway's most famous painting in the style of the national romanticism. It was later parodied as *Oljeferden i Hardanger* (1975; the **Oil** Journey in Hardanger) by Rolf Groven (1943– ), who, with a landscape of oil tanks and garbage, wanted to show that the Norwegian oil **industry** was a threat to both nature and traditional Norwegian values. Herman August Cappelen (1827–52), who belonged to the so-called Düsseldorf School, is known for his nature motifs. Thomas Fearnley (1802–42), a student of Dahl, unites nature with Norwegian history in his most famous painting, *Slindrebirken* (1839; the Slindre Birch), which shows an old birch tree growing on the top of an ancient burial mound. Lars Hertervig (1830–1902) painted nature motifs from the area northeast of **Stavanger**.

When the national romanticism gave way to a more realistic style, Christian Krohg (1852–1925), a student of Hans Gude, chose to paint motifs from everyday life. As he gradually moved in the direction of the naturalism of the 1880s, he depicted prostitutes and poverty, for example, *Kampen for tilværelsen* (1888–89; the Struggle for Existence), which shows a group of hungry children tightly bunched together. Norway's most famous pictorial artist, **Edvard Munch**, who was Krohg's student, made the transition from naturalism to impressionism and expressionism. He has achieved world renown with *Skrik* (1893; Scream), *Madonna* (1894–95), and other works. Another world-famous Norwegian artist is the sculptor **Gustav Vigeland**, who is much admired for the numerous sculptures located in the Frogner Park in **Oslo**.

In the later 20th century, Norway has not produced artists comparable to Munch and Vigeland. The pictorial tradition remained strong, however, with such artists as Per Krohg (1889–1965), who studied with Henri Matisse (1869–1954), was later influenced by cubism, and is known for his large frescoes, including one in the **United Nations** Security Council chambers. Kaj Fjell (1907–89), who was inspired by Munch's work, is known for his vitalism and his emphasis on the female elements of existence. Since the 1960s, Karl Erik Harr (1940– ) has been one of Norway's foremost painters in a new romantic depiction of landscape and life in northern Norway. Odd Nerdrum (1944– ) has rebelled against modernism by creating realistically painted figures, for example, in *Mordet på Andreas Baader*

(1977–78; the Murder of Andreas Baader), in which the head of the Baader-Meinhof terrorist gang is portrayed as a martyr. Many of the contemporaries of these artists have abandoned painting in favor of installations, which break down the boundaries between various art forms, as well as those that separate the audience from the artwork.

**ASBJØRNSEN, PETER CHRISTEN (1812–85).** Norwegian folklorist and author. Born in Christiania (now **Oslo**) on 15 January 1812, Asbjørnsen attended a private course that was to prepare him for matriculation at the university, held at Norderhov, where he met his future collaborator **Jørgen Moe**. While working as a tutor at Romerike, north of Oslo, he started writing down the folktales and legends he heard. Influenced by the ideas of the **national romanticism**, he published many of the legends under the title *Norske Huldre-Eventyr og Folkesagn* (Norwegian Popular Legends and Stories of the Hidden Folk), which came out in 1845, 1848, and 1870. Asbjørnsen wrote stories set in the milieu where the legends flourished, presenting the tellers in fictional form and including the actual legends within these frame stories. The frame stories present rural living in a lifelike manner. Together with Jørgen Moe, he edited and published *Norske Folkeeventyr* (Norwegian Folktales) in 1843 and 1852. Asbjørnsen's academic studies centered on botany and zoology, about which he was well informed. For example, he published a popular article about Charles Darwin in 1861. He also worked as a forester and traveled widely. His primary legacy is in the area of folklore, however, and his contributions to Norwegian **literature** exist primarily in his lively descriptions of nature and his use of oral and popular **language**.

# – B –

**BÅHUSLEN.** Part of Norway until the peace treaty signed in Roskilde, **Denmark**, in March 1658, Båhuslen (the Fief of Båhus) was ceded to **Sweden** by the Danish king Frederik III (1609–70), along with two other Norwegian provinces, Trøndelag and Møre, as well as several Danish possessions. The treaty concluded the first of two wars commonly referred to at the Karl Gustav wars, from the name of Karl X Gustav (1622–60), king of Sweden. The cause of the war was Denmark's 1657 attack on the territory belonging to the Duke of Gottorp, one of the political rivals of the Danish king. The Swedes withdrew subsequent to the treaty of Roskilde but then attacked Copenhagen in July 1658. When Holland, Poland, and Saxony came to Denmark's aid, the second Karl Gustav war was concluded through another peace treaty, signed in Copenhagen on 27 May 1660. Most of the Roskilde treaty was allowed to stand, but Trøndelag and Møre were returned to Norway.

**BASTESEN, STEINAR (1945– ).** Norwegian politician. Born in Dønna, Nordland County, on 26 March 1945, Bastesen qualified for a license to operate coastal vessels (*kystskippereksamen*) in 1967 and worked in **fishing** and **whaling**. A resident of Brønnøysund, he represented the **Conservative Party** in local politics. He was first elected to the *Storting* in 1997 on the ticket of a new party called *Tverrpolitisk Folkevalgte* (Cross-Spectrum Elected) and reelected in 2001 as a representative of the **Coastal Party**, which he formed in 1999. He lost his seat in 2005. Bastesen was the head of the Coastal Party until 2005, when he was thrown out of office at a turbulent party convention. Many observers believe that his political career is over. During his time on the national stage, he was a colorful presence in Norwegian politics and strongly argued in favor of the whaling **industry**. He also liked to wear articles of seal-fur clothing at public appearances.

**BERG, PAAL OLAV (1873–1968).** Norwegian legal scholar, politician, and resistance leader. Born in Hammerfest on 18 January 1873, Berg studied law at the University of **Oslo** and graduated in 1895. He first served as a judge at a city court and became a Supreme Court justice in 1913. Representing the **Liberal Party**, he served as minister of social work form 1919 to 1920 in **Gunnar Knudsen**'s second government and then as minister of justice in **Johan Ludwig Mowinckel**'s first government, starting in 1924. He became chief justice of the Supreme Court in 1929, and in this capacity, he led the efforts to establish a provisional government for Norway subsequent to the German attack and occupation in 1940. In 1943, he was asked by the Norwegian exile government in London to assume leadership of *Hjemmefronten* (the Home Front), which conducted Norwegian resistance to the occupiers, was fully operational only by 1944, and was preparing to assume temporary control of Norway after the capitulation of the Germans. *See also* WORLD WAR II.

**BERGE, ABRAHAM THEODOR (1851–1936).** Norwegian politician. Born on 20 August 1851 in Lyngdal, Vest-Agder County, Berge was a member of the *Storting* (**Parliament**) from 1892 to 1894 as well as from 1898 to 1912. He first represented the **Liberal Party** but left it for the **Liberal Left Party** when it was formed in 1909. He served as minister of finance under **Christian Michelsen** from 1906 to 1907 and as minister of ecclesiastical affairs under **Jørgen Løvland** from 1907 to 1908. He again served as minister of finance under **Wollert Konow** from 1910 to 1912 and in the same position in the second government of **Otto Bahr Halvorsen** in 1923. When Halvorsen died unexpectedly after less than three months in office, Berge took over as prime minister, serving in that capacity from 1923 to 1924, with a continuing coalition of the **Conservative Party** and the Liberal Left Party. A vexatious issue in Norwegian politics at the time was how to maintain Norway's ban on heavy wine and liquor in the face of possible and actual **trade** sanctions from three traditional exporters of alcoholic beverages, France, Spain, and Portugal. The prohibition against heavy wine had been abandoned by Halvorsen's government, and Berge wanted to also cancel the ban on liquor and to do it without a referendum, which the Liberal Party wanted. That decision led to a vote of no confidence against his government in the summer of 1924, and it was succeeded by **Johan Ludwig Mowinckel**'s first government. Berge was later impeached for having provided government support to a bank without consulting the *Storting* but was acquitted.

**BERGEN.** The name *Bergen* comes from the Old Norse name *Bjørgvin*, meaning "a meadow among mountains." Founded by King Olav Kyrre (c. 1050–93) in 1070, it was the capital of Norway until 1299, when **Oslo** took over. The city is located on the southwestern coast of Norway and is surrounded by seven mountains, which makes it a very rainy place, but it also gives it a mild climate, at least by Norwegian standards. The annual rainfall is 88 inches, but it is not uncommon to have temperatures above 10 degrees Celsius in the middle of the winter. Bergen has a maritime climate thanks to the Gulf Stream, which brings warm water across the North Atlantic from the Gulf of Mexico.

Bergen is a municipality within Hordaland County and is Norway's second-largest city, after Oslo. It is governed by an elected city council with 67 members, from which an executive city government, *Byrådet*, is selected. The system of government is **parliamentary**, so the executive council is responsible to the city council. Because Bergen has almost a quarter of a million inhabitants, the city bureaucracy is substantial.

Historically dependent on **trade**, the Port of Bergen is the largest port in Norway and a center of coastal traffic, as well as an important port of call for cruise ships. Bergen is also the home of a significant **fishing** fleet, and it supplies much of the off-shore **oil industry**. Bergen is served by a major international airport and is the terminus of a railroad line leading to Oslo and from there to other parts of Norway, as well as **Sweden** and the European continent. Car ferries run from Bergen to **Denmark**, Great Britain, Iceland, and the Faeroe Islands. **Education** is also a major activity, as Bergen hosts the University of Bergen, the Bergen University College, and many other educational institutions. The city is also the center for government administration and health care delivery in western Norway.

Bergen was severely affected by the **Black Death** in 1349. In the wake of the disaster, however, it became one of the most important trade centers for the **Hanseatic League**, which exploited the early Norwegian fishing industry, buying stockfish from coastal fishermen and exporting it throughout Europe. There was a persistent struggle between the Hansa merchants and the local royal administrators, but the Hansa managed to hold on to their position until the early modern period. Even though they lost their trade hegemony around 1750, the trade with northern Norway remained an important basis for Bergen's **economic** life. Bergen retained a royal monopoly on trade with northern Norway until 1789.

The largest city in Norway until the 1840s, Bergen grew less rapidly than Oslo during the second half of the 1800s and throughout the 1900s, but its borders were gradually enlarged through annexation of a number of surrounding communities. Before and during **World War I**, it was a major center for Norwegian **shipping**. There was, however, a devastating fire in the city center in 1916. On 9 April 1940, Bergen was occupied by German troops and sustained a great deal of damage during **World War II**. During the postwar period, it has experienced a tremendous amount of growth, both in trade and in higher education, and it remains a forward-looking and vibrant city of great charm and beauty.

Not surprisingly, tourism is a major industry in Bergen. Among its many attractions are *Bryggen*, the old Hanseatic wharf, including its open-air fish market. The Håkon's Hall was built during the reign of Haakon IV Haakonsson (1217–63), and both the Bergen Cathedral and the Mary Church date back to medieval times. The Rosenkrantz Tower was an important part of the old Bergenhus Fortress. Bergen also has a number of museums, including the open-air museum Gamle Bergen (Old Bergen).

**BERGGRAV, EIVIND JOSEF (1884–1959).** Norwegian theologian and bishop. Born in **Stavanger** on 25 October 1884, Berggrav, whose last name originally was Jensen, then Berggrav-Jensen, and finally just Berggrav, studied theology at the University of **Oslo**, from which he graduated in 1908. He was later ordained a State Church minister, although he also worked as a teacher and editor of the journal *Kirke og Kultur* (Church and Culture). During **World War I**, he was working as a journalist and wrote a book about the psychological effects of war and how to harmonize a **religious** attitude toward life with being a soldier. Having visited the western front, he was particularly concerned about man-to-man fighting with bayonets. Berggrav served as bishop in the Hålogaland bishopric from 1928 to 1937 and wrote a book titled *Spenningens land* (1937; Land of Suspense) about his life there. He later served as the bishop of Oslo (1937–51), which entailed being the leader of the college of bishops and the *primas* (foremost leader) of the church.

During **World War II**, Berggrav led the resistance of the church against the occupiers' attempted Nazification of Norwegian life, including the church. A highly principled man, Berggrav was interested in cooperation with other groups of believers. He successfully allied the church with the Christian lay movement in Norway during the war years and was the main force behind the statement "Kirkens grunn" (Foundation of the Church) which was read from the pulpits throughout Norway at Easter 1942 and led the ministers to resign the portion of their duties that pertained to their positions as government appointees. Berggrav felt that he had a moral duty to speak out against the refusal of the Nazis to honor freedom of religion; also, they wanted to change the liturgy of the church by deleting the reference to the king from the Common Prayer and substituting the names of Nazi leaders. Furthermore, the Nazis wanted to remove the priest–penitent confidentiality privilege so as to be able to use ministers as informers. Berggrav was arrested and placed at the Grini concentration camp but was later confined to his cabin for three years, guarded by a detail of *Hirdsmenn* (**Vidkun Quisling**'s specially trained soldiers) that was frequently rotated so that none of the soldiers would be influenced by his anti-Nazi beliefs.

**BERNADOTTE, JEAN-BAPTISTE JULES (1763–1844).** French marshal, later king of Norway under the name Karl III Johan and of **Sweden** under the name of Karl XIV Johan. Born the son of a French local administrator on 26 January 1763, Bernadotte rose from private in the French army to one of Napoleon's 18 marshals. Very successful on the field of battle, he had an outstanding career before being elected crown prince of Sweden and adopted by Sweden's King Karl XIII. At this time, he was also made supreme commander—generalissimo—of the Swedish armed forces. At the **Treaty of Kiel**, he realized one of Sweden's long-term foreign policy objectives, as **Denmark**'s King Frederik VI ceded Norway to Sweden as a consequence of having been on the losing side in the Napoleonic wars. When Norway called a **constitutional** convention and claimed independence from both Denmark and Sweden, Bernadotte—now under the name Karl Johan—conducted a brief war against Norway. A diplomatic realist who knew that Europe's Great Powers preferred to see the matter settled without additional hostilities, he negotiated a resolution of the conflict that allowed Norway to keep its constitution mostly intact, as only the changes required by the union were made. The king of Norway and Sweden from 1818 to 1844, he was greatly admired in both countries.

**BJØRNEBOE, JENS INGVALD (1920–76).** Norwegian novelist and dramatist. Born in Kristiansand on 9 October 1920, Bjørneboe was profoundly influenced by the culture of continental Europe. Deeply affected by the experience of **World War II**, Bjørneboe wrote his first novel, *Før hanen galer* (1952; Before the Cock Crows) about medical experiments performed by Nazi doctors on concentration camp prisoners. His next novel, *Jonas* (1955; tr. *The Last of These*, 1959), offers a portrait of a dyslexic little boy and attacks the Norwegian school system, while *Under en hårdere himmel* (1957; Under a Harder Sky) portrays Norway's treatment of Nazi wartime collaborators. Other novels followed, after which Bjørneboe returned to the war experience and its connection with the problem of evil. A trilogy commonly referred to as "The History of Bestiality" discusses crimes committed by the European nations and America, mostly during the 20th century. Bjørneboe wrote several dramas, of which *Fugleelskerne* (1966; tr. *The Bird Lovers*, 1993) is set in an Italian village and presents the affects of World War II on both the natives and the former German occupiers. *See also* LITERATURE.

**BJØRNSON, BJØRNSTJERNE (1832–1910).** Norwegian novelist, dramatist, poet, and cultural leader. Born in Kvikne, Hedmark County, on 8 December 1832, Bjørnson was considered Norway's most important writer during his lifetime. In fact, his significance to Norwegian **literature**, culture, and society cannot be overestimated; for half a century, he used his preeminence as a writer to provide both political and artistic leadership. The son of a Lutheran minister, Bjørnson grew up among farmers and became thoroughly familiar with most aspects of rural life. After schooling in Molde and Christiania (now **Oslo**), he started writing cultural journalism for the Christiania paper *Morgenbladet* (Morning Post) in 1854. He had a tremendous amount of energy and involved himself in a variety of causes, including Norway's first worker's movement and the struggle to establish a Norwegian theater, as well as liberal politics in general.

Starting in 1857, when he published both the historical drama *Mellem Slagene* (tr. *Between the Acts*, 1941) and a *bondefortelling* (peasant tale) titled *Synnøve Solbakken* (tr. 1858), Bjørnson produced a series of works influenced by the ideas of the **national romanticism**. In the 1870s, he helped introduce realistic drama to Norway, criticizing contemporary business practices, journalism, and even the monarchy. After abandoning his Christian faith in favor of a worldview inspired by the works of Charles Darwin (1809–82), he wrote an important drama that probes the psychology of faith, *Over ævne I* (1883; tr. *Pastor Sang*, 1893). He also got heavily involved in the so-called morality debate of the 1880s, in which he argued that men should be held to the same standards as **women** in matters of sexual conduct. Most of Bjørnson's works from the latter part of his career have not withstood the test of time, but many of his best poems have become part of Norway's national patrimony.

**BLACK DEATH.** The Black Death is a highly communicable disease that initially hit Europe from 1347 to 1351 and returned from time to time thereafter. Usually thought of as the bubonic plague because of the apparent abscesses of the lymph nodes that were characteristic of it and spread by rats and their fleas, it hit Norway for the first time in 1349, when it appeared in **Bergen**. It may also have arrived overland from the east, possibly appearing in **Oslo** in 1348. Its effects in Norway were devastating, likely killing between one half and two thirds of the population. Reliable estimates are difficult to make, but according to tax records, a large proportion of Norwegian farms were still uninhabited as late as around 1520. With the decline in the population, land values fell precipitously and land rents even more so. The Norwegian landed nobility were thus hit particularly hard.

**BLEHR, OTTO ALBERT (1847–1927).** Norwegian politician. Born in Stange, Hedmark County, on 17 February 1847, Blehr received a law degree and entered political life as a member of the **Liberal Party**. He served as a member of the *Storting* (**Parliament**) from 1883 to 1888 and again from 1895 to 1900 and was the Norwegian prime minister in Stockholm from 1891 to 1893. This meant that he was in effect Norway's top representative to its union partner, and it fell to Blehr's lot to present the consular service bill to King Oscar II in 1892. He also served as Norway's prime minister from 1902 to 1903 at the height of the struggle that led to the **dissolution of the union with Sweden** in 1905. Still at issue was the long-standing disagreement about Norway's demand for its own consular service, but in addition, Norway wanted its own minister of foreign affairs. Blehr managed to negotiate a possible solution to the conflict in March 1903, according to which each of the two countries was to have its own consular service, but the matter of the minister of foreign affairs was partly left unresolved. Blehr's government had to resign when the Liberal Party lost the 1903 parliamentary election to the Unity Party, a combination of the **Conservatives** and some right-leaning Liberals, and was succeeded by a Unity Party government led by **Francis Hagerup**.

Blehr next served as a county administrator in Kristiania (now Oslo) from 1905 to 1917 but came back to national politics when **Gunnar Knudsen** declined the post of prime minister in 1921. Blehr's government lasted until 1923 but foundered on the question of how to deal with Portugal's demand that Norway should continue importing its alcoholic beverages in spite of the Norwegian prohibition against heavy wine. This was essentially the same issue that had felled **Otto Bahr Halvorsen**'s government two years earlier, and the matter was resolved only when Norway abandoned its prohibition against heavy wine later in 1923.

**BOJER, JOHAN KRISTOFFER (1872–1959).** Norwegian novelist. Bojer was born 6 March 1872 in Orkdal, Sør-Trøndelag County, but grew up in Rissa next to the **Trondheim** fjord. A very prolific writer, Bojer is remembered for those of his novels that depict the lives of common people from his home community, foremost among them *Den siste viking* (1921; tr. *Last of the Vikings*, 1923). The story of a group of fishermen from Trøndelag who travel to and participate in the great Lofoten cod fisheries, it is a novel of great cultural and historical significance. The novel *Folk ved sjøen* (1929; tr. *Folk by the Sea*, 1931), also has Rissa as its setting. *Vor egen stamme* (1924; tr. *Emigrants*, 1925) is a narrative of the Norwegian **emigration** to America and was written in competition with **Ole Edevart Rølvaag**'s *I de dage* (1924) and *Riket grundlægges* (1925), which were translated by Lincoln Colcord and published together as *Giants in the Earth: A Saga of the Prairie* (1927). *See also* LITERATURE.

**BONDEVIK, KJELL MAGNE (1947– ).** Norwegian politician. Born in Molde in northwestern Norway on 3 September 1947 as the son of an educator, Bondevik studied theology at *Menighetsfakultetet* (MF Norwegian School of Theology), a divinity school located in **Oslo**, earning his degree in 1975. He was ordained a minister in the Norwegian Evangelical-Lutheran Church (the State Church) four years later. A member of the **Christian Democratic Party**, he was first elected a member of the *Storting* (**Parliament**) in 1973, serving until his retirement from politics in 2005, subsequent to the defeat of his coalition government in that year's parliamentary elections. During five different periods of time, he also functioned as the leader of the Christian Democratic parliamentary caucus and party leader from 1983 to 1995. From 1983 to 1986 Bondevik served as minister of church and **education** in the government headed by **Kåre Willoch**, and in 1989–90, he was minister of foreign affairs under **Jan P. Syse**. In 1997, Bondevik became the prime minister in a minority coalition government consisting of the Christian Democrats, the **Center Party**, and the **Liberal Party**, which remained in power until 2000, when its commitment to clean generation of electricity from natural gas (*see* OIL AND NATURAL GAS) was not supported by a parliamentary majority. It was succeeded by a **Labor Party** government headed by Jens Stoltenberg, which experienced a heavy setback in the parliamentary elections of 2001. Bondevik then formed a second minority coalition consisting of the **Conservative Party**, the Christian Democrats, and the Liberal Party.

**BORTEN, PER (1913–2005).** Norwegian politician. Born on 3 April 1913 in Flå, Melhus in Sør-Trøndelag County, Borten was trained at the Norwegian **Agricultural** University and later worked as a local agricultural extension representative. He had joined the Agrarian Party, which later became known as the **Center Party**, and served as mayor of his home community from 1945 to 1955. He became a member of the *Storting* (**Parliament**) in 1949, retiring in 1977. From 1955 to 1967, he was also the head of the Center Party and was instrumental when it changed is name from *Bondepartiet* (Agrarian Party) to *Senterpartiet* (Center Party) in 1959. In 1965, he became prime minister in a Center–Right coalition but resigned in 1971. The hottest political issue at the time was whether Norway should join the **European Economic Community** (EEC), later known as the **European Union**, about which a referendum was held on 25 September 1972. The Center Party was opposed to Norwegian membership in the EEC, and Borten was accused of having given confidential documents related to the issue to an organization that led the fight against joining. It later became clear that one of Borten's associates was behind the leak.

**BRATLIE, JENS KRISTIAN MEINICH (1856–1939).** Norwegian politician, legal scholar, and military officer. Born on 17 January 1856 in Nordre Land, Oppland County, to the lawyer and sheriff Erik Bratlie (1814–90), Bratlie's conservatism was of rural rather than urban origin. After graduating from the Military Academy in 1880, Bratlie studied law at the university in Christiania (now **Oslo**), then served in the Ministry of Defense and as the chief legal officer of the Norwegian army. As a young man, Bratlie belonged to the wing of the **Conservative Party** that was friendly toward the union with **Sweden** and believed that the Norwegian army should be a mobile force that could assist Sweden in defending the **Scandinavian** Peninsula. Elected to the *Storting* (**Parliament**), Bratlie had a powerful influence on the changes that were made to the organization of the Norwegian Army in 1909. He served as the leader of the Conservative Party from 1911 to 1919 and became prime minister in 1912, when **Wollert Konow** had to resign because of his positive comments about *nynorsk* (New Norwegian), which gave the Christiania Conservatives in his government a pretext for rebelling against him. Bratlie's rural background meant that he did not have the same animosity toward *nynorsk* as his urban colleagues, and he wanted to unite the conservative and centrist forces in Norwegian political life. He resigned when the election in 1912 gave the **Liberal Party** a majority in the *Storting*, and **Gunnar Knudsen** took over as prime minister.

**BRATTELI, TRYGVE (1910–84).** Norwegian politician. Born the son of a small farmer on 11 January 1910 in Nøtterøy, Vestfold County, Bratteli worked on a **whaling** vessel while yet in his teens and later did construction work. He served in several positions in *Arbeidernes Ungdomsfylking* (the youth division of the **Labor Party**) and as an editor of the Labor press in Kirkenes and **Oslo**. After engaging in resistance work, he was arrested by the Germans during **World War II** and imprisoned in the concentration camps Sachsenhausen and Natzweiler, weighing a scant 103 pounds when he was released in 1945 as part of a humanitarian mission led by the **Swede** Folke Bernadotte. A member of the *Storting* (**Parliament**) from 1949 to 1981, he led the Labor Party caucus during three periods, 1964–71, 1972–73, and 1976–81. Bratteli was also vice chair of the Labor

Party from 1945 to 1965, as well as its leader 1965 to 1975. He served as minister of finance under **Oscar Torp** and in **Einar Gerhardsen**'s third government, as well as minister of transportation in Gerhardsen's third and fourth governments. When **Per Borten** resigned as prime minister in 1971, Bratteli was thus the obvious choice to form the Labor Party minority government that served until shortly after the European Community (EC; *see* EUROPEAN ECONOMIC COMMUNITY [EEC]) referendum on 25 September 1972. Bratteli was strongly in favor of Norwegian membership in the EC and had been conducting negotiations in Brussels, and the 1972 victory of the anti-EC forces were a serious political blow. He formed a second minority government subsequent to the parliamentary elections of 1973 and remained prime minister until he was succeeded by **Odvar Nordli**, also of the Labor Party, in 1976. Bratteli has also served as both a long-time member and president of the *Nordisk Råd* (Nordic Council).

Bratteli's strength as a politician was his command of the issues and his ability to find practical solutions to problems associated with the management of Norwegian society, including its **economy**. He was a superb communicator, and his integrity was never in question. Once the more pressing social and economic problems of postwar Norway had largely been solved, however, he had a perhaps less-than-perfect understanding of the nonmaterial and values-related considerations that informed those who opposed his drive toward Norwegian membership in the EC.

**BRUNDTLAND, GRO HARLEM (1939– ).** Norwegian politician. Known simply as "Gro" by most Norwegians, Brundland was born in Bærum on the outskirts of **Oslo** on 20 April 1939 to Gudmund Harlem, a member of **Einar Gerhardsen**'s third and fourth governments. Brundtland became a very popular prime minister of Norway, first for a brief stint in 1981 and then during two additional periods, 1986–89 and 1990–96. She was educated as a medical doctor at the University of Oslo (1963) and also received a master of public health degree from Harvard University (1965). A lifelong member of the **Labor Party** (she joined its children's organization at age seven), she served as party chairperson from 1981 to 1992 and first functioned as a cabinet member—she was minister of the **environment**—from

1974 to 1979. As prime minister, her ability to further her party's political agenda was hampered by the fact that none of her governments had the support of a **parliamentary** majority. One of her most significant setbacks came when a proposal for Norwegian membership in the **European Union**, which she strongly supported, was voted down in a 1994 referendum.

Brundtland has also had a distinguished international career. She chaired the World Commission on Environment and Development, generally known as the Brundtland Commission, which was established by the **United Nations** in 1983 and the report of which was published in 1987. Charged with examining the increasing deterioration of the world's human environment, including the depletion of natural resources and its consequences for the social and **economic** future of the planet, the commission defined the concept of sustainable development and outlined policy changes that would make it possible. Brundtland was also named director general of the World Health Organization in 1998, serving until 2003. She stressed the significance of violence as a public health issue and received much praise for her coordination of the world's response to the SARS epidemic. In 2007, she was chosen to serve as a United Nations special envoy for climate change.

**BRUUN, CHRISTOPHER ARNT (1839–1920).** Norwegian theologian and educator. Born in Christiania (now **Oslo**) on 23 September 1839, Bruun studied theology and enlisted as a private in the **Danish** army, fighting the Prussians in 1864. A man of strong emotions, his life was changed when he became acquainted with the ideas of the Danish clergyman Nicolaj Severin Frederik Grundtvig (1783–1872), whose form of Christianity emphasized the uniqueness of every single human being and who had developed a perspective on life that allowed him to hold the history of his country and Christianity in a single vision. Bruun was particularly taken with Grundtvig's Folk High School, which emphasized the student's native tongue and history in its curriculum and where oral interaction and singing often took the place of reading as a form of study. When he returned to Norway, Bruun started a school in the Grundtvigian spirit at Raamundgard in Sel parish in Norway's central valley, Gudbrandsdalen, in 1867. He dressed and lived like a farmer and wanted to renew Norwegian society by drawing strength from rural life and the written form of Norwegian called *nynorsk* (New Norwegian), the language of **Ivar Aasen** and **Aasmund Olafsson Vinje**. In 1875, his school was moved to Vonheim, close to Aulestad in Gausdal not far from Lillehammer. Bruun systematized his ideas in his book *Folkelige Grundtanker* (1878; Fundamental Popular Ideas).

**BULL, OLE BORNEMANN (1810–80).** Norwegian violinist and composer. Born to a **Bergen** druggist on 5 February 1810, Bull was a highly gifted violinist and Norway's first internationally known musical performer. His father wanted him to study theology at the university in Christiania (now **Oslo**), but he was unable to focus on his studies, as he was obsessed with the ideas of **national romanticism** and promoted Norwegian folk music. He also was a leading light in creating the first theater in Norway at which the actors spoke Norwegian rather than **Danish**. The communal socialist ideas of his day also attracted his interest, and he tried to establish a colony named Oleanna in Pennsylvania. Bull was greatly admired by many of his contemporaries and had tremendous success as a concert violinist, especially in the **United States**. Many of his compositions have been lost because he memorized them and did not write them down. He is, however, remembered for "Sæterjentens Søndag" (The Sunday of the Dairymaid), the musical setting of a poem by **Bjørnstjerne Bjørnson**, and "I ensomme Stunde" (In Solitary Moments), for which the philosophy professor **Marcus Jacob Monrad** wrote the lyrics. He is also remembered as a mentor for **Edvard Grieg**.

## – C –

**CAPPELEN, ANDREAS ZEIER (1915– ).** Norwegian politician. Born in Vang, Hedmark County, on 31 January 1915, Cappelen was trained as a lawyer and served as prosecuting attorney during the trials of Nazi collaborators after **World War II**. He began his government career as the minister of local government and labor under **Einar Gerhardsen** from 1958 to 1963 and served as Gerhardsen's minister of finance from 1963 to 1965. When the **Labor Party** returned to power in 1971, **Trygve Bratteli** named Cappelen his minister of foreign affairs, and from 1979 to 1980, he served as **Odvar Nordli**'s minister of justice. In 1972, Cappelen experienced a major political setback when the Labor government's proposal for Norwegian membership in the European Community (*see* EUROPEAN ECONOMIC COMMUNITY [EEC]) was defeated in a nationwide referendum.

**CASTBERG, JOHAN (1862–1926).** Norwegian politician and legal scholar. Born in Brevik, Telemark County, on 21 September 1862, Castberg served as a representative in the *Storting* (**Parliament**) for the **Worker-Democrats**, a nonsocialist liberal party with strong ties to the **Liberal Party**, during the periods of 1901–9, 1913–21, and 1924–26. He served as minister of justice in **Gunnar Knudsen**'s first government from 1908 to 1910, as well as both minister of **trade** (1913) and minister of social affairs (1913–14) in Knudsen's second government. Somewhat to the left of the Liberal Party, Castberg argued in favor of a republican rather than a monarchical form of government in 1905. In Norwegian history, his name is associated with two groups of laws, the natural resources laws and the child laws. The former, passed in 1909, regulated how natural resources were to be used in the development of **hydroelectric power** and applied to both Norwegian and foreign interests. A major point was the doctrine of reversion, the rule that the ownership of waterfalls, power stations, and electrical distribution networks was to revert to the state after a certain period of time. The child laws, passed in 1915, specified that children born out of wedlock were to have the right to inherit from their paternal relatives and established the rules used when support payments were collected from their fathers.

**CENTER PARTY.** *Senterpartiet* (Sp) dates to 1920, when it was formed at the behest of the *Norges Bondelag* (Norwegian Farmer Association) as its political arm under the name *Bondepartiet* (Agrarian Party). During the first years of its existence, it fought for issues that were of interest to the agrarian class, such as better conditions for Norwegian grain producers, support for the cultivation of new farmland, lower taxes for the farmers, and protective tariffs for **agricultural** products. The party garnered 15 percent of the popular vote in the 1921 **parliamentary** election, the first election in which it participated. During the 1920s and the 1930s, the Agrarians continued to receive significant support and possibly so because the party departed from the classic **economic** liberalism that had been the mainstay of its two primary rivals, the **Conservative Party** and the **Liberal Party**. Some of the ideas of the British political economist John Maynard Keynes found resonance among the Agrarians, who came to favor a mixed economy with significant state intervention. There was, therefore, a basis for cooperation between the Agrarians and the other Norwegian class-based party, Labor, and in 1935, the two parties made a crisis agreement, according to which the **Labor Party** government, headed by **Johan Nygaardsvold**, would receive the support of the Agrarians, who in turn received Labor's support for some of their farm policies. This event is of significance as the beginning of the Labor Party's overwhelming dominance in Norwegian politics, which lasted well into the years after **World War II** and went virtually unchallenged until 1965.

During the years leading up to World War II, while Fascism and Nazism were on the march in Europe, there were some Agrarians who were taken with these ideologies. One of them was **Vidkun Quisling**, who served as minister of defense in Agrarian Party governments headed by **Peder Kolstad** (1931–32) and Jens Hunseid (1932–33). Hunseid later joined the Norwegian National Socialist Party. After World War II, the Agrarians increasingly distanced themselves from the Labor Party, demanding economic equality between the rural and the urban portions of the population while resisting Labor's call for capital-intensive **industrialization** and its corresponding centralization, including the depopulation of the countryside. The party changed its name to the Sp in 1959 as a reflection of the fact that it was no longer a party just for farmers but one that wanted to maintain a stable population throughout the entire country. In 1965, the party supplied the prime minister in a broad Center–Right coalition government that, for the first time since 1935, showed that Norway had a genuine alternative to government by the Labor Party.

The flagship issue of the Sp since 1970 has been resistance to Norwegian membership in the **European Union** (EU), an organization that was earlier known as the European Community (EC) and the **European Economic Community**. The success of the "No to EC" faction at the time of the 1972 referendum did not show up at the ballot box in the 1973 parliamentary election, however, as the Sp gained only one additional seat in the *Storting* (Parliament). In October 1975, flush from the victory in the referendum, the Sp joined with the **Christian Democrats** and the Liberal Party and established a Center coalition led by **Lars Korvald** of the Christian Democrats. This government lasted for only one year.

During the 1970s, the Sp shifted its focus significantly, adopting **environmental** protection as its new focus. Environmentalism went well with the party's old emphasis on decentralization and the quality of rural life. During the 1970s, the early years of Norway's **oil** bonanza, it warned against materialism and wanted to slow down the country's economic growth. This issue cost the party dearly in the 1977 parliamentary election, when it lost 10 seats. In the 1980s, it participated in two Center–Right coalitions led by the Conservative Party, and its support eroded until the next battle about Norway's relationship with Europe arrived, the referendum about membership in the EU held in 1994. Speaking for those opposed to membership, the party came through the 1993 parliamentary election as the second-largest party in the *Storting*. After the opponents had won the 1994 referendum, however, support for the Sp declined again, as it participated in the Center coalition led by **Kjell Magne Bondevik** of the Christian Democratic Party. In 2005, it joined the Labor Party and the **Socialist Left Party** in a so-called red–green coalition, which represents both a kind of return to its collaboration with Labor in 1935 and a departure from many of its policies since World War II.

**CHRISTIAN III (1503–59).** King of **Denmark** and Norway. The son of King Frederik I of Denmark and Norway, Christian III was born on 12 August 1503 in Gottorp, Denmark. His earliest teachers were of the Lutheran faith, and Christian became very impressed with Martin Luther, whose defense before the Diet of Worms in 1521 he witnessed. His **religious** convictions were strongly at variance with the Roman Catholicism still subscribed to by most Danish noblemen and royals. When his father, King Frederik I, died in 1533, the Catholic-controlled council of the realm was reluctant to name Christian III king because of his Lutheran beliefs, and he refused to accept the offer of the throne from the council's Lutheran minority. However, when the city of Lübeck, a key member of the **Hanseatic**

**League**, attacked Denmark in 1534 in order to restore to the throne King Christian II, who had been deposed in 1523, Christian III allowed himself to be named king by the Danish nobles on 4 July 1534. He fought the Lübeck forces successfully, gradually bringing all of Denmark under his control and finally taking Copenhagen on 29 July 1536. He had fought with the aid of hired German mercenaries, however, and needed money to pay them, and these funds could be obtained if he were to confiscate the properties of the church. So, on 12 August 1536, King Christian III arrested three Catholic bishops who were members of the council of the realm, thus in effect both carrying out a coup d'état and bringing about the Danish **Reformation**.

**CHRISTIAN IV (1577–1648).** King of **Denmark** and Norway. The grandson of King **Christian III** and the son of King Frederik II, Christian IV was born on 12 April 1577 and reigned as king of Denmark and Norway from 1588 to 1648. A man of great energy and capacity for work, he is known to Norwegian history chiefly as the founder of Christiania (now **Oslo**), which he located close to the fortress of Akershus after a devastating city fire in 1624. He also carried out an adventurous foreign policy, for which he was ill suited, conducting hostilities against **Sweden** during the Kalmar War (1611–13), German Catholics during the Thirty Years War (1618–48), and the Netherlands during another war with Sweden (1643–45). When a peace treaty was signed at Brömsebro on 8 February 1645, Christian IV had to cede parts of his Danish possessions as well as two Norwegian provinces, Jemtland and Herjedalen. In Norway, he also established the city Christiansand (now Kristiansand) and the mining town Kongsberg.

**CHRISTIAN AUGUST (1768–1810).** Prince of the house of Augustenborg, military commander in Norway. Born at Augustenborg, Als, Denmark on 9 July 1768, Christian August was named major general and commander of Fredriksten Fortress in eastern Norway on 10 June 1803, and in 1807, he became the head of a separate Norwegian provincial government. When England destroyed **Denmark**'s fleet in 1807 and Denmark entered the Napoleonic wars on Napoleon's side, the British blockade made it impossible to administer Norwegian affairs from Copenhagen. A temporary government commission was therefore established in Christiania (now **Oslo**), followed by separate financial and judicial institutions. It was the first time since the council of the realm had been disbanded in 1536 that Norway had its own national governing bodies. Christian August served as the president of the government commission from its first meeting on 1 September 1807 until 28 December 1809. During the hostilities with **Sweden** in 1808, he was the successful commander of the Norwegian troops and became very popular among the Norwegians as well as highly respected by the Swedes. In 1809, the Swedish *Riksdag* (national assembly) elected him crown prince of Sweden, and he accepted on the condition that there was to be an end to the hostilities between Sweden and Denmark. One reason for his election was that the Swedish leaders hoped that his popularity in Norway might lead the Norwegians to want to become united with Sweden, which some Norwegian patriots, for example, **Herman Wedel Jarlsberg**, had been advocating. Christian August was adopted under the name of Karl August by Sweden's childless king, Karl XIII, but died on 28 May 1810.

**CHRISTIAN DEMOCRATIC PARTY.** *Kristelig folkeparti* (KrF) was founded in Hordaland County in 1933, mostly by former **Liberal Party** voters who were concerned about the erosion of traditional Christian values, and has been viewed by some as a successor to the **Moderate Liberal Party**. An expression of pietistic and low-church perspectives abundantly present in western Norway at the time, before **World War II**, its operations were limited to the county in which it had been founded. With 0.8 percent of the popular vote in the 1933 **parliamentary** election, it nevertheless secured one seat in the *Storting* (Parliament), and it was—and this is fairly typical for the Christian Democrats—occupied by the leader of a small bible school. In 1936, 1.3 percent of the popular vote gave it two seats. The parliamentary elections of 1945, however, provided its national breakthrough, as the party garnered almost 8 percent of the vote and received eight seats in the *Storting*, in spite of its lack of a national apparatus. Its popularity peaked in 1987, when it got 13.7 percent of the popular vote and 25 seats. Since 1963, it has participated in seven Center and Center–Right governments, and it has supplied Norway's prime minister for a total of almost eight years. Its Christian heritage and commitment to the inviolable dignity of human beings gives it a strong conservative slant, but it differs from most conservative parties in its commitment to families, particularly children, the disadvantaged, and the poor. The Christian Democrats are opposed to a **woman**'s right to choose to have an abortion and want strict legislation governing biomedical research.

**CHRISTIAN FREDERIK (1786–1848).** Norwegian king (briefly) in 1814, later king of **Denmark**. Born in Copenhagen on 18 September 1786 to Heir Presumptive Frederik, the half-brother to Denmark's mentally ill King Christian VII and the later King Frederik VI, Christian Frederik was sent to Norway as viceroy by his father in 1813, during the height of the Napoleonic wars. After the **Treaty of Kiel** on 14 January 1814, in which Frederik VI ceded Norway to **Sweden**, Christian Frederik became a focal point in a movement to establish a Norwegian **constitution**. The members of the constitutional convention held at Eidsvold signed the constitution of 17 May 1814 and elected Christian Frederik king of Norway. A man with a romantic and artistic personality, Christian Frederik was a valuable source of inspiration for the Norwegian patriots. He was also a skilled negotiator who did much, including sacrificing his personal claim to Norway's throne on 14 August 1814, in order to ensure that Norway was given the best possible terms in its union with Sweden. He later reigned as king of Denmark from 1839 to 1848.

**CHRISTIANIA.** *See* OSLO.

**CHRISTIE, WILHELM FRIMANN KOREN (1778–1849).** Norwegian politician and legal scholar. Born in Kristiansund on 7 December 1778, Christie studied law at the University of Copenhagen, earning his degree in 1799. He first worked for the **Danish** chancery, after which he became a regional government administrator in Norway. During the political ferment of early 1814, he belonged to a group of people that held discussions about how the Norwegian **constitution** should be shaped. Christie was in favor of the constitutional form of government found in the **United States**, Great Britain, and France. Elected to the constitutional assembly held at Eidsvoll later in the spring, Christie preferred Norwegian independence rather than a union with **Sweden** but wanted a strong and effective government and to leave legislation in the hands of experts, so he preferred to give the *Storting* (**Parliament**) solely an advisory role.

Christie's most significant contribution, however, was made during the extraordinary meeting of the *Storting* in the fall of 1814, when the details of the union with Sweden were being negotiated. As the president of the *Storting*, Christie provided clear and insightful presentations of the issues, showing the members what was at stake and how to proceed. He is credited with preventing other changes to the constitution than those that had been made necessary by the union. He also insisted that the **Treaty of Kiel** should not be considered the basis for the union with Sweden and that it was essential that Christian Fredrik be recognized as Norway's legal king from his election on 17 May 1814 to his abdication, which had been accepted by the *Storting* later that year. Highly respected as a statesman, Christie declined King Carl Johan's invitation to join his cabinet. After a few more years of service as a member of the *Storting*, his health forced him to withdraw from politics.

**COASTAL PARTY.** The *Kystpartiet* (KP) is a regional party with most of its support in the counties of Nordland and Troms. While it has considerable influence in local politics in northern Norway, on the national level, it has had only one representative in the *Storting* (**Parliament**), **Steinar Bastesen**. He was first elected to the *Storting* in 1997 on the ticket of a new party called the *Tverrpolitisk Folkevalgte* (Cross-Spectrum Elected), which for a time included the *Frihetspartiet mot EF-unionen* (Freedom Party Opposed to the Union with the European Community [EC]), started in 1992 under the name of an older minor party, the *Frie Folkevalgte* (Free Popularly Elected), until its name change in 1993. The KP was started in 1999, and Bastesen was reelected on its ticket in 2001; however, the party got no seats in the *Storting* in the 2005 election. The KP stresses traditional Christian values and **environmental** protection. It has been plagued by internal dissent and a very harsh tone and turbulent proceedings at many of its meetings.

**COLLETT, CAMILLA (1813–95).** Norwegian novelist and early feminist. Born in Kristiansand on 23 January 1813, Collett was the daughter of the theologian and cultural leader **Nicolai Wergeland** (1780–1848) and sister of the well-known Norwegian poet **Henrik Wergeland** (1808–45). After receiving a traditional **education** for upper-class girls, Camilla fell in love with the poet **Johan Sebastian Welhaven** (1807–73), an enemy of her brother and father, who rejected her. Her **literary** efforts were encouraged by her husband, Peter Jonas Collett, whom she married in 1841. Widowed in 1851, she focused increasingly on her literary work and soon published *Amtmandens Døttre* (1854–55; tr. *The District Governor's Daughters*, 1992), which, based on her personal experience, depicted the familial and social oppression suffered by **women** at the time.

Collett followed up the success of *Amtmandens Døttre* with a book of memoirs, *I de lange Nætter* (1862; During the Long Nights), which tells about her youth and offers vivid portraits of her father and brother. Most of her other writings from her later years were highly polemical; a representative title is *Fra de Stummes Leir* (1877; From the Encampment of the Mute), which criticizes what she sees as the almost universal denigration of women by male writers. *See also* LITERATURE.

**CONSERVATIVE PARTY.** The *Høyre* was formed on 25 August 1884 under the name of *De Conservative Foreningers Centralstyre* (Executive Committee of the Conservative Associations). Formed as a response to the **Liberal Party**, which had successfully pushed through the beginning of **parliamentarism** in 1884 by impeaching the king's conservative cabinet, it was Norway's second political party. During the earliest decades of its existence, it did well in the parliamentary elections, particularly in 1894, when it got almost half of the votes cast. The party declined during the interwar period, however, when other parties, including the Agrarian Party and the **Christian Democratic Party**, were established. When not in opposition, which has been its usual lot, it has usually supplied the "Right" portion of a Center–Right coalition, usually in cooperation with the Christian Democrats and the **Center Party**, sometimes also with the Liberal Party. An exception to this rule was **Kåre Willoch**'s first government (1981–83), which was a minority government staffed by the Conservatives alone. Willoch also served as prime minister from 1983 to 1986 but in a coalition with the Christian

Democratic Party and the Center Party. Other Conservative Party prime ministers since **World War II** include **John Lyng** (briefly in 1963) and **Jan P. Syse** (1989–90).

The Conservative Party has attracted true conservatives, who, when faced with problems, are disposed to seek solutions by looking to tradition, prefer gradual change rather than sudden upheavals, and stress established institutions as a means of promoting social stability. Other Conservatives have been market liberalists who have promoted relatively unfettered capitalism but tempered by the programs of the welfare state. Civil liberties, democracy, and property rights are central to the philosophy of the Conservative Party. Since 1973, when the **Progress Party** (FrP) was formed, it has been the custodian of some of the liberalist thought formerly associated with the Conservatives.

**Erna Solberg** has been both the party leader and head of the Conservative parliamentary caucus since 2004. With only 14.1 percent of the popular vote in the 2005 parliamentary election, the party received only 23 seats, was overtaken by the FrP, and ended up as number 3 in the *Storting* (Parliament). The election result was the poorest ever for the Conservatives.

**CONSTITUTION.** Norway's constitution was signed in Eidsvoll on 17 May 1814 and was changed on 4 November 1814 in order to allow for Norway's union with **Sweden** under a common king. Those changes were undone at the **dissolution of the union with Sweden** on 7 June 1905. Other changes have since been made, most recently on 20 February 2007, and those changes will take effect on 1 October 2009.

The Norwegian constitution was inspired by the American Declaration of Independence made in 1776, the French Revolution of 1789, and the constitutions of the two countries. It takes into account the ideas of Charles-Louis de Secondat Montesquieu (1689–1755) concerning the division of powers between the three branches of government, as well as other Enlightenment ideals. Two of its differences from the constitution of the **United States** are that Norway is a constitutional monarchy and that it has a state establishment of **religion**, the Norwegian Lutheran Church.

The constitution is the supreme source of law in Norway. When the most recent amendments made to it take effect, it will specify that

Norway is governed according to the principles of **parliamentarism**, which by convention has been in force since 1884.

## – D –

**DAHL, JOHAN CHRISTIAN KLAUSSON (1788–1857).** Norwegian painter. Also known as I. C. Dahl and J. C. Dahl, Dahl was born the son of a **Bergen** fisherman and rower on 24 February 1788. As his talent unfolded, he received financial assistance that allowed him to study **art** at the University of Copenhagen. He later moved to Dresden in Germany, where he became a professor at the art academy. Norway's first painter of international stature, he is known for his landscape paintings in the mode of the **national romanticism**, which he pioneered in pictorial art. Two of his best-known paintings are *Fra Stalheim* (1842; From Stalheim) and *Bjerk i storm* (1849; Birch in a Storm).

**DASS, PETTER (c. 1647–1707).** Norwegian poet. Born to Peiter Dundas in Herøy, Nordland County, in 1647 (possibly 1646), Dass is Norway's most significant writer of the Baroque period and is known chiefly for his long descriptive poem *Nordlands trompet* (1739; tr. *The Trumpet of Nordland*, 1954). He attended the cathedral school in **Bergen** and studied theology at the University of Copenhagen, later serving as a minister in the Helgeland district of northern Norway. He also wrote **religious** poetry designed to edify his parishioners, most notably *Katechismus-sange* (1714; Catechism Songs). With their down-to-earth presentation of religious doctrines, Dass's songs reached a large audience. Dass was thoroughly acquainted with life among the fishermen and small farmers of Helgeland, and although educated both at the cathedral school in Bergen and at the University of Copenhagen, he never lost touch with his origins. Much loved and respected by the people to whom he ministered, he was regarded as a leader spiritually, **economically**, and socially. *See also* LITERATURE.

**DENMARK.** Norway's closest neighbor to the south, Denmark has for centuries served as Norway's gateway to continental Europe. In

**Viking** times, when Danish chieftains vied with their Norwegian counterparts for control of southern Norway, there was little difference between Danes and Norwegians, who all spoke the same **language**. Medieval politics led to a union of Denmark, Norway, and **Sweden** in Kalmar in 1397, but there were still hostilities, particularly involving Danes and Swedes. After Sweden left the **Kalmar Union** around 1520, the numerous wars between Denmark and Sweden spilled over into Norway as well.

As the Protestant **Reformation** was introduced in Denmark and Norway in 1536, King **Christian III** of Denmark and Norway abolished the Norwegian council of the realm, which meant that Norway ceased to exist as a separate country, and its territory became part of Denmark. As the Danish kings ruled Norway from Copenhagen, the Norwegian rural population showed a great deal of loyalty to them, accepting their laws while generally resisting changes in taxation. Before the events of 1814, most Norwegians did not wish to be separated from Denmark, although there were some who realized that Denmark's and Norway's strategic needs and mercantile interests were fundamentally different. Norway's suffering during the Napoleonic wars made that quite clear.

The end of the Napoleonic wars led to the **Treaty of Kiel**, in which Norway was taken away from Denmark and given to the Swedish king. Norway had essentially no choice in the matter but used the opportunity to establish its own **constitution**. It is probably safe to say, however, that the constitution was regarded more as protection in the relationship with Sweden than as an expression of dissatisfaction with Denmark. After the union between Norway and Sweden had solidified, the cultural connections with Denmark were at least as close as before. Throughout most of the 1800s, the written language used in Norway was largely the same as that used in Denmark, books by Norwegian writers were published in Copenhagen, and to a great extent the two countries comprised a single intellectual marketplace.

Denmark experienced significant political and **economic** progress during the decades following the events of 1814, culminating in the establishment of a free constitution on 5 June 1849, when it became a constitutional monarchy. There was a flowering of Danish cultural life as well, with such important figures as the philosopher Søren Kierkegaard (1813–55) and the writer Hans Christian Andersen (1805–75).

War returned in 1864, however, when Prussia attacked and forced Denmark to cede Schleswig and Holstein. This defeat led the Danes to both embark on a policy of neutrality and to turn more of their remaining territory into productive **agricultural** land. Both efforts were successful, as Denmark made rapid economic progress and managed to stay out of **World War I**, at the close of which some of its lost territory was restored to it.

Denmark was invaded by Germany on 9 April 1940 and remained occupied until 1945. It then became a founding member of both the **North Atlantic Treaty Organization** and the **United Nations** and joined the **European Economic Community** in 1973. It has since become the home of a sizable immigrant population that has been only partially integrated into Danish society.

Even though the close cultural connections between Norway and Denmark have become much looser during the 20th century, many Danes still have a sense of kinship with Norway. Norwegians see Denmark both as an important trading partner and a wonderful place to go on vacation.

***DET NORSKE ARBEIDERPARTI.*** *See* LABOR PARTY.

**DISSOLUTION OF THE UNION WITH SWEDEN.** When Norway entered into a union with **Sweden** in 1814, it was the result of the wishes of the European Great Powers rather than any kind of desire on the part of the Norwegians. Once the union was a fact of life and had proven relatively benign, in that Norway seemed to develop just fine both **economically** and culturally—for example, **Henrik Ibsen**'s fame as a dramatist did not seem to be rivaled by any Swedish writer—many Norwegians were mostly unconcerned about it. Predictably, those who had something to gain from the union liked it more than those who did not. Most members of the *embedsmann* (public official) class, which tended to be conservative, very likely felt some degree of kinship with their Swedish counterparts and were generally friendly toward the union, while cottagers and small farmers, who were opposed to the privileged position and relative opulence that characterized the lives of the officials, were usually more critical of it.

There was, however, a difference of opinion between Norwegians and Swedes about what the union entailed. The Norwegians tended to see it as a personal union in which the same individual was the king of both countries, while the Swedes regarded it as a real union in which the two countries were, so to speak, joined at the hip. There was some reason to hold the latter view inasmuch as foreign affairs—the consular and diplomatic services—were firmly under the control of the king in his capacity as king of Sweden. He appointed the Swedish cabinet, including its minister of foreign affairs, who supervised the Foreign Office. The consular service, a division of the Foreign Office, was controlled by a body jointly representing the Norwegian and the Swedish governments and had as its primary responsibility to look after Norwegian and Swedish business interests abroad, particularly interests related to **shipping**. The members of the diplomatic corps, on the other hand, were appointed by a Swedish government body, called the ministerial cabinet; however, after 1835 a Norwegian cabinet member was to be present when matters related to Norway were being discussed. While Norwegians and Swedes had equal access to appointments as consuls, most diplomats were Swedish aristocrats.

As long as Norway was governed by a cabinet appointed by the king and generally consisting of members of the *embedsmann* class, this arrangement did not seem to pose too big a problem. Between 1814 and 1884, most of the disagreements between Norway and Sweden relating to the union had been about symbolic matters, as, for example, the **flags** used in the two countries or how to formulate the title of the king used on Norwegian coins. In the 1860s, there had even been a movement, known as **Scandinavianism**, toward greater ties between all of the three Scandinavian countries, including a strengthening of the union between Norway and Sweden. When **parliamentarism** was introduced in Norway in 1884, however, and the control of cabinet appointments was vested in the *Storting* (**Parliament**), the situation changed. The radical forces had long had their eye on questions concerning the union—for example, **Johan Sverdrup** and **Ole Gabriel Ueland**'s **Reform Association** had greater equality with Sweden on their agenda as early as 1859—but they had not had the power to do something meaningful about it. After Sverdrup's great electoral victory in 1882, and especially after the successful impeachment of the government in 1884, they had at least enough power to attempt to bring about change.

The union issue first came to the fore in 1885, when the Swedes changed the procedures for supervising the diplomatic service. The ministerial cabinet, the body that made the appointments, was enlarged by one member (from two to three, plus the Norwegian representative when invited) as well as put under the supervision of the Swedish parliament. This clearly made it look like the Swedish parliament was running Norwegian affairs, which was demeaning to members of the *Storting* as well as to other patriotic Norwegians. Sverdrup's government entered into negotiations with the Swedes, and it was agreed that the number of Norwegian representatives in the ministerial cabinet would be increased to three. This decision was to be codified as part of the Union Law (*riksakten*), which governed the relationship between Norway and Sweden. Then Sverdrup and his ministers in Stockholm agreed that they would also demand that this change was to be included in the Norwegian **constitution** by the *Storting*. This was, of course, totally unacceptable to the Swedes, who maintained that the *Storting* had no power to unilaterally change the parts of the constitution that related to the union. In addition, Sverdrup tried to renege on a concession he had earlier made to get his three members of the ministerial cabinet. This concession was that the minister of foreign affairs would always be a Swede, and it was a point that deeply hurt Norwegian national pride. It was unacceptable to the *Storting*, and the negotiations came to an end in 1886 without any changes to a system that the Norwegians felt to be humiliating.

Sverdrup resigned as prime minister in 1889, and **Emil Stang** of the **Conservative Party** became his successor. Stang wanted to improve relations with Sweden, which had recently changed its thinking about the free **trade** between the two countries. The trade law was weakened against Norway's interests—Sweden was becoming protectionist, the shipping nation Norway still held on to the idea of free trade—and this was by itself perceived as a threat to the union. When Stang reopened the negotiations about the constitution of the ministerial cabinet, the provisional agreement reached was still deemed unacceptable to the *Storting*, and Stang resigned in 1891. His successor, **Johannes Steen** of the **Liberal Party**, had been obligated by his party's program to press for a separate Norwegian minister of foreign affairs, while the Conservatives hoped for a joint minister of foreign affairs who could be either a Norwegian or a Swede. Leading figures in Swedish political life were, however, talking about the possibility of using military power against Norway, so Steen moved in a different direction by proposing that Norway should establish its own separate consular service, which made sense in view of Norway's significance as a shipping nation. The Liberals regarded this move both as a step toward a separate Norwegian Foreign Office and as a means of eventually getting the union dissolved. The *Storting* passed the consular service bill in 1892, but King Oscar II refused to sign it into law and agree to the expenditures associated with creating the service. The mood in Sweden was becoming increasingly bellicose, and on 11 May 1895, the Swedish parliament canceled the free trade arrangements with Norway. The Swedes also increased their military expenditures and seemed to be preparing for war.

Norway thus had a choice between a war with Sweden, for which it was not prepared, and the humiliation of having to continue negotiating. On 7 June 1895, the *Storting* took a vote that amounted to eating humble pie, promising to continue the negotiations with Sweden, but Norway also started building up its defenses. Several warships were acquired, and a series of forts were built along the Swedish border. There was also continued growth in the country's democratic development. Universal male suffrage was introduced in 1898, the school system was reformed, and the people as a whole was becoming better informed and increasingly united in favor of significant changes in the relationship between the two countries.

The negotiations continued on and off between 1895 and the winter of 1905, but the Swedish demands were unacceptable, and on 8 February 1905, the *Storting* was informed that the negotiations had collapsed. On 18 February, the *Storting* established a special committee in which all the political parties were represented, and this committee voted that a Norwegian consular service was to be established by 1 April 1906. The sitting government of **Francis Hagerup** resigned, paving the way for a government headed by **Christian Michelsen**, who on 15 March 1905 promised the *Storting* that he would carry out the decision of the special committee. On 5 April, the Swedish crown prince regent offered a proposal that might have solved the crisis concerning the specific matter of the consular service, but the Norwegians regarded it as a smokescreen and an attempt to sow disunity in their parliament. The Norwegians seemed to be intent on dissolving the union, come what may.

On 18 May 1905, the *Storting* passed the legislation prepared by the special committee, and the bill was presented to King Oscar II for his signature in Stockholm on 27 May. When he refused to sign it into law, the cabinet resigned on the spot. With Michelsen as the primary strategist, the plan of the Norwegians was that the cabinet would turn its power over to the *Storting*, which would then request that it continue to function on a temporary basis. Simultaneously, the *Storting* was to ask King Oscar II to select a prince of the Swedish royal family to become Norway's new king. The purpose of this move was to make the dissolution of the union look like a less radical act than it in fact was and to make it possible for the Conservative Party to support the breakup. On 7 June 1905, Michelsen proposed to the *Storting* that because the cabinet had resigned subsequent to King Oscar II's refusal to sign the consular service bill and because the king had proved incapable of supplying the country with a new cabinet, King Oscar II had in essence stopped functioning as the king of Norway. The union with Sweden, which the Norwegians regarded solely as a personal union, was thus dissolved. The *Storting* was to formally transfer to the (now former) cabinet the authority that was vested in the king by Norway's constitution and laws. The proposal was accepted unanimously by the *Storting*, which then voted to ask for a Swedish prince to serve as king.

The Swedish parliament met in an extraordinary session on 21 June 1905, and King Oscar II expressed his dismay at Norway's unilateral decision. He discouraged the use of military power, however, and the Swedish government expressed its desire to find terms of dissolution that would prevent hostilities. Certain segments of the Swedish population, on the other hand, wanted Sweden to respond forcefully, but other groups, for example, the socialists, were vocal in their demand for reason and peace. The Swedes did, however, demand that Norway conduct a referendum on the dissolution, and the result was overwhelmingly in favor; less than 200 people voted against. The Swedish government also insisted that the union was not just a personal one but a real one and that the Swedish parliament needed to abolish the Union Law before the dissolution would be official. During the negotiations conducted in the Swedish town of Karlstad in September 1905, Norway agreed to tear down most of its forts along the border, and the agreement was signed on 23 September 1905. The Swedish parliament voted to rescind the Union Law, and King Oscar II formally relinquished the Norwegian throne. The dissolution of the union was official. The **Danish** prince Carl was offered the throne of Norway; he accepted on the condition that a referendum would be held concerning the matter and became the new king of Norway under the name **Haakon VII**.

**DØRUM, ODD EINAR (1943– ).** Norwegian politician. Born to Odd Werge Dørum and Edith Donner on 12 October 1943, Dørum first lived in a middle-class home in **Oslo** and then in **Bergen** and **Trondheim**, where he attended secondary school and later studied history at the university. As a youth, he was exposed to the ideas of the **Liberal Party**, enthusiastically participated in its youth organization, and gradually rose through the party ranks. He was also trained as a social worker while simultaneously serving on the Trondheim City Council. He has since taught social work at the college level as well as worked as a consultant in this field. He served as the leader of the Liberal Party from 1982 to 1986 and 1992 to 1996. He was first elected a member of the *Storting* (**Parliament**) in 1977, serving until 1981, and was elected a second time in 1997 and again in 2001 and 2005. He was minister of transport and communications in a coalition government headed by **Kjell Magne Bondevik** from 1997 to 1999, when he became Bondevik's minister of justice, serving until 2000. He also served as minister of justice in Bondevik's second government from 2001 to 2005. Dørum is noted for his participation in the Mardøla protest, where a group of **environmentalists** tried to stop a **hydroelectric** project and in which he was arrested for civil disobedience along with the philosopher **Arne Næss** and others.

**"DRAUMKVEDET."** The greatest of the Norwegian ballads collected during the heyday of the **national romanticism**, "Draumkvedet" (the Dream Ballad) is an example of both the traditional ballad and medieval visionary **literature**. Recorded mostly in the county of Telemark starting in the late 1830s, it exists in a number of reasonably complete variants. Telling about a young man named Olav who falls asleep on Christmas Eve not to awaken until the 13th day of Christmas, the ballad gives details of the journey of his soul through the afterlife, where it observes the condition of both the righteous and the wicked. The need to show charity in this life if one's soul is to escape torment after death is the most important theme of the ballad. For example, those who have cared for the poor will be given shoes by the Virgin Mary as protection against brambles, those who have given grain to the poor will not have to face ferocious bulls while crossing the bridge into the afterlife, and those who have given bread to the poor will themselves be provided for. Rather than being an expression of an Old Testament ethics of retribution and reward, however, the ballad emphasizes the idea of grace found in the New Testament. As Olav, as well as the listener or reader, watch while Michael the Archangel weighs the souls of the dead, adding grace where needed to qualify them for salvation, it becomes clear that the ballad's message is primarily one of healing and reconciliation.

**DUNKER, CARL CHRISTIAN HENRIK BERNHARD (1809–70).** Norwegian lawyer. Born in Germany in 1809 to Wilhelm and Conradine Dunker, née Hansteen, Dunker earned a law degree at the university in Christiania (now **Oslo**) in 1834. He belonged to the circle around **Johan Sebastian Welhaven** and **Anton Martin Schweigaard**, favored the union between Norway and **Sweden**, and opposed expanding such democratic institutions as trial by **jury**. Later in his life, his social and political views became more liberal, and he promoted the **dissolution of the union with Sweden**.

– E –

**ECONOMY.** With a combination of free market capitalism and government involvement, the Norwegian economy is in exceptionally good health. Endowed with plentiful natural resources, including **hydroelectric power**, **fish**, farm and forest land, minerals that can be **mined**, and **oil and natural gas**, Norway has sustained high levels of employment, a favorable balance of **trade**, and a high per capita gross domestic product (GDP).

According to the *CIA World Factbook*, the Norwegian GDP for 2006 was estimated at $264.4 billion, which translates into a per capita GDP of $46,300. The GDP real-growth rate was a satisfying 4.6 percent. With a labor force of 2.42 million workers, the unemployment rate was a scant 3.5 percent, well below what most economists consider full employment. In spite of such indicators of a high level of economic activity, the rate of inflation was kept at 2.6 percent.

Almost three fourths of all Norwegian workers, or 74 percent, were employed in the service sector, which accounts for 56.3 percent of the GDP. **Industry** employed 22 percent of the workforce and accounted for 41.4 percent of the GDP, while the corresponding numbers for the **agricultural** sector were 4 percent of the labor force and 2.3 percent of the GDP. The industrial production growth rate was 1.8 percent. Coupled with Norway's very high investment rate of 19.1 percent of GDP, such numbers presage a healthy economy for years to come, and it is no wonder that the **Organization for Economic Cooperation and Development** (OECD) tends to be complimentary of Norway in its annual economic assessments.

The Norwegian economy is nevertheless not without its weaknesses. The effective retirement age for Norwegian workers is below 60 years of age, and the OECD has pointed out that it is desirable to increase this number. Also, the economy is heavily dependent on oil and natural gas, which account for one third of all Norwegian exports. Norway is thus highly sensitive to international petroleum prices. The health of the oil and gas sector is still very good, though, for gas production is rising even though the output of oil peaked in 2000. Norway has also squirreled away a large amount of its excess oil and gas revenues in a pension fund, the value of which is above $250 billion. With proven oil reserves of 8.5 billion barrels and natural gas reserves of 2.085 trillion cubic meters, Norwegians have every reason to trust that the fund will continue to grow.

In 2006, public revenues stood at $195.8 billion, while expenditures, including capital expenditures, were $133.1 billion. The public debt was 44.8 percent of the GDP, and the external debt was $350.3 billion; however, Norway is a net external creditor. Norway's foreign exchange and gold reserves were $49.62 billion.

In addition to the oil and gas sector, hydroelectric power is very significant to Norway's economy. In 2004, 108.9 billion kilowatt hours of total power were generated, and 99.3 percent of it was hydropower. Norway is nevertheless a net importer of electric power, as its consumption stood at 112.8 billion kilowatt hours. The Norwegian **shipping** fleet remains significant; in 2001, it counted for 4.3 percent of the gross tonnage of the world fleet. Norwegians also regard **whaling** to be of economic significance, especially to the coastal population. *See also* EUROPEAN INTEGRATION; WILLOCH, KÅRE.

**EDUCATION.** In pre-Christian Norway, what little education there was took place in the home. If the parents knew how to read and write, they would pass these skills on to their children if they were able. After the coming of Christianity, those who entered the priesthood would have an opportunity for some learning and perhaps especially those who were intellectually gifted. During the High Middle Ages, cathedral schools were started in some of the most important population centers: Nidaros (now **Trondheim**) in 1152, **Oslo** (later known as Christiania and still later again known as Oslo) in 1153, **Bergen** in c. 1153, Hamar in 1153, and **Stavanger** in 1260. These schools originally had as their chief mission to prepare their students for the priesthood. Three of them—those in Bergen, Trondheim, and Hamar—were founded by Nicolaus Breakspeare, later Pope Hadrian IV, when he visited Norway on behalf of the pope in 1152–53.

The **Black Death**, striking Norway in 1349, affected all aspects of life in the country, including education. A large part of the educated portion of the population died, including much of the medieval Norwegian nobility. When the **Reformation** took place starting in 1536, some education could still be had at the cathedral schools, but most people had to make do with whatever scant private instruction was available.

In the 1500s, the cathedral school in Bergen was the most important one in the country, and for a time, it had on its faculty a very talented lecturer, Absalon Pederssøn Beyer (1528–75), who had studied in Copenhagen and Wittenberg. Other Norwegian theologians had studied in Rostock or Cologne, but they were exceptions to the rule. Not even the great humanist Peder Claussøn Friis

(1545–1614), who taught at the cathedral school in Stavanger, ever traveled outside the country.

The most important event in the early history of education in Norway was the Reformation. Lutheranism emphasizes the individual's personal relationship to deity, and reading the Bible and other goodly books is considered essential to developing one's relationship to God, thereby securing one's salvation. The Lutheran ministers were made responsible for seeing to it that young people were taught the fundamental truths of the church before they were allowed to go to communion. Motivated by the **pietism** of the early 1700s, confirmation was introduced in 1736. Two laws about education, given in 1739 and 1741, established usually ambulatory schools in every parish, and both the financing and the control of these schools were local. Even though the local people were often opposed to the time and expenses associated with the schools, there was some progress throughout the following decades. Poor children benefited more than those from a more prosperous background, as their opportunity to learn to read and write was no longer a function of whether their parents could afford to provide them with instruction.

The principles enshrined in the laws of 1739 and 1741—children had a duty to attend school, and the community was obligated to provide it—continued in force after the union between Norway and **Denmark** came to an end in 1814. A new elementary school law was passed in 1827, but the school was still ambulatory, there were few school days per year, and the teachers were poorly paid and prepared. There was an improvement in the later 1830s, when teacher training courses were instituted. The biggest problem was where to get the money for the schools.

As the modernization of social and **economic** life in Norway accelerated after 1850, there was a widely shared understanding that the system of primary education needed to be improved. In 1848, a law about primary schools in the cities was passed, and a corresponding law for the rural areas took effect in 1860. While reading, writing, and **religion** had been the traditional elementary school subjects, the subject coverage was now increased. The school should not normally be ambulatory, so school houses were to be built. Some state funds could be used, but local funds were still predominant. The philologist

Ole Hartvig Nissen (1815–74) and Grundtvigian Ole Vig (1824–57) were driving forces behind these improvements.

There was also a modernization of the old Latin school, which had traditionally been used to prepare the sons of the ***embedsmann*** (public official) class for university studies and careers in the state administration. A law passed in 1869 established a system where students attended middle school from ages 9 to 15, followed by *Gymnasium* (High School) for another three years. There were two tracks, one that emphasized the study of Latin all the way through and one that emphasized the study of English on the middle-school level, followed by mathematics and science in high school. Both of the tracks qualified a person for study at the university. Folk high schools established according to religious ideas or, as in the case of **Christopher Bruun**, Grundtvigian principles, provided additional education but did not lead to higher education. This was also the case with the so-called *amtsskoler* (county schools).

The next series of significant school reforms were instituted after the **Liberal Party** had gained control of the government by instituting the beginnings of **parliamentarism** in 1884. Laws relating to both urban and rural schools were passed in 1889, and the basic principle was that children from the different social classes should all attend the same schools together. Elementary school was divided into two grades, for younger and older children, respectively, and was to be suitable preparation for secondary school, which again was to prepare the students for university study. Such additional subjects as history, geography, and natural science became mandatory, while drawing, woodworking, and physical education were considered desirable. Elected local government representatives were to choose the members of the school boards.

The secondary school system was further reformed through legislation passed in 1896 and 1920. Latin was no longer to be taught in middle school, while such subjects as Norwegian, German, English, and practical mathematics were given increased attention. This made the middle school a suitable basis for various practically oriented educational programs, including vocational schools. With the exception of a few high schools aimed at future theologians, Latin was excluded from the preparation for university study. Also in 1920, the high school part of secondary education was expanded by a year. The educational structure was further refined in the 1930s. A seven-year elementary school was to be followed by either a three-year middle school that prepared students for further vocational training or a five-year curriculum of university preparation; however, the first two years were identical in the two sequences. The elementary school curriculum was strengthened, but the school year was still shorter in rural areas than in the cities, where English was introduced as a subject in elementary school. On all levels, competition among the students became increasingly fierce.

The next big step forward came in 1959, when a nine-year elementary school was made elective, and in 1969, when it was made mandatory. A law that took effect in 1974 gave all youth the right to three years of further schooling in a program of their choice, be it vocational or preparatory for university studies. There was a general sense in the country that investments in education were both worthwhile and necessary. While the **Labor Party** governments tended to view public education as a way to promote social equality, the nonsocialist parties saw it as a way to promote economic development and supply business and **industry** with an effective and reliable workforce.

Higher education in Norway also made giant strides forward throughout the 20th century. The Royal Frederik's University had been established in Christiania (now **Oslo**) in 1811 (it changed its name to the University of Oslo in 1939). While theology and law had been its major subject areas, the growth in Norwegian secondary education, as well as the departure from the study of the classics, meant that there was an increasing demand for graduates in foreign languages, natural sciences, and social studies. There was also a significant growth in the study of medicine, as the national health care delivery system was being strengthened. Higher education in the areas of **agriculture**, engineering, and teacher training were being made available in specialized institutes outside of the university.

Norway's second university was established in Bergen in 1946, with the scientific milieu at Bergen's Museum as its nucleus. In 1968, a university in Trondheim was established when its already-existing polytechnic graduate school was combined with a graduate teacher training academy. The same year, a university was established in **Tromsø**. Norway's fifth university, located in Stavanger, came into existence on 1 January 2005, based on an already-existing university college. The same year, Norway's graduate agricultural college was given university status. Finally, the University of Agder was created on 10 August 2007, when an existing university college, located in Kristiansand, was given university status.

The beginning of the regional university colleges dates to 1969, when an attempt was made to reduce the pressure on the universities by establishing smaller and less expensive additional institutions that would offer coverage of the most common subjects. Later, traditional normal schools were expanded to offer instruction in additional subject areas and given the status of university colleges. The result is that there is now in place a quite well-established mechanism whereby additional universities can be created. When a university college has grown to the point that a certain number of stable doctoral programs has been established, the institution may be changed into a university. This is, in fact, what happened when the previously existing Stavanger University College became the University of Stavanger in 2005 and when the University of Agder was created in 2007. Other likely candidates for this kind of institutional promotion are the current university colleges in Bø, Hamar, and Bodø. Supple and flexible, the higher education system in Norway rests on a solid foundation of elementary and secondary education and is well equipped to provide for the country's educational needs. Other specialized schools continue to offer instruction in a wide variety of subject areas.

**EGEDE, HANS (1686–1758).** Norwegian missionary to the native Greenlanders. Born at the Harstad farm in Hinnøy in northern Norway on 31 January 1686, Egede served as a State Church minister in the district of Lofoten from 1707 to 1718. Fascinated with the history of Old Norse settlements in Greenland, he contacted the bishop of **Bergen**, who had ecclesiastical jurisdiction over Greenland, about traveling there in order to convert the Norsemen possibly still living there from Roman Catholicism to the Lutheran faith. Nothing came of this suggestion, but in 1717, Egede resigned from his living and, with the permission of King Frederik IV, traveled with his family to

Greenland in 1721. Founding the colony Godthaab (now Nuuk), he started missionary work among the Inuit, remaining in Greenland for 15 years. Although he found no surviving Norsemen, he gathered much valuable information both about the **language** and culture of the natives and about the local geography and natural history. He was named bishop of Greenland in 1740.

**EIRIK BLOODAXE (c. 895–954).** Norwegian **Viking** king. The oldest son of King **Harald Fairhair**, Eirik most likely received his nickname from killing several of his brothers. He also went on Viking raids in northern Russia, sailing down the northern Dvina River. He married Gunhild, daughter of the **Danish** king Gorm the Old and who has a reputation in the sagas for being a very powerful witch. Eirik was driven out of Norway in 934, when his youngest brother Haakon, who had been raised in England, organized the Norwegian chieftains in opposition to the very harsh Eirik. Eirik fled to Orkney Island, later settling in York in England, where he was to defend Northumbria against the marauding Scots and Irish on behalf of King Athelstan. Eirik was seemingly unable get along with anybody, however, and he was betrayed and killed in 954.

*EMBEDSMANN.* Essentially a public official, an *embedsmann* is a person who occupies a position to which he or she has been appointed by the king in one of his regular meetings with the cabinet. Such an appointee can only be fired by court order and is thus free to speak and act without fear of reprisals. Owing to the memory of royal abuses during the period of **absolute monarchy** in **Denmark** and Norway—for example, *Kongeloven* (the Royal Law) of 1665 was kept secret until 1709—the *embedsmann* was given considerable protection by the Norwegian **constitution**. Many of Norway's political leaders in the 1800s and early 1900s belonged to this class of people, who included government officials, State Church ministers, and professors. As a group, this segment of the population had interests in common with large landowners and businessmen. Their families tended to intermarry, they were usually conservative, and they jealously guarded their social position. Until the introduction of **parliamentarism** (1884), their political influence was grossly out of proportion to their numbers.

**EMIGRATION FROM NORWAY TO AMERICA.** Prior to 1825, only a few individual Norwegians traveled to America. One of them was a man from Tysvær parish in southwestern Norway named Klein Pedersen Hesthammer, who was later to be known as Cleng Peerson (1783–1865) and who was associated with a group of Quakers in **Stavanger**. Acting as their scout, he secured land for them in Kendall, New York, and then went back to Norway, only to lead a group of 52 emigrants, who left Stavanger on 4 July 1825, to New York City onboard the sloop *Restaurationen*. They settled in upstate New York but later moved west, establishing a settlement in the Fox River Valley southwest of Chicago, Illinois. They appear to have been motivated by a desire for greater **religious** freedom than what they were granted by the form of religion practiced in Norway at the time.

Additional emigrants followed the Sloopers, as they are called, particularly after the middle of the 1830s. Early Norwegian emigration statistics are incomplete, but it is generally believed that approximately 15,000 Norwegians emigrated prior to 1850. By 1893, roughly 500,000 people had emigrated, which is approximately one fourth of Norway's population in 1875, when a nationwide census was taken. By 1915, about 250,000 more had made the journey.

Traveling to America was expensive, especially in the beginning of the period of emigration, so the very poor did not leave. As the Norwegian immigrant population in the **United States** grew, there was a flow of both information and money going back to the old country. An American relative would provide a ticket that the emigrant would work for after his or her arrival.

Norwegian immigrants settled mostly in the Midwest, although Cleng Peerson himself spent the last years of his life in Bosque County, Texas. They worked on farms or in logging and settled in such cities as Chicago and Minneapolis. Many of them acquired farms under the Homestead Act, and others became newspaper men, preachers, or educators. Shortly before and after 1900, many of them traveled to the West Coast, particularly Seattle, Washington. Many of these immigrants worked in **fishing**.

After **World War I**, the Norwegian emigration to America slowed to a trickle, and the descendants of earlier immigrants gradually became assimilated. Many of these second-, third-, and fourth-generation immigrants still remember their Norwegian roots, however. Some of them learn a bit of Norwegian, research their family history, belong to Norwegian American cultural or fraternal organizations, visit Norway occasionally, and enjoy various dishes associated with the old country.

**ENGELBREKTSSON, OLAV (c. 1480–1538).** Norwegian archbishop. After studies at the university in Rostock, Engelbrektsson came to Norway in 1515 and became dean of the priests associated with the cathedral in Nidaros (now **Trondheim**). He was chosen archbishop in 1523, at a time when the **Reformation** had already started in northern Europe. In this position, he was also the head of the Norwegian council of the realm, and he saw it as his task to preserve both the Norwegian independence provided for within the **Kalmar Union** and to protect the Roman Catholic Church against loss of position and property. In 1525, he built a fortress at Steinvikholmen in the Trondheim fjord, but it was militarily obsolete by the time it was completed. Engelbrektsson was strongly opposed to **Christian III**, who believed in Lutheranism, had become the king of **Denmark** in 1534, and was the choice of the Danish nobles as the king of Norway. As the head of Norway's council of the realm, he wanted a king who would consent to the same terms as the previous king, Frederik I (1471–1533), who had agreed that only Norwegian-born individuals were to command fortresses and receive high administrative appointments in Norway. Engelbrektsson, therefore, conspired with Christian III's enemies and arranged for the killing of Christian III's representative Vincents Lunge (c. 1486–1536), who acted for Christian III during negotiations conducted in Nidaros at the end of 1535. He had hoped for a popular rebellion against Christian III, but this rebellion did not come to pass, and Engelbrektsson had to flee Norway for the low countries, where he died.

**ENVIRONMENT.** Norwegians have traditionally been very close to nature, which played a major role in the nation-building project of the 19th century through the ideology of the **national romanticism**. Often avid skiers, fishermen, or hunters, Norwegians tend to agree that the natural environment should be preserved and restored through the conservation of natural resources and actions aimed at preventing or reducing pollution. In 1972, Norway became the first country in the world to establish a cabinet-level appointment in environmental protection when the botanist Olav Gjærevoll (1916–94) was named minister of the environment.

Environmental activism has often been linked to the causes of indigenous peoples. Norway's **Sámi** population has fought valiantly for control of its traditional lands and waters, some of which were restored to them through the Finnmark Act passed by the *Storting* (**Parliament**) in 2005. The spirit of this law represents a significant departure from the way the Sámi population of Finnmark County was treated as recently as the 1970s and the early 1980s, when the Norwegian authorities pushed through a **hydroelectric** project in the Alta River against the wishes of 10,000 demonstrators.

Another major environmental battle took place at Mardøla in Møre and Romsdal County in 1970, when civil disobedience was used to prevent hydroelectric development of a scenic river and waterfall. One of those arrested was the philosopher **Arne Næss**, who is known as one of the most significant theoreticians behind the environmental movement not only in Norway but throughout the world. His concept of "deep ecology" entails that all species have a right to continue their existence and that human beings should be considered on a par with other living things.

Norway has a number of environmental organizations. The oldest one, the *Norges Naturvernforbund* (Friends of the Earth Norway), was founded in 1914 and is moderate in its approach by promoting a healthy balance between human activities and the need for environmental protection. The *Norges Miljøvernforbund* (Green Warriors of Norway), on the other hand, was established as recently as 1993 and takes a more radical tack; for example, it warns against the dangers of wi-fi networks and cell phones. The *Bellona*, established in 1986 and with a long record of direct action against "environmental criminals," a concept it pioneered and succeeded in having written into Norwegian law, has a strongly scientific and interdisciplinary approach to environmental protection.

The political parties of Norway vary greatly in their attitude toward environmental protection, although all of the major parties state that they are in favor of the concept. The **Progress Party** claims to have a commitment to reasonable environmental protection but is very conscious of its costs. The **Conservative Party** finds that environmental protection is necessary but believes that it can be done without significantly affecting established patterns of consumption. The **Christian Democratic Party** is willing to make significant **economic** sacrifices in order to preserve the earth, which is viewed as a divine creation. The **Center Party** has environmental protection as one of the major planks in its platform. The **Liberal Party** has a strong proenvironmentalist stance and a long record of supporting environmental causes. The **Labor Party** is in principle in favor of environmental protection but would like to balance the needs of the environment against those of working men and **women**. The **Socialist Left Party** wants Norway to be a pioneer in environmental protection and to set an example for the rest of the nations of the earth.

Norwegian politicians can be counted on to hew close to the party line with regard to the environment, and specific disagreements usually come to the fore only when concrete issues are being discussed. For example, all major parties are in favor of maintaining a reasonable population of such large predatory animals as bears and wolves, but disagreements tend to surface when it is a question of how to practically manage their populations, especially vis-à-vis the farm animals on which they prey. *See also* DØRUM, ODD EINAR (1943– ).

**EUROPEAN COMMUNITY (EC).** *See* EUROPEAN ECONOMIC COMMUNITY (EEC).

**EUROPEAN ECONOMIC AREA (EEA).** The EEA is the result of an agreement between the **European Union** (EU) and the **European Free Trade Association** (EFTA) that makes three of the remaining four members, Iceland, Norway, and Lichtenstein, full participants in the EU single market without having to join the EU. The single market program was first established in 1986 for the purpose of removing barriers to the free movement of goods, services, capital, and labor among its participants, while the Maastricht treaty, which in 1992 established the EU, formally made the European Community (*see* EUROPEAN ECONOMIC COMMUNITY [EEC]) a single market. The agreement creating the EEA was signed on 2 May 1992 and ratified by the Norwegian *Storting* (**Parliament**) on 16 October 1992. It formally went into effect on 1 January 1994. The EEA agreement entails some transfer of sovereignty to the EFTA Surveillance

Agency and the EFTA Court of Justice, which investigate and adjudicate claims that the EEA agreement may have been violated. Two Norwegian political parties, the **Center Party** and the **Socialist Left Party**, opposed Norwegian EEA membership, partly because of a concern about loss of sovereignty. The EEA agreement was renegotiated prior to the addition of 10 new EU new member countries in 2004, and the *Storting* overwhelmingly approved it on 29 January 2004. *See also* EUROPEAN INTEGRATION; TRADE.

**EUROPEAN ECONOMIC COMMUNITY (EEC).** The EEC was the first name for a **trade** organization that resulted from the Treaty of Rome in 1957 and has since developed into the **European Community** in 1967 and then the **European Union**. It was preceded by the European Coal and Steel Community, established by the Treaty of Paris in 1951 and in which the future EEC states created a common market for their coal and steel. In 1972, after a bitter political struggle that preceded the referendum of 25 September, Norway chose not to join the community. *See also* EUROPEAN INTEGRATION.

**EUROPEAN FREE TRADE ASSOCIATION (EFTA).** The EFTA was organized in Stockholm, **Sweden**, in 1960. Founded by Great Britain, **Denmark**, Norway, Sweden, Austria, Switzerland, and Portugal, it later was joined by several other states, including Finland, Iceland, and Lichtenstein. *See also* EUROPEAN INTEGRATION; TRADE.

**EUROPEAN INTEGRATION.** Norway has always been dependent on free international **trade**, and its most important trading partners have been other European countries, including the rest of **Scandinavia**. For this reason, Norway joined the **General Agreement on Tariffs and Trade** in 1947, as well as the **Organization for European Economic Cooperation** (OEEC) in 1948 (the OEEC became the **Organization for Economic Cooperation and Development** in 1961). When the Treaty of Rome was signed in 1957, creating what was then known as the **European Economic Community** (EEC), it meant that the EEC countries—France, West Germany, Italy, Belgium, the Netherlands, and Luxembourg—had entered into a trade alliance that excluded Norway but also that there was a possibility that the group of "the inner six," as they were sometimes called, or the common market, would be enlarged and perhaps include all of Europe. Norway's immediate need, however, was to protect its free trade interests in the face of the newly formed block, so Norway happily participated in the 1960 negotiations in Stockholm that led to the formation of the **European Free Trade Association** (EFTA). Consisting of seven countries, the EFTA's founders were Great Britain, **Denmark**, Norway, **Sweden**, Austria, Switzerland, and Portugal, which were sometimes referred to as "the outer seven." Most of the Norwegian parties, including the **Labor Party** and the **Conservative Party**, were hoping that the two trade blocks would unite into one association, and this wish was expressed as a plank in the platforms of both parties prior to the **parliamentary** election in 1961.

Norway considered EEC membership in 1962 and 1967, but the concern was what would happen to Norwegian farmers and fishermen if they had to compete with farmers who could grow food in more favorable climates and European **fishing** vessels with more advanced—and also more expensive—equipment. There was a split within the Labor Party concerning these issues as early as 1961. On the other hand, Labor Party policy was to transfer workers from less productive industries to more productive ones, thus increasing the Norwegian gross national product. This was important to Labor, which saw as its mission to make Norwegians materially better off and did not fully understand the significance of such intangible values as family roots and other long-term social relations. Those values were dispensable in Labor's quest for material progress.

When Britain, Ireland, and Denmark expressed an interest in joining the **European Community** (EC) in the early 1970s—the former EEC became known as the EC as of 1967—the Norwegian government entered into negotiations about possible Norwegian membership. The government had earlier made it clear that there would be no Norwegian membership in the EC unless the people as a whole, through a referendum, expressed its support. The purpose of its negotiations with the EC was to allow the people to know precisely what to expect if Norway were to become a member. Most Norwegian business leaders, newspaper editors, and **economic** experts had already made up their minds that it was essential to Norway's future welfare to join the EC.

The referendum was set for 25 September 1972, and for a period of about six months prior to this date, Norway experienced more political tension than ever before in the post–World War II era. The only parties that clearly opposed membership were the **Center Party** and the **Socialist People's Party**. Separate organizations opposing and promoting membership were formed, and the rhetoric of their exchanges was very heated. The opponents accused the proponents of wanting to sell Norway for money, and the proponents accused the opponents of being foolish and naïve. The vote went against joining, and it revealed some interesting divisions within the country. Northern Norway was strongly opposed, while **Oslo** and the surrounding area were strongly for EC membership. On a whole, the cities were in favor, while the rural areas were opposed. It is telling, however, that if the three northernmost counties had not been part of Norway, the rest of the country would have voted to join the EC in 1972.

After the referendum, there was general agreement that EC membership could not be placed on the public agenda for many years to come. When Britain, Ireland, and Denmark left the EFTA for the EC in 1973, however, there was an obvious need for some mechanism of cooperation between the EFTA and the EC. Negotiations resulted in an agreement between the EFTA, the EC, and the individual members of the EC (or **European Union** [EU] as it was called after the Maastricht treaty of 1992) that created the **European Economic Area** (EEA) on 2 May 1992, which the *Storting* (Parliament) ratified on 16 October 1992. The EEA agreement gave the EU significant influence over Norwegian policy decisions; however, it did not amount to a transfer of national sovereignty to the EU.

When the Norwegian Labor Party government led by **Gro Harlem Brundtland** decided to hold another referendum on Norwegian membership in the EU on 28 November 1994, the successful conclusion to the EEA negotiations was a major source of motivation. This second referendum is referred to as an *omkamp*, or rematch, indicating that the losing side in 1972 thought that it somehow deserved a second chance at winning. The timing of the referendum was very carefully chosen, for it was held shortly after both Finland and Sweden had voted to join the EU, but the arguments for and against were largely the same as in 1972, and the result was almost the same as well, essentially postponing another consideration of EU membership for quite some time.

In the meantime, European integration has been moving forward in spite of a few bumps in the road here and there, but the attitude of the Norwegians is still not entirely clear. Norway's remarkable **oil** wealth is perhaps the major reason it has been able to remain outside the EU this long. Only the future can tell if a sufficient number of Norwegians will change their minds so that the wishes of their economic and political leaders will be fulfilled. *See also* AGRICULTURE.

**EUROPEAN UNION (EU).** The EU was established by the Maastricht treaty of 1992. It grew out of the **European Economic Community** (EEC), which was created by the Treaty of Rome signed in 1957. The EEC, which subsequently became the European Community (EC) in 1967, was a trade organization consisting of France, West Germany, Italy, Belgium, the Netherlands, and Luxembourg. Often known as the common market, it was also called the "six" and later on the "inner six" as it began to expand. In 1958, President Charles de Gaulle of France refused to consider a British proposal that the EEC should be integrated into an extended European free trade area, and the **European Free Trade Association** (EFTA) was subsequently formed in Stockholm in 1960. Originally consisting of seven states, it was later expanded with additional members. Two EFTA countries, Great Britain and **Denmark**, joined the EC in 1973 (other EFTA countries joined later). Ireland joined the EC with Great Britain in 1973; Greece in 1981; Spain and Portugal in 1986; and Austria, Finland, and **Sweden** in 1995.

An additional 10 countries—Cyprus, Czech Republic, Estonia, Hungary, Latvia, Lithuania, Malta, Poland, Slovakia, and Slovenia— were admitted to the EU in 2004, as well as Bulgaria and Romania in 2007. Under the direction of the Norwegian government and with the strongest possible encouragement of Norwegian business interests, Norway sought to join in both 1972 and 1994, but on both occasions, the negative result of a referendum halted the process. *See also* EUROPEAN INTEGRATION.

**EVANG, KARL (1902–81).** Norwegian physician and health care administrator. The primary architect of the Norwegian public health system, Evang was born in Kristiania (now **Oslo**) on 19 October 1902. He held radical political views throughout his life and was a Communist in his youth. Later he became a member of the left wing of the Norwegian **Labor Party** and finally ended up in the **Socialist Left Party**. Led by the insight that doctors should treat not only individual patients but address illness and health from a social perspective as well, Evang tirelessly promoted the dissemination of health-related information, with a special emphasis on sex education. Motivated by his concern that working-class **women** were getting worn out by too many pregnancies, he championed family planning, even to the point of performing illegal abortions. As the head of the Norwegian Directorate of Health from its establishment in 1938 until his retirement in 1972, his influence on Norwegian health policy was profound and included an early emphasis on treatment rather than incarceration of drug addicts.

Evang's international service included participation in efforts during **World War II** that lead to the founding of the Food and **Agriculture** Organization of the **United Nations** in 1945. After the war, he was one of the founders of the World Health Organization.

– F –

**FALKBERGET, JOHAN (1879–1967).** Norwegian novelist. Born in Rugelsjøen near Røros on 30 September 1879, Falkberget spent much of his childhood and youth working in the copper **mines** at Røros. His numerous novels and stories are centered on the history of mining in the area, as well as the conflicts between the various segments of its population. A careful researcher, Falkberget created a body of **literature** that has both historical and artistic value.

Falkberget's first book of any significance was the novel *Svarte Fjelde* (1907; Black Mountains), which combines detailed descriptions of mining life with expressions of his love of the mountain landscape. Many other novels about hard-working people and their **economic** struggles—as well as their trials in various love relationships— followed, one of the more notable being *Lisbet paa Jarnfjeld* (1915; tr. *Lisbeth of Jarnfjeld*, 1930). His first truly significant novel, however, was *Den fjerde nattevakt* (1923; tr. *The Fourth Night Watch*, 1968), which is a novel centered on sin, guilt, and redemption. Its protagonist is the proud and ambitious minister Benjamin Sigismund, who serves as the Røros community's pastor early in the 19th century.

Two multivolume series of novels, both of them dealing with mining life, are considered Falkberget's greatest achievement. *Christianus Sextus* (1927–35), in six volumes, gets its title from a copper mine that is the unifying element in an otherwise episodic narrative. *Nattens brød* (1940–59; Bread of the Night), in four volumes, is centered on An-Magritt, a strong-willed **woman** of the people who leads a life of suffering and toil.

**FALSEN, CHRISTIAN MAGNUS (1782–1830).** Norwegian statesman. Born to Enevold de Falsen (1744–1808) in Christiania (now **Oslo**) on 14 September 1782, Falsen studied law and then served as a circuit judge. Elected to the **constitutional** assembly held at Eidsvoll in 1814, Falsen brought with him a proposed constitution modeled on the French constitution adopted in 1791. He chaired the constitution committee starting on 12 April 1814 and at times also chaired the assembly itself. Known as the father of the constitution, Falsen was the leader of the faction that wanted complete independence rather than a union with **Sweden**. When Falsen was elected to the *Storting* (**Parliament**) in 1821, however, he wanted to change the constitution so as to reduce the growing influence of the farmers in Norwegian political life, thus protecting the interests of the *embedsmann* (public official) class, to which he belonged. Falsen served as *amtmann* (district governor) in western Norway starting in 1814 and as the country's attorney general from 1822 to 1825, when he became prefect in **Bergen** and was named head of Norway's Supreme Court in 1827; however, illness prevented him from serving.

**FEUDALISM.** A somewhat controversial concept among modern historians, feudalism as a means of social organization during medieval times presupposes the existence of lords, vassals, and fiefs. In return for military service or other types of aid, a lord provides a fief to a vassal, who swears allegiance to the lord. Vassals may then in turn act as lords to a lower level of vassals who are given smaller fiefs.

This system of organization and government was not well suited to conditions in Norway. During the **Viking** period, Norwegian society had a strong tradition of equality, as kings and other leaders were largely elected and sustained by the consent of those whom they led. The practice was contrary to the ideas of the church; for example, the church quite consistently pressed for a system of royal succession that honored the principles of legitimacy and primogeniture, with the king's oldest son being the automatic heir to the throne.

Some elements of feudalism can be detected in the **Danish** state administration from the High Middle Ages down to the early modern period. Terms like *len* (fief), *lensherre* (lord of the fief), and *lensmann* (fiefman; vassal) were used. A *len* could be given by the crown on the condition that military service was rendered in return, it could be given in exchange for a specific annual payment, or the recipient could be responsible for rendering a financial accounting, being able to cover his expenses but also being obligated to turn over whatever profit was left from the management of the *len*. Those who held a *len* were responsible for collecting the rents and fixed taxes owed to the crown as well as duties and fines. These forms of income were collected in kind as well as in money, so the holder of a *len* would ideally be a gifted manager. The system came to an end in the 1550s, when royal appointees were allowed to keep only a certain amount of their collections to cover expenditures and as wages for themselves.

**FISHING.** Norway's earliest coastal population made fishing a part of its livelihood as early as shortly after the Pleistocene, and coastal Norwegians have fished pretty much continuously ever since. The **trade** in fish and such fish products as fish oil and cod roe took off during the medieval period, however, when the **Hanseatic League**, through its trading station in **Bergen**, exported stockfish throughout Europe. When the power of the Hansa traders declined in early modernity, Norwegian merchants based in Bergen gradually gained control of this trade.

Stockfish was cod that had been caught with hand lines, long line, or nets, both during the great winter fisheries in the Lofoten area and elsewhere along the coast; dried during the cold part of the year, when flies would not infest it with maggots; and freighted to Bergen onboard locally owned and generally small vessels. Some of the cod was also salted before it was dried. Herring was another major product; it was cured with salt and transported by the barrel. Herring was caught with gill nets and seines, which were strung across shallow bays or inlets, preventing the herring from escaping. The 1860s and 1880s were especially good years for the herring fisheries. The purse seine was not used in Norway until the 1890s, when it became possible to catch herring with a seine far from land. Driftnets had earlier been used for this purpose, however.

Until the latter part of the 1800s, fishing was done with open square-rigged boats that were rowed when there was no favorable wind. As the steam engine was developed, however, larger and more capital-intensive vessels were used, and the availability of the internal combustion engine gradually caused the entire fishing fleet to become motorized. A vivid portrait of the Lofoten cod fisheries, including the early use of motorized vessels, is given in **Johan Bojer**'s novel *Den siste viking* (1921; tr. *Last of the Vikings*, 1923). Costly fishing boats and equipment were a significant threat to most coastal fishermen, who could not afford them.

After **World War II**, there was rapid technological change in the Norwegian fishing **industry**. Such vessels as deep-sea factory trawlers and large purse-seine boats with power blocks (*kraftblokk*) rather than dories made fishing so efficient that the stocks were seriously threatened. They also enabled Norwegian fishermen to increasingly fish in international waters. As the industry was further capitalized, the number of coastal fishermen decreased, however, and many formerly vibrant fishing communities experienced a significant loss of population. In the 1980s and 1990s, fishing quotas and licenses were introduced to prevent overfishing, and although most Norwegian vessels obeyed the regulations, others did not always do so, and the Norwegian Coast Guard has had to impound vessels and catches to bring about compliance with national and international regulations. *See also* ECONOMY.

**FLAG.** Medieval Norwegian rulers used a variety of symbols, including an eagle and a lion holding an ax. The latter is now displayed on the Royal Standard of Norway and is similar to the lion found on Norway's coat of arms. National flags as such did not exist, and when they came into use around 1500, Norwegians used the **Danish** flag. During the brief period of Norwegian independence in 1814, a Danish flag with the lion from the coat of arms in the upper left field, next to the hoist, was introduced. After the union with **Sweden** became official, however, the Swedish flag was used, with a white cross against a red background in the upper left field as the military flag and the merchant flag used in distant waters.

The current Norwegian flag was designed by Fredrik Meltzer (1779–1855), a member of the *Storting* (**Parliament**), and adopted by the *Storting* on 21 July 1821. According to **Scandinavian** tradition, it featured a Christian cross, but Melzer also used the colors red, white, and blue to signify democracy (please refer to the flag on the cover of this volume). The colors red and white maintained the connection with the Danish flag, while the color blue was found on the flag of Sweden. For **constitutional** reasons, it could not be used in military contexts.

In 1844, both Norway and Sweden introduced flags that combined the respective national flags with a union badge consisting of the Norwegian and Swedish colors. Placed next to the hoist, the badge was nicknamed "the herring salad." This flag, which emphasized the equality of the two countries within the union, was initially well liked in Norway. But in 1898, when the union had become very unpopular, the *Storting* removed the union badge from the Norwegian merchant flag, although it remained on the military flag. The union badge was completely removed following the **dissolution of the union** between Norway and Sweden in 1905.

**FLØGSTAD, KJARTAN (1944– ).** Norwegian novelist, poet, and short-story writer. Fløgstad was born on 7 June 1944 in the **industrial** town of Sauda in Rogaland County and is the most significant postmodernist in Norwegian **literature**. His first two published books were poetry collections, but he soon found his narrative voice. Writing in **nynorsk** (New Norwegian), Fløgstad's books were written to be read by common people and were not just for specialists in literature.

Fløgstad's first postmodern work, the novel *Dalen Portland* (1977; tr. *Dollar Road*, 1989), became his definitive literary breakthrough and also garnered him the Nordic Literary Prize. The book mixes features of popular literature with the conventions of belles lettres, intermingles old-fashioned literary conventions with modernist ones, alternates segments of realistic narration with outlandish fantasy, and tells its story of industrialization in western Norway through a veritable chorus of sometimes competing voices. Many other novels, set in the fictional industrial community Lovra, deal with similar themes, for example, *Fyr og flamme* (1980; Fire and Flame) and *Kniven på strupen* (1991; The Knife to the Throat). The latter offers a portrait of life under late capitalism, when factory workers have mostly been replaced by machines and the traditional work ethic of the people has given way to greed and crime. Fløgstad returned to the industrial heritage of Lovra/Sauda in *Grand Manila* (2006).

**FOLKEPARTIET NYE VENSTRE.** *See* NEW LEFT PEOPLE'S PARTY.

**FOYN, SVEND (1809–94).** Norwegian **whaling** pioneer. Born in Tønsberg on 9 July 1809, Foyn started out as a seal hunter but made a name for himself in the whaling **industry**. Hunting large whales off the coast of Finnmark in the 1860s, he perfected the harpoon cannon, which shot a harpoon attached to a line and caused a grenade to penetrate into the body of the whale, where it exploded. Foyn's invention, patented in 1870, enabled the development of large-scale whaling in the open sea, made Norway the foremost whaling nation on earth, and created tremendous wealth for his home district, particularly the towns of Tønsberg and Sandefjord.

**FREETHINKER.** The word *fritenker* (freethinker), borrowed from English, was a term of abuse popular with Norwegian conservatives during the turbulent 1870s and 1880s, particularly with reference to those who questioned the doctrines and dogmas of received **religion**. It was often treated as synonymous with *vantro* (unbeliever/unbelieving) and had a political as well as a religious aspect, as some of the people on the Left who helped form the **Liberal Party** in 1883 objected to the use of religion as a means whereby socioeconomic power could be maintained or enhanced. The conservatives, in turn, associated freethinking (*fritenkeri*) with everything that they objected to in early modernity, be it government (**parliamentarism**), science (Darwinism), **literature** (**Bjørnson** and **Ibsen**), or society (feminism). The writer **Arne Garborg** has detailed the social and emotional force of the concept in his first significant literary effort, the short novel *Ein Fritenkjar* (1878; A

Freethinker), in which he shows what kind of prejudice meets a sincere individual who wants to build his personal worldview on reason rather than dogma. By 1900, there were several freethinker associations in Norway, first and foremost the *Fritænkerklubben* (Freethinker Club) in **Bergen**.

*FREMSKRITTSPARTIET. See* PROGRESS PARTY.

*FRISINNEDE VENSTRE. See* LIBERAL LEFT PARTY.

**FRYDENLUND, KNUT (1927–87).** Norwegian politician. Born in Drammen on 31 March 1927, Frydenlund studied law at the University of **Oslo**, from which he received his degree in 1950. In 1952, he entered the Norwegian Foreign Service and had several significant assignments. He also served as the personal secretary of **Halvard Lange**, the long-serving minister of foreign affairs. Elected a member of the *Storting* (**Parliament**) on the **Labor Party** ticket in 1969, Frydenlund was chosen by Prime Minister **Trygve Bratteli** to serve as the minister of foreign affairs in 1973, continuing until 1981, and served under **Odvar Nordli** and in **Gro Harlem Brundtland**'s first government as well. He also served as minister of foreign affairs in Brundtland's second government, from 1986 until his death. Frydenlund thus had a rare opportunity to contribute to the shaping of Norwegian foreign policy, including the security policy, which at times was at variance with the interests of the **United States**, particularly under Republican administrations. Frydenlund was also strongly in favor of Norwegian membership in the European Community (*see* EUROPEAN ECONOMIC COMMUNITY [EEC]) and was a particularly vocal supporter of the failed membership campaign that culminated in the 1972 referendum. His views of Norway's place in the international community were expressed in numerous books and articles.

– G –

**GARBORG, ARNE (1851–1924).** Norwegian novelist and poet. Born on 25 January 1851 in Time in the district of Jæren south of

**Stavanger** as the oldest son and thus the allodial heir to Eivind Aadneson, Garborg grew up with an extreme form of rural **religious pietism** that long soured him on both religion and rural life. After leaving home in order to become a teacher, he learned at the age of 18 that his father had committed suicide. This gave him deep and lasting feelings of guilt, for he feared that his own rejection of his ancestral farm had contributed to the depression that led to his father's death. After a period of teaching, Garborg went to **Oslo** in order to qualify for admission to the university; he reached this goal in 1875 with superior marks. Around the same time, he abandoned all traces of the conservative religiosity with which he had been raised, becoming increasingly radical in his thinking and writing. One aspect of that radicalism was his choice of **literary** medium; for most of his writing, he choose *Landsmaal* (later known as *nynorsk*, or New Norwegian) rather than the **Danish**-colored standard *Riksmaal* (later known as *bokmål*) of his day. Along with **Ivar Aasen** (1813–96) and **Aasmund Olafsson Vinje** (1818–70), Garborg is credited with creating the *nynorsk* literary tradition.

Garborg's first significant literary effort was the short novel *Ein Fritenkjar* (1878; A **Freethinker**), which details the prejudice that meets a sincere individual who wants to build his personal worldview on reason rather than dogma. During the 1880s, he produced a series of novels and stories in which he championed the progressive causes of his day. Particularly attuned to the experiences of rural youth who had come to the capital in search of higher **education**, he became well known for his novel *Bondestudentar* (1883; Peasant Students), which has been required reading for generations of Norwegian secondary school students. He also intervened in the so-called morality debate of the 1880s, offering a literary diagnosis of the relationship between **economics** and sexual expression both inside and outside of marriage. After his marriage to Hulda Bergersen (1862–1934) in 1887, he spent time in Germany, where he had faithful translators and a considerable audience. In the 1890s, Garborg increasingly turned his attention toward religious themes, which he treated with great insight. He also wrote poetry about the landscape and the people of Jæren in his childhood and youth.

Garborg is one of Norway's finest essayists and offers incisive commentary on the cultural and political issues of his day.

**GENERAL AGREEMENT ON TARIFFS AND TRADE (GATT).** GATT was created in 1947 in order to help the world recover from the effects of **World War II** by reducing barriers to international **trade**. GATT was solely an agreement, and an intended organization called the International Trade Organization did not materialize because its charter was not ratified. In the mid-1990s, the functions of GATT were superseded by the World Trade Organization (WTO). Norway was part of GATT from the beginning and continues as a member of the WTO. *See also* EUROPEAN INTEGRATION.

**GERHARDSEN, EINAR (1897–1987).** Norwegian politician. The son of a minor public official, Gerhardsen was born on 10 May 1897 in Asker near **Oslo** and rose from errand boy and laborer to the position of prime mover behind the development of the Norwegian welfare state. Active in both his labor union and in the youth organization of the **Labor Party**, by the outbreak of **World War II**, he had had several responsible assignments also in the national Labor Party itself, including the position of secretary in 1923 and the post as secretary in the Oslo Labor Party from 1926 to 1936. During World War II, when the occupants forbade him to engage in politics, he briefly served as acting chairman of the Labor Party and as mayor of Oslo. After working in the Resistance, he was arrested, tortured, and imprisoned by the Germans, first in Norway and then in Germany, including in the concentration camp Sachsenhausen. Later transferred back to a Norwegian prison, he was released at the time of the German capitulation.

After the war, Gerhardsen was made chairman of the Labor Party and briefly served as mayor of Oslo. He played a leading role in establishing Norway's first postwar government, which included representatives of all major political parties, and served as prime minister in this government from 25 June 1945 until the fall general elections. These elections gave the Labor Party a majority in the *Storting* (**Parliament**), and he continued to serve as prime minister in this Labor government until 1951. By then, he had shepherded Norway into membership in the **North Atlantic Treaty Organization**.

Gerhardsen resigned his post as prime minister in 1951, stating that he was worn out from both his wartime imprisonment and his postwar leadership responsibilities. He became the leader of the Labor

Party caucus in the *Storting*, trading places with the new prime minister, **Oscar Torp**, and was able to both smooth over tensions in the relationship between the government and the Labor *Storting* caucus and resolve some disagreements between the Labor Party and the trade unions. These internal conflicts in the Labor Party were mostly related to the question of which defense policy to pursue and how to deal with inflationary pressures in the **economy**.

In 1955, Gerhardsen again took over as prime minister after Torp's resignation, and this government lasted until 1963. During the parliamentary elections of 1961, however, the newly formed **Socialist Left Party** (SF), consisting mostly of voters who had broken away from the Labor Party, had gotten two representatives in parliament. The Labor Party and the opposition had 74 representatives each, so Gerhardsen had to secure the continued support of SF to remain in power. A tragic coal **mining** accident at **Kings Bay**, Spitzbergen, led to a no-confidence vote against the Gerhardsen government on 23 August 1963, and the two SF representatives voted with the opposition. A coalition government headed by **John Lyng** of the Conservative Party was formed, but it lasted for only about one month.

Gerhardsen's fourth government took over on 25 September 1963 and lasted until the fall of 1965, when it was replaced by a coalition government headed by **Per Borten** of the **Center Party**. Gerhardsen continued as a member of the *Storting* until 1969, however, when he retired from active participation in politics. He remained a beloved and trusted elder statesman, though, and continued to be influential in Labor Party affairs. He is considered one of Norway's foremost political leaders of all time.

**GODAL, BJØRN TORE (1945– ).** Norwegian politician. Born in Skien on 20 January 1945, Godal studied political science, sociology, and history at the University of **Oslo** and received a bachelor-level degree in 1969. For the next several years, he held various position in the **Labor Party** and its youth organization and acted as a substitute member of the *Storting* (**Parliament**), serving in the place of Prime Minister **Gro Harlem Brundtland** from 1986 to 1989. He then was a regularly elected member of the *Storting* from 1989 to 2001. From 1991 to 1994, he served as minister of **trade** and **shipping** in Brundtland's third government and, from 1994 to

1996, as Brundtland's minister of foreign affairs. He also served in the same position under Prime Minister **Thorbjørn Jagland** from 1996 to 1997 and then as minister of defense in Prime Minister **Jens Stoltenberg**'s first government from 2000 to 2001. Godal has also been Norway's ambassador to Germany. A loyal and versatile Labor team player, Godal is noted for his dissent from party orthodoxy at the time of the 1972 referendum concerning Norwegian membership in the European Community (*see* EUROPEAN ECONOMIC COMMUNITY [EEC]), when he was the most vocal Labor opponent of membership.

**GREAT NORTHERN WAR.** Lasting from 1700 to 1721, the Great Northern War was indirectly a result of **Sweden**'s position as a European Great Power during the decades after the end of the Thirty Years War (1618–48). In control of a Baltic empire, Sweden ruled a large territory centered on the Gulf of Finland as well as several German-speaking provinces. For most of the period of the war, Sweden was led by the great warrior king Karl XII (1682–1718), and the opposite force was made up by a coalition consisting of **Denmark**–Norway, Sachsen–Poland, Russia, Prussia, and Hanover. Even though Karl XII had initial successes with his well-trained army, the opposition was too much for him. Russia beat him decisively at the Battle of Poltava in 1709, and his campaign in Germany went from bad to worse. Having lost his possessions in Germany and the Baltic, Karl went into exile for five years.

Upon his return, he set his sights on Norway, however, which was to be compensation for his losses and which he invaded in 1716. Having initially captured Christiania (now **Oslo**), he was unable to vanquish Akershus Fortress and was forced to withdraw, taking the town of Fredrikstad on his way back to Sweden. The townspeople set fire to their houses, and Karl withdrew, having been unable to take its fortress, Fredriksten. At this time, **Peter Wessel Tordenskjold** captured or destroyed the Swedish fleet, depriving Karl of the guns and ammunition that he needed to retake Fredrikstad. When he again attacked in 1718, a portion of his army invaded Trøndelag, while the bulk of his forces went into eastern Norway, laying siege to Fredriksten. Karl XII was killed while inspecting the work associated with the siege, but it is unknown if the bullet was fired by friend or foe.

The army that had attacked Trøndelag withdrew once the news of the king's death reached it, and many soldiers froze to death during its retreat. Danes and Russians continued their attacks along the Swedish coast, but a peace treaty signed in the town of Nystad in 1721 finally brought the conflict to an end.

**GREPP, KYRRE (1879–1922).** Norwegian politician. Born in Brønnøy, Nordland County, on 6 August 1879, Grepp studied **literature** and medicine. His true vocation was **Labor Party** politics, however, and he succeeded **Christian Holtermann Knudsen** as the leader of the Labor Party in 1918, serving until his death from pulmonary tuberculosis. A fiery speaker, Grepp led the radical wing of Labor, which under his direction joined the Communist International.

**GRIEG, EDVARD (1843–1907).** Norwegian composer. Born on 15 June 1843 in **Bergen** and of Scottish descent, Grieg received piano lessons from his mother and later, on the recommendation of the violinist **Ole Bull**, studied at the conservatory in Leipzig, Germany. He became an excellent pianist but is better known as a composer in the romantic vein who was strongly influenced by Norwegian folk music. Some of his best-known musical pieces are selections drawn from the incidental music he composed for the 1876 Christiania performance of **Henrik Ibsen**'s drama *Peer Gynt* (1867). Two suites, Opus 46 and Opus 55, contain such classics as "Morning Mood," "Solveig's Song," and "In the Hall of the Mountain King." Grieg also wrote songs with texts by the Norwegian writers **Bjørnstjerne Bjørnson**, **Arne Garborg**, and **Aasmund Olafsson Vinje**. His *Lyric Pieces*, written for piano, are also well known, and his three violin sonatas have an honored place in the standard chamber music repertoire.

**GUDE, HANS (1825–1903).** Norwegian painter. Born in Christiania (now **Oslo**) on 13 March 1825, Gude was a child prodigy and began studying **art** in Düsseldorf, Germany, at the age of 16. He was an immensely influential landscape painter who found inspiration in both the mountains and along the coast of Norway and celebrated the greatness of Norwegian nature. His best-known work is *Brudefærden i Hardanger* (Bridal Journey in Hardanger), painted in 1849, on which he collaborated with his colleague **Adolph Tidemand**. Gude painted the landscape, Tidemand the figures. This work is regarded as a high point of Norwegian **national romanticism** and was accompanied by a song written by Andreas Munch (1811–84) and music by Halfdan Kjerulf (1815–68).

**GUSTAVSEN, FINN RUDOLF (1926–2005).** Norwegian journalist and politician. Born in Drammen on 22 February 1926, Gustavsen was a factory worker in his youth before he became a journalist in 1947, working for the **Labor Party** press. When the weekly newspaper *Orientering* (Orientation) was started as a forum for left-wing socialist critique in late 1952, Gustavsen and others, including **Karl Evang**, resisted making the paper a forum primarily for the views of **Norway's Communist Party**. For several years, Gustavsen was the paper's only full-time employee and was named editor in 1959. A critic of Norway's membership in the **North Atlantic Treaty Organization** and other aspects of Labor Party foreign policy, Gustavsen was excluded from the party in 1961. This led to the formation of the **Socialist People's Party** (SF), and Gustavsen was elected a member of the *Storting* (**Parliament**) in 1961, representing the SF until 1969. From 1973 to 1977, he served as a member of the *Storting* as a representative of the SF's successor party, the **Socialist Left Party** (which had grown out of the Socialist Electoral Alliance, on whose ticket Gustavsen was elected in 1973).

Gustavsen is known for his role in the **Kings Bay affair**, when a series of **mining** accidents led to a vote of no confidence against the government led by **Einar Gerhardsen**, the legendary leader of the Labor Party during the years after **World War II**. The SF had gotten 2 seats in the *Storting* in the 1961 election, while Labor and the nonsocialist parties had 74 seats each. When Gustavsen and his SF colleague Asbjørn Holm sided with the nonsocialists in the no-confidence vote, the Labor Party government was briefly replaced by one led by **John Lyng** of the **Conservatives**. (Labor returned to power when Gustavsen and Holm later sided with it in a vote of no confidence against Lyng's government.) This was the first non-Labor government in the postwar era and showed that the nonsocialists could work together and offer a realistic alternative to Labor. Gustavsen also opposed the Labor Party during the struggle about Norwegian membership in the European

Community (*see* EUROPEAN ECONOMIC COMMUNITY [EEC]) in 1972. While many of his fellow opponents did not appreciate his socialist commitments, he was highly respected for his courage and intellectual honesty.

After the end of his political career, Gustavsen did development work in Africa and returned to journalism, working for the weekly paper *Ny Tid* (New Age), which succeeded *Orientering* in 1975.

## – H –

**HAAKON VII (1872–1957).** King of Norway. Born Christian Carl Georg Valdemar Axel on 3 August 1872 as the second son of the future King Frederik VIII of **Denmark**, Prince Carl, as he was known in his youth, was the brother of the future Danish king Christian X, the paternal grandson of King Christian IX of Denmark, and the maternal grandson of King Karl IV of Norway, also known as King Karl XV of **Sweden**. **Christian Frederik**, who was briefly the king of independent Norway in 1814, was his great-granduncle. Prince Carl married his first cousin Princess Maud, the daughter of the future King Edward VII of Great Britain, in 1896. Their only child, Prince Alexander, who later succeeded his father as **Olav V** of Norway, was born in 1903.

With family connections such as these, Prince Carl was well suited to bring a sense of legitimacy to newly independent Norway after the **dissolution of the union with Sweden** in 1905. The fact that he already had a son and that he was married to a member of the British royal family was viewed as particular advantages when Norwegian political leaders considered various candidates for the throne of Norway. He accepted after a Norwegian referendum overwhelmingly approved the government's choice and was crowned in Nidaros Cathedral in **Trondheim** on 22 June 1906.

Even though he never learned to speak Norwegian well—Danish is so close to Norwegian that few individuals succeed in mastering both **languages**—Haakon VII was very popular among the Norwegian people. He was particularly admired for his strong stand against Nazism when Norway was invaded by Germany in 1940. When the invaders demanded concessions from the Norwegian *Storting* (**Par-**

**liament**) and government, the king stated in no uncertain terms that he would abdicate if the government were to yield to the German ultimatum. The Germans next bombed Nybergsund, the place where he was staying, hoping to kill him.

After the king and the government were first conveyed to **Tromsø** by a British cruiser and ultimately taken to safety in Britain onboard the HMS *Devonshire* on 7 June 1940, King Haakon was the central symbol of the Norwegian resistance for the next five years. His return to Norway on 7 June 1945 was a day of great rejoicing. His death on 21 September 1957 at the age of 85—2 years after he had fallen and broken his hip, thereafter being confined to a wheelchair—was a day when deep sorrow was felt in the entire country. *See also* WORLD WAR II.

**HAAKON THE GOOD (c. 920–61).** Norwegian king. The youngest son of Harald Fairhair, Haakon was brought up by King Athelstan of England, who taught him the Christian **religion**. After his father's death, Haakon went to war against his older brother, **Eirik Bloodaxe**. Enlisting dissatisfied Norwegian chieftains and promising tax relief, he drove Eirik away but later had to fight his sons. He died from a wound he received at the Battle of Fitjar in western Norway. *See also* VIKINGS.

**HAAVARDSHOLM, ESPEN (1945– ).** Norwegian novelist and short-story writer. Born on 10 January 1945 in **Oslo**, Haavardsholm started out with a focus on modernist themes. A semidocumentary collection of seven texts, *Zink* (1971; Zinc), directly argues in favor of a Marxist-Leninist revolution in Norway, however. *Grip dagen* (1973; Seize the Day) centers on Norway's European Community (*see* EUROPEAN ECONOMIC COMMUNITY [EEC]) referendum of 25 September 1972 and argues that Norwegian society is sacrificing its traditional values of liberty and equality in favor of **economic** growth at any price. *Historiens kraftlinjer* (1975; The Power Lines of History) offers Albania as an example of an ideal society. Like many other radical writers in Norway at the time, however, Haavardsholm began to depart from orthodox Marxism-Leninism in the 1980s and has since produced less ideologically strident work. *See also* LITERATURE.

**HAGEN, CARL IVAR (1944– ).** Norwegian politician. Born on 6 May 1944 in **Oslo**, Hagen was educated as an **economist** and spent his early career with the sweetener company Tate and Lyle (1970–74). His influence on Norwegian political life has frequently been felt to be acerbic, however, and Hagen has often been tarred with the right-wing nationalist brush. As the chair of the ultraconservative **Progress Party** from 1978 to 2006, Hagen has been a highly controversial figure in Norwegian politics. He was first elected a member of the *Storting* (**Parliament**) on the Reform Party ticket in 1974, having earlier served as a deputy representative for the Reform Party's parent party, Anders Lange's Party. The Reform Party/Anders Lange's Party changed its name to the Progress Party in 1977, and since 1981, Hagen has represented it in the *Storting*. He ultimately rose to the position of parliamentary vice president. While Hagen never succeeded in becoming a cabinet member—let alone prime minister—he led his party to a position of great strength; at times, the Progress Party has been Norway's second-largest party, as only **Labor** has received more votes. While the **Conservatives** have mostly regarded Hagen as a spoiler and consistently refused to enter into any kind of close cooperation with his party, he has been too far to the right to make any kind of meaningful relationship with the centrist parties a reality, as some of the neoliberal policies advocated by the Progress Party advocates entail both greater social inequality and more severe limits to immigration.

**HAGERUP, GEORG FRANCIS (1853–1921).** Norwegian politician and legal scholar. Born in Horten on 22 January 1853, Hagerup studied law at the university in Christiania (now **Oslo**), receiving a doctorate in 1885, and was professor of law from 1887 to 1906. A member of the *Storting* (**Parliament**) representing the **Conservative Party** from 1901 until 1906, he first served as the minister of justice under **Emil Stang** from 1893 to 1895. He first served as prime minister from 1895 to 1898, when the crisis in the relationship with **Sweden** brought about by the proposal of an independent consular service made it desirable to have a Norwegian prime minister who was capable of successfully carrying out the delicate negotiations concerning the matter. Hagerup again served as prime minister in a Unity Party government from 1903 to 1905, but he was a man of negotiations and careful deliberation rather than decisive action and was replaced by **Christian Michelsen** on 11 March 2005, just as the struggle over the **dissolution of the union with Sweden** was entering its concluding phase. Hagerup's talents were put to use later during his many years as a diplomat and legal scholar. He was deeply interested in international law, particularly the law of the sea, and in 1920, he led the Norwegian delegation to the first meeting of the **League of Nations**.

**HALVORSEN, OTTO BAHR (1872–1923).** Norwegian politician and legal scholar. Born on 28 May 1872 in Christiania (now **Oslo**) to Otto Hellen Halvorsen (1840–1921), Halvorsen got his matriculation certificate in 1890 and received a law degree from the university in Christiania in 1896. He then practiced law and was active in the **Conservative Party**, both locally and nationally. Elected to the *Storting* (**Parliament**) in 1913 and serving until his death, he became caucus leader in 1919. He first served as prime minister from 1920 to 1921, when he had the unpleasant experience of trying to enforce Norway's prohibition against alcohol in the face of strong pressure from France, Spain, and Portugal to continue importing wine and spirits at pre–**World War I** levels. There was little confidence in Halvorsen's ability to successfully protect Norwegian exports against the wine producers' **trade** retaliation, so his government was voted out in the summer of 1921, and **Otto Albert Blehr** led a **Liberal Party** government for the next two years. Halvorsen formed his second government in 1923 but died in office after three months.

**HAMBRO, CARL JOACHIM, SR. (1885–1964).** Norwegian politician. Born in **Bergen** to Edvard I. Hambro on 5 January 1885, Hambro received a university degree in 1907 and went to work as a journalist for the conservative daily *Morgenbladet* (Morning Post) in **Oslo**. Elected to the *Storting* (**Parliament**) in 1919, he served as a member until 1957, much of the time as its president. It was in that capacity that Hambro seized the mantle of leadership and organized the escape of King **Haakon VII**, the royal family, and the government from Oslo after the attack by Germany on 9 April 1940, first to Hamar and then to Elverum. Understanding more clearly than most of his contemporaries what Germany's true intentions were, he also made certain that the *Storting* transferred its authority to the government, so that there would be a solid legal basis for the Norwegian exile government during **World War II**. Hambro spent the war in **Sweden**, Great Britain, and the **United States** furthering Norway's cause.

During the postwar era, Hambro was a clear-headed observer and commentator; for example, he understood that **Einar Gerhardsen**'s notion of cooperation during the period of postwar reconstruction was not cooperation among the various political parties but cooperation between the government, on the one hand, and **trade** and **industry**, on the other. He also perceived that the **Nordic Council**, established in 1952, would most likely bring about much practical cooperation among the Nordic countries. His service to international organizations included working with the **League of Nations** and serving as a delegate to the **United Nations** General Assembly.

**HAMSUN, KNUT (1859–1952).** Norwegian novelist. Born on 4 August 1859 in Lom, Oppland County, to Peder Pedersen Garmostrædet, Hamsun is one of the few Norwegian writers that truly belong to world **literature**. When he was a young boy, his family moved to Hamarøy in northern Norway, where they lived on a farm called Hamsund, the name of which, minus its final letter, gave him the name under which he is known. Many of his early experiences, including hard work in a variety of jobs, are reflected in Hamsun's long and varied oeuvre.

Early in his life, Hamsun decided that he wanted to become a writer and self-published his first story at the age of 18. Success long eluded him, however, and it was only after a very difficult winter in Christiania (now **Oslo**) and two stints in America that he had his first literary success, the psychological and autobiographical novel *Sult* (1890; tr. *Hunger*, 1899). Other novels in a similar vein followed, the best known of which are *Mysterier* (1892; tr. *Mysteries*, 1927) and *Pan* (1894; tr. 1920).

While his early works were groundbreaking not only in Norwegian letters but in European literature as a whole, Hamsun later made a reactionary turn as he embarked on such themes as industrialization and the evils of modernization. For example, his novel *Markens grøde* (1917; tr. *Growth of the Soil*, 1920), for which he won the Nobel Prize in 1920, tells about a homesteader whose virtuous ways are threatened by the encroaching modernity. Other works from the 1920s and 1930s show indications of what became the major tragedy of Hamsun's life, his assent to Nazism before and during **World War II**. After the war, he was convicted of collaboration and given a heavy fine. True to form, however, these experiences were used as material for his final book, the autobiographical narrative *Paa gjengrodde stier* (1949; tr. *On Overgrown Paths*, 1967), the artistic qualities of which show that the aged Hamsun had not lost his creative touch.

**HANSEATIC LEAGUE.** A federation of German **trade** guilds, the Hanseatic League had its center of gravity in the town of Lübeck, but its interests extended across the Baltic and North Sea areas from Russia in the east to England in the west. Its interests in Norway were centered in **Bergen**, where a *Kontor* (office) or trading post was established in 1360. This is shortly after the **Black Death**, when the loss of a large segment of the population perhaps gave the Hansa traders an opportunity for expansion. Approximately 1,000 Germans settled in Bergen and took over most of the warehouses along the wharf. They kept mostly to themselves, even to the point of having their own dispute resolution system and prohibiting intermarriage with the Norwegians. Their extensive network of international trade gave them a strong competitive edge with regard to imported goods, and their strong capital base made it possible for them to make their Norwegian suppliers dependent on them through the extension of credit. Their most lucrative trade in Norway was the stockfish trade (*see* FISHING). During the spring and early summer, fishermen from northern Norway would bring their dried fish and other fish products to market in Bergen and return home with grain, salt, and other necessities. The Hansa merchants also used their strong capital position to get control of the local trade.

There can be no question that the presence of the Hanseatic League in Norway furthered the development of the Norwegian **economy**, but it is also a fact that their dominant position retarded the growth of the indigenous middle class. They had a reputation for ruthlessness, and jealously guarded their position, even to the point of using force against would-be competitors. The long-lasting dependencies established through their extension of credit also worked against the interests of the individual fishermen who got caught in their web of economic power.

**HANSEN, GERHARD HENRIK ARMAUER (1841–1912).** Norwegian physician. Born in **Bergen** on 29 July 1841, Hansen studied medicine at the university in **Oslo**, receiving his degree in 1866. In 1873, he announced the discovery of *Mycobacterium leprae* as the cause of leprosy, a disease that was prevalent in Norway at the time and that was thought to be hereditary. Hansen's discovery eventually led to a notable decline of the disease.

**HANSEN, MAURITS CHRISTOPHER (1794–1842).** Norwegian novelist and short-story writer. Born in Modum, Buskerud County, on 5 July 1794, Hansen is one of Norway's earliest prose writers in modern times. Often forced to write under pressure in order to supplement his income as a teacher, however, few of his works are of lasting value. He was influenced by German romanticism, and some of his stories are reminiscent of the Gothic novel. The short story "Luren" (1819; The Shepherd's Horn) inaugurated the peasant tale and was later popularized by **Bjørnstjerne Bjørnson**. It also exhibits many of the characteristics of the **national romanticism**, such as a focus on Norwegian nature and the connections between the rural people of Hansen's day and the virtues of **Viking**-age Norway. *See also* LITERATURE.

**HARALD FAIRHAIR (c. 850–c. 933).** Norwegian king. Born to Halfdan the Black, a regional king in the area of Vestfold County, Harald is credited with uniting many small local chiefdoms and earldoms into one national kingdom through various battles as well as his great victory at the battle of Hafrsfjord near **Stavanger** in 872 CE. Because there are but two contemporary sources that mention Harald, both of them skaldic poems, most information comes from later and less reliable writings, for example, the sagas of **Snorri Sturluson**. The precise extent of Harald's realm is unknown, but it was probably limited to the coastal areas of southeastern and western Norway. He is reported to have had a large number of children, to whom he assigned administrative responsibilities, but his favorite son and intended successor was **Eirik Bloodaxe**. *See also* VIKINGS.

**HAUGE, HANS NILSEN (1771–1824).** Norwegian **religious** leader. Hauge was born at the Hauge farm in Østfold County on 3 April 1771. While working in the fields one day in 1796, he had a spiritual experience that made him conscious of his personal need for divine grace. Although given a religious upbringing, he did not have a deeply personal relationship with the divine. In the Norwegian Lutheran State Church, rationalism was the order of the day, and most people found little nourishment for their souls there.

Hauge immediately began sharing his insights with others and encouraged them to develop a personal relationship with God. He traveled around, holding meetings in the homes where he was given shelter. This kind of activity was illegal, for there was an ordinance called the *Konventikkelplakaten* (Conventicle Notice) that regulated religious assemblies and stated that no meeting could be held without the express permission of the local State Church minister. Having traveled continually from 1797 to 1804, he was arrested for violating the religious assembly ordinance, and it surely did not help that he kept attacking the ministers, both orally and in writing. Hauge's **pietism** simply could not look the other way when confronted with the rationalism of the State Church.

The movement founded by Hauge was a typical peasant-class movement and did not appeal to the rich and the educated. In addition, Hauge was a man of practical talents who started many and varied business ventures that were financed with monetary contributions from his believers and managed by some of his most trusted associates. His business and mercantile activities also violated the laws that favored the existing merchant class. As his movement spread throughout the country and he became Norway's best-selling writer, he was frequently mocked and criticized by those whose interests were threatened by his success.

After his arrest, he was kept imprisoned for many years without being charged with any crime but was eventually sentenced to two years of hard labor. His movement flourished, however; for example, there were three *Haugianere* (Haugeans) present at the **constitutional** convention in 1814. The Haugeans remained a strong force in

Norwegian politics throughout the 19th century, making a significant contribution to the struggle that eventually eviscerated the power of the *embedsmann* (public official) class, many members of which had been among Hauge's most severe critics.

**HEYERDAHL, THOR (1914–2002).** Norwegian explorer, adventurer, ethnologist, and experimental archaeologist. Born in Larvik on 6 October 1914, Heyerdahl early became fascinated with zoology, which he later studied at the university in **Oslo**. He also read everything he could find about the islands of the Pacific and developed a strong interest in anthropology. His first expedition was a stay with his wife, Liv, in the Marquesas Islands in 1937–38; most of the time was spent studying animal life on the island Fatu Hiva. In 1939–40, he spent time among the Native Americans on the coast of British Columbia, Canada. **World War II** got in the way of further scientific work, however, and Heyerdahl was trained as a paratrooper, serving in the Norwegian brigade in Scotland and attaining the rank of lieutenant.

Heyerdahl became famous for his theory that the islands of the Pacific had been populated by migrations from the American continent. The Kon-Tiki expedition, which in 1947 sailed a raft made from balsa logs 4,300 miles from Peru to the Tuamotu Islands, was undertaken in order to demonstrate that such prehistoric migrations were possible. While there is some evidence that supports Heyerdahl's theory, it remains controversial in the scientific community, where it is generally held that the Pacific islands were populated by migrations from Asia. Heyerdahl's later expeditions to the Galapagos Islands (1952) and Rapa Nui (Easter Island) from 1955 to 1956, while groundbreaking in their own right, did little to influence general scientific opinion about the origins of the Polynesians.

The two *Ra* expeditions, undertaken in 1969 and 1970, similarly had as their purpose to show that prehistoric crossings of the Atlantic Ocean were possible. Built according to ancient drawings found in Egypt, *Ra I* and *Ra II* were reed boats similar to those used in many ancient cultures. While *Ra I* broke apart, *Ra II* sailed from Morocco and landed in Barbados 57 days later. A voyage with another reconstruction of an ancient vessel, the *Tigris*, was undertaken in the Gulf of Persia and the Indian Ocean in 1977. Its purpose was to demonstrate that it had been possible to engage in long-distance **trade** in ancient times.

In his later years, Heyerdahl carried out archeological digs in several places, including the Maldive Islands in the Indian Ocean, Túcume in Peru, Tenerife in the Canary Islands, and Azov near the Black Sea. All of these investigations had as their purpose to demonstrate that ancient cultural similarities were the result of migrations rather than parallel independent developments. The Azov project was particularly controversial, as its aim was to show that **Snorri Sturluson** was correct when claiming that the ancient **Scandinavian** gods were in reality people who had migrated from Asia Minor to **Sweden**.

While considered largely unscientific by specialists, Heyerdahl's expeditions caught the attention of large numbers of people. His books were widely translated and sold very well. Heyerdahl also received numerous civic and academic honors.

**HOEM, EDVARD (1949– ).** Norwegian novelist, playwright, and poet. Born on 10 March 1949 in Fræna, Møre and Romsdal County, Hoem studied philosophy and **literature** at the university. Considered one of the foremost stylists in contemporary Norwegian literature, he started out as a poet but has devoted most of his energy to the theater and the novel. A Marxist-Leninist in the 1970s, he early wrote a novel titled *Anna Lena* (1971) that depicted the exploitation of low-paid workers in the Norwegian countryside. Capitalism's push for centralization of the rural population is the related theme of *Kjærleikens ferjereiser* (1974; tr. *The Ferry Crossing*, 1989), which is highly critical of the policies of the Norwegian government. As in **Dag Solstad**'s *Arild Asnes, 1970*, published three years earlier, the book ends as the Marxist-Leninist paper *Klassekampen* (Class Struggle) is being sold door to door.

The play *Tusen fjordar, tusen fjell* (1977; A Thousand Fjords, a Thousand Mountains) argues in favor of maintaining the rural population, even in small communities. The historical play *Der storbåra bryt* (1979; Where the Big Wave Breaks), set at the end of the Napoleonic wars, depicts people's reactions to the new ideas of liberty. Among many other themes, Hoem's later works express his disenchantment with Marxism-Leninism.

**HOLST, JOHAN JØRGEN (1937–94).** Norwegian politician. Born in **Oslo** on 29 November 1937, Holst received his secondary schooling there and studied Russian in the Norwegian military. He then attended Columbia University, where he obtained a B.A. in 1960. During and after graduate studies in political science at the University of Oslo, he held various research appointments, including one at Harvard University (1962–63). He was also the head of research at the *Norsk Utenrikspolitisk Institutt* (Norwegian Foreign Policy Institute), a think tank devoted to issues regarding politics and **economics**, from 1969 to 1976, as well as its director from 1981 to 1986. He used his academic background for the benefit of the **Labor Party** as speech writer and adviser, as well as through his work as a government employee in both the Ministry of Defense and the Ministry of Foreign Affairs. Holst served as minister of defense in **Gro Harlem Brundtland**'s second government from 1986 to 1989, in the same position in Brundtland's third government from 1990 to 1993, and then as minister of foreign affairs, also in Brundtland's third government, from 1993 to his death in 1994. Both through his academic work and on account of his public service, Holst had an extraordinary influence on the development of Norwegian foreign policy under these Labor Party governments. He was also strongly in favor of Norwegian membership in the European Community (EC; *see* EUROPEAN ECONOMIC COMMUNITY [EEC]), serving as head of the *Europabevegelsen* (Europe Movement), an organization devoted to securing Norwegian membership in the EC, from 1982 to 1986. His foremost political accomplishment is undoubtedly his contribution to the Oslo Accords in 1993, the confidential negotiations that resulted in an agreement by the State of Israel and the Palestine Liberation Organization to acknowledge one another as valid parties in peace negotiations.

**HORNSRUD, CHRISTOPHER (1859–1960).** Norwegian politician. Born in Øvre Eiker, Buskerud County, on 15 November 1859, Hornsrud was a farmer active in local politics and served as mayor of Øvre Eiker. After service on the **Oslo** City Council, he was elected a member of the *Storting* (**Parliament**) in 1912 until his resignation in 1936. Subsequent to the reunification of *Det norske Arbeiderparti* (The Norwegian **Labor Party**) and *Norges Socialdemokratiske Ar-*

*beiderparti* (**Norway's Social-Democratic Labor Party**) in 1927, Labor won a considerable victory—it received 37 percent of the votes—in that year's parliamentary elections, and Hornsrud formed a Labor government that lasted for a little more than two weeks. It was the first Labor Party government in Norwegian history.

*HØYRE. See* CONSERVATIVE PARTY.

**HUNDSEID, JENS (1883–1965).** Norwegian politician. Born on 6 May 1883 in Vikedal, Rogaland County, Hundseid represented the Agrarian Party (*see* CENTER PARTY) in the *Storting* (**Parliament**) from 1924 to 1940 and was also the Agrarians' caucus leader (1931–33 and 1934–40). His political life changed when **Peder Kolstad**, who had been the leader of a weakly supported Agrarian Party government from 1931 to 1932, died while in office. King **Haakon** then asked Hundseid if the Agrarians were willing to continue as the party providing the government. Hundseid reported to the party leadership that the king had asked him to become the new prime minister and then told the king that the party wanted him to be the new government's head.

This intrigue set the tone for his time in office, which was characterized by much internal squabbling, especially between Hunseid and **Vidkun Quisling**, Kolstad's minister of defense, who continued in the same position under Hundseid. When in 1933 the *Storting* accepted a proposal from **Johan Ludwig Mowinckel** that departed from the traditional liberalist principle of cutting expenses in order to keep the government from meddling in **economic** life, Hundseid resigned and was succeeded by a government headed by Mowinckel. Two years later, however, the Agrarian Party, still under Hundseid's leadership, entered into an agreement with the **Labor Party** that entailed precisely the kind of thinking that Mowinckel had suggested.

In 1940, Hundseid joined the Norwegian National Socialist Party, possibly to protect himself from retaliation by his old nemesis, Quisling. After the war, he received a 10-year prison sentence but served only until 1949, when he was pardoned.

**HYDROELECTRIC POWER.** With its long coastline and tall mountains facing the North Atlantic, Norway receives abundant rainfall.

After the modern water turbine had been developed in 1849, it became possible to attach it to an electric generator, thus producing electric current. Norway's first hydroelectric power plant that provided electricity to subscribers was built by **Gunnar Knudsen** in Skien in 1885. As foreign interests bought up and developed Norwegian waterfalls with hydroelectric potential, **Johan Castberg** took the lead in introducing licensing laws in 1909. While these laws were not always strictly enforced (for example, in the 1920s there was concern that they might prevent foreign investment necessary to modernize Norwegian society), they specified that after a certain time, ownership of the resources would revert to the state. An important early industrial use of electricity was in the production of nitrogen, for which the raw material was basically just air.

After **World War II**, there was rapid development of Norwegian hydropower, which was needed in the aluminum **industry** and in the production of various alloys. Throughout the 1950s and 1960s, the production of electricity increased almost fourfold, and aluminum plants were built all over the country. Some aspects of this development have been chronicled by the novelist **Kjartan Fløgstad**. Foreign capital provided most of the investments and reaped the largest share of the profits in a manner reminiscent of classic colonialism. Raw materials (ore) were imported from third-world countries and smelted by the use of Norwegian power, after which the metals were used in production in other industrialized countries.

With a growing awareness of the need to preserve scenic areas from development, however, resistance against government-mandated hydroelectric development manifested itself. The first major incident took place in 1970 in Mardøla, Møre and Romsdal County, where civil disobedience was used as a tool to keep a power plant from being built. The philosopher **Arne Næss** and the future minister of justice **Odd Einar Dørum** were among those arrested. Later in the same decade, there was also significant resistance to the development of hydroelectric power in the Alta River in Finnmark County, where 10,000 people demonstrated against the government decision. The government won the battle, however.

The traditional rule in Norwegian hydroelectric development has been that bigger is better. During recent years, however, small power plants producing less than 10 megawatts have become increasingly common, with some of them producing less than 100 kilowatts. These power plants are usually built by the landowner, and the power is primarily for his or her own use, while the surplus is sold to local utility companies. Increasingly, hydroelectric power is being replaced by the use of **oil and natural gas**. *See also* ENVIRONMENT.

– I –

**IBSEN, HENRIK JOHAN (1828–1906).** Norwegian dramatist and poet. Born on 20 March 1828 to Knud Ibsen in the town of Skien, Telemark County, Ibsen is recognized as one of the world's greatest dramatists. During his lifetime and especially in his native Norway, he was considered a notable poet as well. While his family belonged to the upper middle class, Ibsen lost the social and **economic** advantages of his birth through his father's financial reversals while yet a small boy. **Education** beyond elementary school was out of the question, and at the age of 16, he had to leave home to earn a living as a druggist's apprentice in the nearby town of Grimstad.

While in Grimstad, Ibsen fathered an illegitimate child by one of his employer's maids, a woman 10 years his senior, which brought him both social and pecuniary embarrassment. Perhaps through his work for the druggist, he also hit on the idea of pursuing a career in medicine. This necessitated passing his university matriculation examinations, for which he prepared by self-study. He also wrote poetry, and when studying his Latin curriculum, he came across the account of the Roman rebel Catiline and was so taken with this story that he shaped it into a play, *Catilina* (1850; tr. *Catiline*, 1900).

In 1851, Ibsen was given an appointment at the recently founded Norwegian theater in **Bergen**. One of his duties was to provide an original play each year, and Ibsen's time in Bergen became an opportunity for him to thoroughly learn his craft. First in Bergen and later at the Norwegian Theater in Christiania (now **Oslo**), Ibsen wrote a long series of plays on historical, mythological, and folkloric topics, most of which are now read only by scholars. After leaving Norway for Italy in 1864, however, he wrote two verse dramas, *Brand* (1866; tr. 1891) and *Peer Gynt* (1867; tr. 1892), which together catapulted him to fame. His improved income allowed him to remain abroad, and he lived in Italy and Germany until 1891. A series of dramas followed, Ibsen's own favorite being the nine-act play *Kejser og Galilæer* (1873; tr. *Emperor and Galilean*, 1876).

Ibsen's international reputation rests on 12 modern prose dramas, beginning with *Samfundets støtter* (1877; tr. *The Pillars of Society*, 1888) and including such titles as *Et dukkehjem* (1879; tr. *A Doll's House*, 1880), *En folkefiende* (1882; tr. *An Enemy of the People*, 1888), *Vildanden* (1884; tr. *The Wild Duck*, 1890), *Hedda Gabler* (1890; tr. 1891), and *Bygmester Solness* (1892; tr. *The Master Builder*, 1893). His prose plays were very critical of contemporary social life and castigated all manner of hypocrisy and deception. On the cultural and political Right, Ibsen was regarded as a dangerous radical, while the more liberal saw him as a leader in the struggle for social justice. It is a testimony to the power and enduring value of his plays that they continue to be performed all over the world and have affected the public debate, not only in Europe and North America, but in such places as China, Bangladesh, and Africa as well. *See also* LITERATURE.

**IBSEN, SIGURD (1859–1930).** Norwegian politician, diplomat, and pioneering sociologist. Born to the dramatist **Henrik Ibsen** in Christiania (now **Oslo**) on 23 December 1859, Ibsen spent his childhood and youth in Italy and Germany. After earning a doctorate of law degree in Rome in 1882, Ibsen had a significant career as a politician and diplomat. From 1885 to 1889, he was employed by the Swedish-Norwegian Foreign Service, being stationed in Stockholm; Washington, D.C.; and Vienna. From 1902 to 1903, he had a ministerial appointment in the **Liberal Party** government of **Otto Albert Blehr**, serving in Stockholm. He served as the Norwegian prime minister in Stockholm under **Francis Hagerup** from 1903 to 1905, which meant that he, in essence, was the Norwegian government's top representative to **Sweden**, its union partner. In a series of newspaper articles in 1891, Ibsen argued that Norway should have its own minister of foreign affairs, its own Ministry of Foreign Affairs, and its own diplomats. This was a radical proposal, as the two union partners had always had a single—and always Swedish—minister of foreign affairs and a foreign service from which Norwegian nationals were largely excluded.

It was not typical of Ibsen to be that daring, though, as he preferred negotiation to drastic action. For example, while **Christian Michelsen**, Norway's prime minister during the **dissolution of the union with Sweden** in 1905, presented the Swedes with a situation where they would either have to go along or go to war, Ibsen wanted to dissolve the union by having the *Storting* (**Parliament**) vote to withdraw from the Union Law, which specified the terms of the relationship with Sweden, and then requesting that the Swedish parliament do the same. During the crucial process of deciding whether Norway should remain a monarchy or become a republic, however, this sense of caution stood the country in good stead, as Ibsen persuaded other Norwegian cultural leaders—his father-in-law **Bjørnstjerne Bjørnson**, **Arne Garborg**, and **Fridtjof Nansen**—that they should support the monarchy.

Ibsen was also a significant thinker and essayist who published several collections of philosophical, political, and sociological essays. His intellectual background and interests suited him very well for a professorship in sociology at the Royal Frederik's University (now the University of Oslo), and he was invited to give a series of lectures that were essentially an extended job talk. For political reasons, several conservative professors were opposed to the appointment, however. One of them, **Marcus Jacob Monrad**, stated that he found the term *sociology* to be in bad taste.

**IHLEN, NILS CLAUS (1855–1925).** Norwegian politician. Born in Christiania on 23 July 1855, Ihlen received an advanced degree from the university there in 1873. Later the owner of a foundry, he was elected to the *Storting* (**Parliament**) on the **Liberal Party** ticket in 1906. He first served as minister of work in **Gunnar Knudsen**'s first government from 1908 to 1910. Starting in 1913, he became the minister of foreign affairs in Knudsen's second government, serving until 1920. Ihlen's significance in Norwegian history is that he helped Norway navigate the treacherous waters presented both literally and figuratively during **World War I**. While Ihlen's personal sympathies lay with the Allies, he kept his opinions mostly to himself and was a clever negotiator. It fell to his lot to inform the German government about Norwegian policy decisions that were just barely within the bounds of the neutrality that Norway successfully claimed for itself during the war. While under pressure from the Allies to withhold from Germany fish and copper ore that would help the country weather the British blockade, Ihlen had to find a way to offer the Germans enough concessions to keep them from attacking Norway while simultaneously maintaining Norwegian access to commodities necessary to Norwegian life. He is remembered for succeeding on both counts, thus managing to keep Norway out of the war.

**INDUSTRY.** In ancient times and throughout the Middle Ages, most commodities produced in Norway were made at home. During the reign of King **Christian IV**, however, some efforts were made, through the granting of privileges, to encourage production in primitive factories. Sawmills as well as glass- and ironworks operating throughout the 1700s and early 1800s may also be regarded as industrial enterprises.

True industrialization began to take off only in the 1840s, however. Steam-powered sawmills and planers improved the quality of the lumber produced, and wood pulp mills were established. Textile mills were built, for example, *Hjula Veveri* (the Wheels Textile Mills), which was established in 1849 and in 1916 became part of *De forenede Ullvarefabrikker* (United Woolen Mills). Foundries and engineering workshops also arose. Most of the machinery was imported, but thousands of jobs were created. Data provided by the 1875 census show that there were 5,000 factory jobs in the textile mills alone.

The forest products industry expanded at a tremendous rate in the 1880s, and Norwegian paper products became among the best in the world and accounted for a large share of Norwegian exports. The development of **hydroelectric power** furthered such power-hungry industries as the production of nitrogenous fertilizer, the foundation for Norsk Hydro, established in 1905. Because electrical power was lost when transmitted to locations far from where it was generated, factory towns were established near the generating plants. The dislocations associated with **World War I** and the **economic** downturn during the 1930s significantly hampered the nation's industrial development.

After **World War II**, there was an urgent need for commodities, however, and because import controls limited what could be brought into the country, the demand led to an unprecedented industrial expansion in such areas as the food and drink industry, textiles, shoes, electronics, and home furnishings. There was also significant growth in such export-oriented industries as aluminum works, the state-owned Steel Works (*Jernverket*) in Mo i Rana, and an ammonia plant in Glomfjord, Nordland. The **Labor Party** had as its policy to move workers from low-value employment in the rural areas to the large and capital-intensive factories located in what often amounted to company towns, where they could make a greater contribution to Norway's gross national product, thus increasing the general standard of living. Mo i Rana serves as a good example of what this policy resulted in. Like a magnet under a sheet of paper sprinkled with iron filings, the Mo i Rana Steel Works pulled people in from the surrounding areas, depopulating some and diminishing social life in most of them. An even more graphic example can be found in the history of Sauda in western Norway, where the Electric Furnace Products Company, a wholly owned subsidiary of Union Carbide, used both locally generated hydroelectric power and local labor to refine imported ore. The industrial and social conditions present in Sauda have been superbly analyzed and recreated in the fictional works of **Kjartan Fløgstad** and **Tor Obrestad**.

The industrial expansion came to a halt in the early 1970s, partly caused by the **oil** crisis of 1973 but also because of increasingly automated production processes. The development of the off-shore oil industry occupied some of the displaced manpower, but the country had to tolerate higher unemployment levels for a number of years. As Norway was approaching the beginning of the third millennium, a strong knowledge-based economy was emerging, partly replacing the country's earlier reliance on industry.

– J –

**JAABÆK, SØREN PEDERSEN (1814–94).** Norwegian politician. Born on 1 April 1814 in Holum, Vest-Agder County, Jaabæk was the oldest son of a poor farmer with nine children. He was intellectually gifted and read voraciously, and at the age of 16, he determined that he would become a schoolmaster. He also assisted the local State Church minister as a sexton, got involved in local politics and served as mayor of his community. He was elected a member of the *Storting* (**Parliament**) in 1845 and served until 1890, which makes him Norway's longest-serving member of the parliament.

In his ideology, Jaabæk was a classic **economic** liberalist in the spirit of Adam Smith (1723–90) and Frederic Bastiat (1801–50). He believed that Norway's economy suffered from excessive regulation and wanted the government to get out of the way and allow people to manage as best they could. Restrictions on buying, selling, and occupational choice left over from the **Danish absolute monarchy** needed to be done away with. Taxes—many of them paid by Jaabæk's constituents, the small farmers—should be drastically lowered, and Norway's public indebtedness reduced or eliminated. This could only be accomplished if the *Storting*, empowered to allot funds for all government projects, would act decisively to eliminate waste and make saving its watchword. Jaabæk was perceived as stingy, especially by members of the *embedsmann* (public official) class, whose lives he considered frivolous, whose salaries he wanted to keep low, and whose pensions he tended to vote against. The reduction in prices and general economic crisis that hit Norwegian farmers toward the end of the 1860s made his ideas music to the ears of many and catapulted him into a position of national leadership. When he started his paper *Folketidende* (People's News) in 1865, he laid the foundation for a national movement known as *bondevennene* (friends of the farmers), with local associations or chapters. According to a table published in *Folketidende* on 12 July 1871, there were associations in every county except Finnmark, and the grand total was 271. Jaabæk was elected leader of the movement in 1868, and *Folketidende* garnered a higher circulation than any other Norwegian publication at the time.

Jaabæk's greatest historical significance, however, lies in his support of the policies of **Johan Sverdrup** and his role in the development of Norwegian political parties, particularly the **Liberal Party**. Sverdrup pushed for annual sessions of the *Storting* and **jury** trials. At first, Jaabæk was wary of these proposals because of their potential costs, but the improvements in Norway's economy that took place in the 1870s allowed him to set his misgivings aside, and he remained Sverdrup's loyal supporter for the rest of his political career.

**JAGLAND, THORBJØRN (1950– ).** Norwegian politician. Born in Drammen on 5 November 1950 and educated as an **economist**, Jagland held a number of positions of trust in the **Labor Party** and its youth organization before being elected a member of the *Storting* (**Parliament**) in 1993. He was the leader of the Labor Party from 1992 to 2002, when **Jens Stoltenberg** took over after an acrimonious struggle. After **Gro Harlem Brundtland** resigned as prime minister in 1996, Jagland formed a minority government based on the 67 Labor Party representatives in the *Storting* out of a total of 165. He resigned after the parliamentary elections of 1997, when the support for the Labor Party declined relative to the elections four years earlier, and **Kjell Magne Bondevik** took over as the prime minister in a minority coalition government consisting of the **Christian Democrats**, the **Center Party**, and the **Liberal Party**. He also served as minister of foreign affairs in Stoltenberg's first government (2000–2001). He became president (speaker) of the *Storting* in 2005. While Jagland has had an outstanding career as a politician, he has, like other Labor leaders, failed to reach one of his foremost goals, Norwegian membership in the **European Union**.

**JENSEN, SIV (1969– ).** Norwegian politician. Born in **Oslo** on 1 June 1969, Jensen was trained as an **economist**. She was elected a member of the *Storting* (**Parliament**) on the **Progress Party** ticket in 1997, after serving as substitute representative the previous four years. She also served on the Oslo City Council from 1995 to 1999. Well known for her strongly conservative views and friendliness toward the policies of the **United States**—for example, she has been in support of the war in Iraq—she has a long record of service in her party and succeeded **Carl I. Hagen** as caucus leader in 2005. She became party leader in 2006, when Hagen declined reelection.

**JOHNSON, GISLE CHRISTIAN (1822–94).** Norwegian theologian. Born in Halden on 10 September 1822, Johnson grew up in Kristiansand and studied theology at the university in Christiania (now **Oslo**), earning his degree in 1845. He was a brilliant student and was early marked for a scholarly career. After a year in Germany, he became a lecturer at the university, and in 1860, he became a professor.

He taught systematic theology, dogmatic history, and church history. A personal crisis of faith had caused him to develop a strong **pietistic** and darkly serious view of his relationship with God, and his work as an evangelist dovetailed nicely with the low-church tradition back to **Hans Nilsen Hauge**. Riding the wave of the **religious** awakening of the 1850s, he organized the *Christiania Indremissionsforening* (Christiania Society for the Inner Mission) in 1855. In 1868, he founded *Den norske Lutherstiftelse* (The Norwegian Luther Foundation), which in 1891 changed its name to *Det norske lutherske Indremisjonsselskap* (The Norwegian Lutheran Society for Inner Mission), commonly just known as the Inner Mission. He also founded the periodical *Luthersk Kirketidende* (Lutheran Church News) in 1863.

Both these institutions and his academic position gave Johnson a power base from which to turn popular pietistic beliefs into the doctrine of the church as a whole. His teachings were strict and particularly opposed to the Grundtvigianism found in the Norwegian Folk High School movement as represented by **Christopher Bruun**. He felt that people should avoid everything that did not directly lead them to God, not just those things that might lead them astray. Johnson therefore condemned the theater, joking, luxuries, and card games, and he had a special talent for making the punishments of hell seem both frightening and realistic. He had a puritan outlook and advised parents to keep their children in ignorance about anything related to procreation. Through his students—a better term may be *disciples*—his influence was further spread throughout the land.

**JURY LAW.** Passed in 1887 and taking effect on 1 January 1890, the jury law (*juryloven*) provided for a system of trial partly by lay judges. It thus transferred some of the responsibility for criminal justice from the *embedsmann* (public official) class to the people and was therefore a significant step in Norway's process of democratization. The **absolute monarchy** had been founded on the understanding that sovereignty rested with the monarch, who in all areas, including the dispensation of justice, ruled through his appointed representatives. While the establishment of the **constitution** of 1814 shows that the concept of the absolute sovereignty of the monarch had been replaced by the idea of popular sovereignty,

Norway's administrative and legal system had not yet caught up with the new understanding. Social development in Norway was hampered by the power of the *embedsmann* class, whose representatives were largely in control of the state administration until the introduction of **parliamentarism** in 1884. Like parliamentarism, the jury law was part of **Johan Sverdrup**'s efforts to reform and modernize Norwegian society.

## – K –

**KALMAR UNION.** The work of Queen Margareta of Norway, the Kalmar Union was a series of personal unions that brought **Denmark**, Norway, and **Sweden** together under one head of state. Margareta, the daughter of King Valdemar IV Atterdag (c. 1320–75) of Denmark, had been married to King Haakon VI Magnusson of Norway (c. 1340–80). At first, she was able to have her son Olav named king of Norway, later also king of Denmark, while she ruled both countries as his guardian. When he died in 1387, she was elected regent by the Danish council of the realm, and the following year, she was also recognized as regent in Norway. After adopting her sister's grandson, known in **Scandinavian** history as Erik of Pomerania (1382–1459), she managed to have him made king of Norway in 1389, with herself as his guardian. She gained control of Sweden by enlisting the aid of a major faction among the Swedish nobility, which controlled part of the country, and going to war against its ruler, Albrecht of Mechlenburg (c. 1338–1412), who was deposed in 1389. Erik of Pomerania then became king of both Denmark and Sweden in 1396.

The Treaty of Kalmar formalized the arrangement on 17 June 1397, stating that Erik and his descendents were to rule the three Scandinavian countries forever. While each country was to be governed separately by its own councils and according to its own laws, the foreign policy was to be in the hands of the king. The result was continual conflict between Denmark and Sweden until Sweden finally broke out of the union in 1523. In 1536, at the time when the **Reformation** was being pushed through in Denmark and Norway, King **Christian III** (1503–59) and the Danish council of the realm declared Norway henceforth to be simply a part of Denmark, and this event marks the formal end of the Kalmar Union. Norway and Denmark remained united until 1814.

**KARL JOHAN.** *See* BERNADOTTE, JEAN-BAPTISTE JULES (1763–1844).

**KIELLAND, ALEXANDER LANGE (1849–1906).** Norwegian novelist, dramatist, and social critic. Kielland was born on 18 February 1849 into a wealthy merchant family in **Stavanger**. He earned a law degree at the university in Christiania (now **Oslo**), married, and purchased a brickworks near his hometown. Dissatisfied with his life, however, he read widely, and in 1878, he left Stavanger for Paris, hoping to become a writer. Encouraged by the **Danish** critic Georg Brandes, Kielland wrote a novel, *Garman & Worse* (1880; tr. 1885), in which he drew heavily on his own family history; the book combines biting satire with a realistic portrait of Stavanger life in a bygone age.

Kielland's purpose was not to write cultural history, however, but to castigate numerous social ills: class distinctions, hypocrisy, the abuse of power by State Church ministers and other **religious** leaders, the stupidity of the school system, and the lack of integrity in business and **industry**. A number of novels placed him among the foremost of the politically radical writers of his time, but he was also a consummate stylist; for example, in a slender volume of short stories titled *To Novelletter fra Danmark* (1882; tr. in *Norse Tales and Sketches*, 1896).

In 1884, Kielland applied for a public grant in support of his creative work. The timing seemed opportune. **Johan Sverdrup**, representing the newly organized **Liberal Party** supported by Kielland and the rest of the radical Norwegian intelligentsia, had just taken over as prime minister after the culture wars of the late 1870s and early 1880s that culminated in the introduction of **parliamentarism** in Norway in 1884. When it turned out that Sverdrup was not quite as liberal as his supporters had assumed and Kielland's request was denied after an acrimonious debate in the *Storting* (Parliament), Kielland felt a strong sense of betrayal, as did most of the other radicals. The negative decision in the Kielland case, as it was called, did much to bring about the internal divisions in the Liberal Party that plagued it for the rest of Sverdrup's time as prime minister.

Three of Kielland's next novels are set in Stavanger. One of them, *Sankt Hans Fest* (1887; St. John's Festival) excoriates religious bigotry and takes to task the clergyman Lars Oftedahl, who had been instrumental in getting his grant application denied. Another personal attack is made in the play *Professoren* (1888; The Professor), which is notable for its unflattering portrait of the ultraconservative philosophy professor **Marcus Jacob Monrad**.

**KINGS BAY AFFAIR.** A political issue that came to the forefront of Norwegian politics in 1963, the Kings Bay affair concerned a series of accidents in a Spitzbergen coal **mine** operated by the Kings Bay Coal Mining Company, which had been wholly owned by the Norwegian government since 1933. After the loss of a total of 71 lives between 1945 and 1963, a commission appointed by the *Storting* (**Parliament**) placed blame on the Norwegian government, headed by **Einar Gerhardsen**. A nonsocialist parliamentary minority of 74 (out of 150, 74 of whom represented the **Labor Party** and 2 represented the **Socialist People's Party**) demanded that Gerhardsen's minister of **industry**, who had had direct oversight of the matter, should resign. Gerhardsen countered that the *Storting* had no jurisdiction in the case, and the result was a no-confidence resolution proposed by the nonsocialists. When the two Socialist People's Party representatives, **Finn Gustavsen** and Asbjørn Holm, also expressed their lack of confidence in Gerhardsen's government, it was replaced by a coalition government headed by **John Lyng** of the **Conservative Party**. The incident is significant because it led to the first nonsocialist government in Norway since the end of **World War II**, a government that served as a harbinger of things to come in Norwegian politics in the next four decades, when Labor Party and nonsocialist governments alternated.

**KNUDSEN, CHRISTIAN HOLTERMANN (1845–1929).** Norwegian politician and printer. Born on 15 July 1845 in **Bergen**, Knudsen was a printer who was the leader of the Norwegian Printers' Union in Christiania (now **Oslo**) starting in 1876. He is credited with giving the impetus to a nationwide federation of printers' unions in

1884. The year 1885 saw the organization of *Den socialdemokratiske forening* (Social-Democratic Association) in Christiania, of which Knudsen was the head and which was an important precursor for the **Labor Party**. When the party was formed in Arendal in 1887, Knudsen again was one of the prime movers. He led the Labor Party during three periods, the last time in 1918, when he was replaced by **Kyrre Grepp**. He also served as a member of the *Storting* (**Parliament**) from 1906 to 1915 and was a member of the Oslo City Council from 1898 to 1925. A confirmed social-democrat, he opposed joining the Communist International.

**KNUDSEN, GUNNAR (1848–1928).** Norwegian statesman and engineer. Born in Saltrød by Arendal on 19 September 1848 to shipowner Christen Knudsen, Knudsen studied engineering in Gothenburg, **Sweden**, completing his degree in 1869. His early career was primarily in **shipping** and **industry**, and he built and operated Norway's first **hydroelectric** generating plant in Skien. In 1891, he was elected to the *Storting* (**Parliament**) on the **Liberal Party** ticket and served as party leader from 1909 to 1927. He was the president of the *Storting* in 1906–9, 1913–15, and 1919–21. He was also the prime minister in a Liberal Party government from 1908 to 1910 and again from 1913 to 1920, including the difficult years of **World War I**. Although fundamentally a liberalist, Knudsen recognized the need for state intervention in the **economy** during the war and used price supports in order to shield wage earners from some of the worst consequences of increased prices and shortages of certain commodities.

A pragmatist as well as a very strong leader, Knudsen realized that the government had to assume increased control over many aspects of social and economic life. This was especially so because Norwegian access to commodities on the world market, as long as the crisis of the war lasted, went through the governments of the countries where these commodities were available. For example, coal and coke could not be purchased from individual suppliers in Great Britain except through agreements involving the British government. Another example is electrolytic copper, which was crucial to the development of Norwegian hydropower and which could be obtained in Britain only on the condition that Norway prohibited the export of copper ore to Germany.

Knudsen's own practical experience in shipping and industry was undoubtedly valuable when he had to assume the ultimate supervision and management of **trade** relationships that had earlier been the exclusive province of the private sector. Some of the restrictions imposed surely seemed drastic, as when the sale of liquor and wine was prohibited because the raw materials used to produce them were needed as food and when only weak beer was allowed to be brewed. The need to avoid any kind of waste meant that only whole-ground flour could be used for bread. The Norwegian population was largely supportive of these and other policies with similar intent, for it was widely acknowledged that in a time of war, everybody had to work together to survive with a minimum of discomfort.

Knudsen's willingness to depart somewhat from strict liberalist economic principles also showed up in his attitude toward the permitting process that was established for hydroelectric development, where he favored restrictions on the owner-developers. Understanding the potential of Norway's many waterfalls, Knudsen wanted the government to buy some of them for future use. This was a good idea because as early as 1906, three fourths of Norway's developed waterfalls were owned by foreign interests, who had usually purchased them from their owners for next to nothing. As a statesman, Knudsen was a practical and pragmatic leader who managed to look beyond traditional ways of thinking as he sought the solutions that would further Norway's true interests.

**KOHT, HALVDAN (1873–1965).** Norwegian politician and historian. Born in **Tromsø** on 7 July 1873, Koht grew up in the family of a high schoolteacher in Tromsø and Skien. A highly gifted and prolific historian, he became professor at the University of **Oslo** in 1910 and joined the **Labor Party** in 1911. His works span Norwegian history from the early Middle Ages to the 20th century and are written from the perspective of the class struggle as a driving force in historical development but also with a view of history as an organic process where newer forms of social organization grow out of older forms. Koht also wrote several biographies, including one on **Henrik Ibsen**, and edited letters and papers of both Ibsen and **Bjørnstjerne Bjørnson**. From 1935 to 1940, he served as minister of foreign affairs in the government headed by **Johan Nygaardsvold** and has been criticized for not taking the German threat of invasion sufficiently seriously. He was also an active participant in the Norwegian **language** debate, and although he wrote in *nynorsk* (New Norwegian) and served as the head of Noregs Mållag (Norway's Language Society), an organization that promoted the use of *nynorsk*, from 1921 to 1925, he wanted to establish a single written form of Norwegian that was based on both urban and rural dialects. Many of Koht's ideas are reflected in the language reform of 1938. After spending **World War II** in the **United States**, Koht returned to academic life in Norway after the war.

**KOLSTAD, PEDER LUDVIK (1878–1932).** Norwegian politician. Born in Borge, Østfold County, on 28 November 1878, Kolstad was prime minister in the first of two Agrarian Party (*see* CENTER PARTY) governments that were in office during the turbulent early 1930s, serving from 1931 to 1932. At the time, the Agrarians were inspired by Keynesian ideas about a mixed **economy** in which the government was an active participant, but Kolstad's minority government had very weak support in the *Storting* (**Parliament**), where the Agrarians held only 25 seats. His government was allowed to remain in power largely because no other party wanted to assume the burden of governing the country under the difficult economic conditions at the time. Kolstad's government is otherwise notable for the fact that its minister of defense was **Vidkun Quisling**. Kolstad became ill and died while in office and was succeeded by **Jens Hundseid**.

**KONOW, WOLLERT (1845–1924).** Norwegian politician. Born in Fana near **Bergen** to Dr. Wollert Konow on 16 August 1845, Konow received his matriculations certificate in 1864, passed the *Examen Philosophicum* at the university in Christiania (now **Oslo**) the following year, and spent some time traveling in Europe. An admirer of the **Danish** Folk High School movement, he led two Norwegian Folk High Schools between 1868 and 1873. Starting in 1880, he served more than 25 years in the local government of Fana, and between 1880 and 1888, he was a member of the *Storting* (**Parliament**), representing the **Liberal Party**. Having left the national political scene for approximately 20 years, he again served in the *Storting* from 1910 to 1912, this time representing the **Liberal Left Party**, which was closer to the **Conservative Party** than the Liberal Party. Even though the Liberal Left Party wanted to establish its independence vis-à-vis both the Conservatives and the Liberals, pressure from **Christian Michelsen** resulted in a coalition government with the Conservative Party as its partner and with Konow as the prime minister (for a month he also served as minister of **agriculture**). Having excluded some of the most experienced and capable members of the Conservative Party from the cabinet, Konow was less supportive of the Conservatives' flagship issues than they liked; for example, he did not seem interested in weakening the licensing laws pushed through by **Johan Castberg** in 1909.

The Conservatives found a reason to rebel in 1912, when Konow gave a speech in which he spoke positively about *nynorsk* (New Norwegian), the written norm established by men like **Ivar Aasen** and **Aasmund Olafsson Vinje** but in 1912 most strongly associated with the name of **Arne Garborg**, a man who was anathema to the Right, both because of his **language** and his history as a leader of the Norwegian radicals. The ministers from the Conservative Party resigned, and Konow was unable to replace them, so he had to resign, too, and his government was succeeded by one from the Conservative Party alone under the leadership of **Jens Bratlie**.

**KORVALD, LARS (1916–2006).** Norwegian politician. Korvald was born on 29 April 1916 in Mjøndalen, Buskerud County, and had his origins in the **pietistic** segment of Norwegian society from which many members of the **Christian Democratic Party** have traditionally been recruited. After doing advanced work in **agriculture**, he became a teacher at and later head of a local agricultural school. He was elected to the *Storting* (**Parliament**) in 1961, retiring from political life in 1981. He served as the caucus leader for the Christian Democrats during two periods (1965–72 and 1973–74) and as party leader from 1967 to 1975 and 1977 to 1979. When the 1972 European Community (EC; *see* EUROPEAN ECONOMIC COMMUNITY [EEC]) referendum resulted in a stern rebuke to the promembership Labor government led by Prime Minister **Trygve Bratteli**, Korvald formed a minority coalition government consisting of the Christian Democratic Party, the **Center Party**, and the **Liberal Party**. This government was succeeded by another government headed by Bratteli approximately a year later, subsequent to the parliamentary elections of 1973.

Korvald was Norway's first Christian Democratic prime minister, and his short-lived government proved that the country had available a viable centrist alternative to a **Labor Party** government. Korvald thus paved the way for **Kjell Magne Bondevik**, whom he mentored and recruited to his administration. It also fell to Korvald's lot to negotiate a **trade** agreement, short of full membership, with the EC after the 1972 referendum and to formulate Norway's first **oil** policy. After his retirement from national politics, Korvald served as the county administrator in Østfold.

**KRISTELIG FOLKEPARTI.** *See* CHRISTIAN DEMOCRATIC PARTY.

**KYSTPARTIET.** *See* COASTAL PARTY.

# – L –

**LABOR PARTY.** Although the full name of the party is *Det norske Arbeiderparti* (DnA; The Norwegian Labor Party), it is commonly known simply as *Arbeiderpartiet* (Ap; the Labor Party). The party arose at a time when the first attempt to create trade unions since the work of **Marcus Thrane** took place. The first union was that of the printers, formed in 1872, and a national federation of trade unions, *Den faglige Landsorganisasjon* (LO; The National Trade Union Association), was organized in 1899. The party was formed on 21 August 1887 in Hisøy near Arendal and has grown from its infancy to become Norway's largest political party. It started out working for the extension of the franchise to all adults, a legal limit to the length of the workday, direct taxation, and support of justified strikes. It presented itself as a socialist party from the beginning.

During the turbulent years in the 1890s, prior to the **dissolution of the union with Sweden**, there was a strong nationalistic tenor in the Labor Party, as it was militantly opposed to the union. The party's appeal was limited to urban workers, however, for the rural population did not like its ideas about collectivization of the farmland. People like **Christopher Hornsrud**, the later Labor Party prime minister, understood that the party needed to become more pragmatic so as to appeal to small farmers and farm workers. The **parliamentary** election held in 1903 gave the party its first four representatives in the *Storting* (Parliament). Progress was made on many of its issues; for example, voting rights for **women** were granted in 1913.

Around this time, there was a faction within the party, led by **Martin Tranmæl**, that argued that revolutionary means were needed to affect social change. At a labor meeting held in **Trondheim** in 1911, Tranmæl expressed opposition to making long-term agreements with employers and supported the use of strikes as well as sabotage to discourage scabs. Tranmæl also wanted the Norwegian **economy** to become nationalized and control of the means of production to be turned over to the workers. These ideas, associated with what was called the Union Opposition within the party, were of interest especially to its younger members, and after the Russian Revolution in 1917, there were some attempts to organize workers' councils and soldiers' councils throughout the country. At the party convention in 1918, the Union Opposition won a decisive victory, and the Labor Party was thenceforth a revolutionary proletarian party, which in 1919 joined the Third International, also known as the Communist International (Comintern), headquartered in Moscow. The Soviet Communist Party considered the Norwegian Labor Party one of its many bridgeheads in capitalist territory.

The moderate members of the Labor Party were unhappy about the party's association with the Comintern and formed a splinter party named *Norges Socialdemokratiske Arbeiderparti* (NSA; **Norway's Social-Democratic Labor Party**) in 1921. When the Labor Party left the Comintern in 1923, its left wing splintered off and formed *Norges Kommunistiske Parti* (NKP; **Norway's Communist Party**). When in 1927 the Labor Party and the NSA merged, the NKP remained a separate party. The 1927 parliamentary election made the new and revisionist (rather than revolutionary) Labor Party Norway's largest political party, with 37 percent of the popular vote and 59 representatives in the *Storting*. The sitting coalition government, under the leadership of Prime Minister **Ivar Lykke** of the **Conservative Party**, resigned in early 1928, and King **Haakon VII** asked Christopher Hornsrud to form a Labor minority government after first trying to get the Agrarian Party and the **Liberal Party** to enter into a coalition.

Hornsrud's program reflected the concerns of Labor's left wing by declaring that his government's intention was to prepare Norway to become a socialist state, however, which led to a vote of no confidence two weeks later, making Hornsrud's government the shortest one in Norwegian history.

The worldwide economic crisis in the late 1920s and throughout the 1930s pulled the Labor Party further away from its revolutionary past as it opted for a mixed economy managed according to certain Keynesian principles. In 1935, the Labor Party formed a minority government with **Johan Nygaardsvold** as the prime minister. A week later, the caucuses of Labor and the Agrarian Party made an agreement that was much to the benefit of both, as it gave the Agrarians support for the farmers and gave the Labor government what amounted to a majority in the *Storting*. While Nygaardsvold's government has been criticized for Norway's lack of military preparedness in 1940, it was a stable government that, while in exile in London, took care of Norway's interests during **World War II**.

During the 20 years between 1945 and 1965, the Labor Party continually governed Norway except for a 4-week hiatus in 1963, when **John Lyng** was the prime minister in a minority coalition government. Mostly, **Einar Gerhardsen** served as prime minister. Labor led the reconstruction made necessary by the war and developed the Norwegian welfare state. Now firmly a social-democratic party, it even supported Norwegian membership in the **North Atlantic Treaty Organization**, which led to a schism in 1961, when the *Sosialistisk Folkeparti* (SF; **Socialist People's Party**) was founded. In 1963, the two SF votes in the *Storting* both brought Lyng's government into power and threw it out again.

The struggle over Norwegian membership in the European Community (*see* EUROPEAN ECONOMIC COMMUNITY [EEC]), culminating in the referendum held in 1972, led to less than the usual stability in Norwegian political life between the mid-1960s and the mid-1980s, when Labor Party governments alternated with Center and Center–Right coalitions. The year 1986 saw the beginning of another Labor era, however, as **Gro Harlem Brundtland** presided over Labor governments for most of the next 10 years. When Brundtland's successor, **Thorbjørn Jagland**, received less support than hoped for in the 1997 parliamentary election, the Labor government gave way to another Center coalition, which fell in 2001, leading **Jens Stoltenberg** to form a Labor government. A Center–Right coalition under **Kjell Magne Bondevik** took over until 2005, when Stoltenberg formed a coalition government consisting of Labor, the **Socialist Left Party** (SV; a successor to *Sosialistisk Folkeparti*), and the **Center Party**.

*LAGTING.* The *Storting*, the Norwegian **parliament**, is largely a unicameral body, but for purposes of considering legislative matters, it is divided into two compartments. The *Lagting* (literally, an assembly that considers laws) functions as a type of upper house in that it consists of one fourth of the members of the *Storting*, elected by their colleagues shortly after a new *Storting* has been chosen by the voters. The *Lagting* receives bills from the *Odelsting* (literally, an assembly of those who possess allodial rights to farmland, consisting of the remaining three fourths of the *Storting*) and gives them further consideration before voting on them. Its members cannot themselves propose bills. The *Lagting* is also the body that, together with the Supreme Court justices, serves as a panel of judges in impeachment proceedings. The *Lagting* was abolished by the *Storting* on 20 February 2007, and this **constitutional** change will take place after the 2009 parliamentary elections.

*LANDSSVIKOPPGJØRET* (**COLLABORATION TRIALS**). When Germany attacked Norway on 9 April 1940, some Norwegians were already members of the Norwegian National Socialist Party (*Nasjonal Samling* [NS]). Others joined during the five years Norway was occupied by the Germans. Some Norwegian men fought for the Nazis on the Eastern Front (*frontkjempere* [front fighters]), while some **women** served as Nazi military nurses. Other Norwegians (for example, **Vidkun Quisling**) committed treason through acts that were primarily political rather than military. Others, like **Henry Rinnan**, actively tortured and murdered Norwegian resistance workers. Many Norwegians made money working for the occupiers.

After the war, approximately 92,000 individuals were charged with various crimes related to their activities during the occupation. Approximately 50,000 received some kind of punishment, ranging from the death penalty to fines. One of those who were fined was the writer **Knut Hamsun**. Approximately 17,000 individuals received prison sentences. Membership in the NS after 9 April 1940 was considered a punishable offense, but most ordinary business dealings with the Germans were not. Many Norwegians felt that those who had made money on the Germans were not punished severely enough. On the whole, the collaboration trials are considered a problematic chapter in Norwegian history.

**LANDSTAD, MAGNUS BROSTRUP (1802–80).** Norwegian folklorist. Born to the State Church minister Hans Landstad on 7 October 1802, Landstad studied theology at the university in Christiania (now **Oslo**), earning his degree in 1827. After a series of appointments in various parts of the country, he succeeded his father as the minister at Seljord, Telemark County, in 1839. Telemark was an area with a rich folkloristic tradition, and Landstad started collecting ballads, collaborating with Olea Crøger (1801–55), who recorded ballads and folk melodies in the area of Heddal, Telemark. Landstad published *Norske Folkeviser* (Norwegian Ballads) in 1852, approximately the same time as the famous publication of legends and folktales by **Peter Christen Asbjørnsen** and **Jørgen Moe**. Landstad is also noted for a significant revision to the Norwegian State Church hymnal.

**LANGE, HALVARD MANTHEY (1902–70).** Norwegian politician. The son of the noted pacifist and **Nobel Peace Prize** winner Christian Lous Lange (1869–1938), Lange was born in **Oslo** on 16 September 1902, earned a university degree in 1929, and worked as a teacher and university lecturer during the 1930s. A member of the **Labor Party** since 1927, he was arrested by the Germans in 1942 and spent the rest of **World War II** in several concentration camps, including Sachsenhausen. In 1946, he became the minister of foreign affairs in **Einar Gerhardsen**'s second government and had the same position under **Oscar Torp** as well as in Gerhardsen's third and fourth governments. In all, he served as minister of foreign affairs until 1965, with the exception of a one-month-long hiatus in 1963, when Erling Wikborg (1894–1992) of the **Christian Democrats** had the post during the administration of Prime Minister **John Lyng**. He was an elected representative to the *Storting* (**Parliament**) from 1950 to 1968.

Lange's greatest historical significance relates to the change in Norwegian security policy during the postwar years. Lange understood clearly that Norway's traditional neutrality, which had kept the country out of **World War I** but had not kept it from being attacked by Germany in 1940, was of no value during the cold war. In contrast to some other Labor Party politicians, he insisted that Norway, which because of its strategic location had little hope of remaining neutral in an armed conflict between East and West, should consider aligning itself with Great Britain and the **United States** by joining the **North Atlantic Treaty Organization** (NATO). Lange kept to his resolve in the face of significant pressure from the Soviet Union, which offered Norway a nonaggression pact in place of NATO membership. When Norway joined NATO as one of its charter members in 1949, the foundation was laid for its peace and complete independence during the cold war era. Lange had an outstanding international reputation as a statesman and was among those who facilitated additional cooperation among the NATO countries, in addition to the primary security mission of the alliance.

**LANGUAGE.** Together with **Danish**, Faroese, Icelandic, and **Swedish**, Norwegian belongs to the Nordic side of the northwest branch of the Germanic language family. Close to the **literary** language found in the medieval Icelandic sagas, Old Norwegian is known from both manuscript sources and runic inscriptions and came into being as a separate language during the **Viking** period.

Old Norwegian was quite stable until about 1350 but changed considerably during the centuries following the **Black Death**. Phonology, grammar, and lexicon were all affected, and it is believed that the decline in population as well as extensive contact with the traders of the **Hanseatic League** may be part of the reason. The spoken form of Old Norwegian ceased to exist and was replaced by a number of different dialects. As the distance between daily speech and the written norm increased, the written language also changed. Furthermore, the union with Denmark led to the use of Danish by government officials, and the **Reformation** made Danish the language of the church. Danish also became the language of the law in Norway, starting with the reign of King **Christian IV** of Denmark and Norway.

Danish remained Norway's written language also after the union with Sweden had come into existence in 1814. While farmers and fishermen spoke their local dialects, members of the *embedsmann* (public official) class and other upper-class people generally spoke Danish but with more or less Norwegian pronunciation. Keeping Danish as Norway's written language was incompatible with the nation-building project of the 19th century, however, and the language debate centered on the question of whether one should quickly create a new national language or opt for a more gradual development that would lead Norwegian to increasingly become different from Danish.

The main spokesperson for the idea that Norway needed a new language right away was the dialectologist and linguist **Ivar Aasen**, who single-handedly created a written form of Norwegian called *Landsmaal* (country language) that was based on the more archaic dialects of western Norway. Influenced by the ideas of the **national romanticism** and in order to promote democracy and education, Aasen wanted the rural population to have a written language that was similar to the speech of the people.

The teacher Knud Knudsen, on the other hand, wanted to gradually create a Norwegian written language on the basis of how members of the upper classes in Norway actually pronounced Danish in their daily speech. While perhaps equally nationalistic as Aasen's project, this way of thinking was both much less democratic and less likely to further popular education. Knudsen's form of written Norwegian was called *Riksmaal* (national language), and later it became known as *bokmål* (book language).

While most Norwegian writers, including **Bjørnstjerne Bjørnson** and **Henrik Ibsen**, hewed close to Knudsen's line of thought, **Aasmund Olafsson Vinje** and **Arne Garborg** consciously worked to develop *Landsmaal*, later known as *nynorsk* (New Norwegian), as a literary language.

In 1885, the *Storting* (**Parliament**) voted to give *Riksmaal* and *Landsmaal* equal status as written forms of Norwegian in all government-related contexts. In 1892, each school district was empowered to determine which form should be used in the local schools. Consequently, **educational** materials are available in both forms of Norwegian, and all Norwegian children are taught to read texts in both forms of the language.

During the first half of the 20th century, government policy, under the leadership of the **Liberal Party** and the **Labor Party**, was focused on uniting *nynorsk* and *bokmål* (the two terms were introduced in 1929) into one form of Norwegian called *samnorsk* (Common Norwegian). Several language reforms were introduced, most notably in 1907, 1917, and 1938. The changes made in 1938 were met with strong resistance, however, as they offended users of both *nynorsk* and *bokmål*, who came to regard *samnorsk* as a common enemy. The government therefore backpedaled significantly during the second half of the 20th century, and reforms in 1959 and 1981 brought back forms of spelling and grammar that had earlier been outlawed, meaning that the idea of *samnorsk* became a thing of the past. The most recent reform took place on 1 July 2005, when a time-honored distinction between "main forms" and "allowable forms" of spelling and grammar was largely abandoned. Also, the spelling of the Norwegian word for *neither*, which had been *verken* since 1959, was again allowed to be the traditional *hverken*.

Since the end of the *samnorsk* project, Norwegian language planning has focused on what to do about new loanwords, especially those borrowed from English. Under the leadership of the *Norsk Språkråd* (Norwegian Language Council), established in 1972, the spelling of loanwords is often changed to reflect Norwegian orthographic conventions. A major spelling reform for loanwords took place in 1996. Another current issue in the Norwegian language debate concerns the status of education in *nynorsk* for users of *bokmål*.

The various **Sámi** languages used in Norway, Sweden, Finland, and Russia comprise a separate language group within the Finno-Ugric language family. Northern Sámi is used as a language of administration in several municipalities in Finnmark County. On 1 January 2006, Tysfjord municipality in Nordland County made Lule-Sámi equal to Norwegian as a language of municipal administration, and five other municipalities in the counties of Troms, Nordland, and Nord-Trøndelag are studying whether to institute similar changes to the status of the local Sámi language.

**LEAGUE OF NATIONS.** The League of Nations grew out of the Versailles treaty following **World War I** and was primarily the brainchild of U.S. President Woodrow Wilson. Its purpose was to promote disarmament, prevent war through collective security, seek diplomatic solutions to conflicts, and promote the general welfare among the nations. Both Germany and Russia were excluded, however, and the **United States** refused to ratify the agreement. Some nonsocialist Norwegian political leaders were skeptical regarding an organization that had so little support from the major players in the international community, while others were in favor of joining. The **Labor Party**, which was still in its revolutionary phase, regarded the league as a capitalist plot. The biggest problem for Norway was the part of the agreement that stated that member states were to cancel all **trade** relations with an aggressor state and otherwise support those attacked, for this was viewed as a threat to Norwegian neutrality.

When Norway joined in spite of its reservations, it consistently advocated in favor of German membership, which was allowed in 1926, and promoted agreements among states to submit to the binding arbitration of conflicts. While the league had some successes, it had no power of its own with which to back up its resolutions. Depending on the member states for enforcement and particularly on the Great Powers, it proved unable to prevent Fascist and Nazi aggression in the 1930s. After **World War II**, it was replaced by the **United Nations**.

**LIBERAL LEFT PARTY.** Formed on 1 March 1909, the *Frisinnede Venstre* answered to needs similar to those that had been met by the **United Party** (*Samlingspartiet*) six years before. Its prime mover was **Christian Michelsen**, and it drew away a large part of the less radical members of the **Liberal Party**. Politically quite successful during the 1910s and 1920s, it cooperated closely with the **Conservative Party**. In 1933, it changed its name to the Liberal People's Party (*Frisinnede Folkeparti*) but received little support and was formally discontinued in 1945.

**LIBERAL PARTY.** *Venstre*, Norway's Liberal Party, was formed in early 1884 during the political struggle that, under the leadership of **Johan Sverdrup**, led to the introduction of **parliamentarism** through the impeachment of the sitting cabinet. After King Oscar II repeatedly refused to sign into law a bill that obligated his cabinet members to attend parliamentary meetings and that had been passed three times by the *Storting* (Parliament) in 1873, 1876, and 1879, a vote in the *Storting* on 9 June 1880 simply declared that the bill was to be considered law. During the extraordinary political turmoil that took place both before and after the vote on 9 June, *Venstreforeninger* (Liberal associations) were formed all over Norway, and in early 1883, Sverdrup's supporters in the *Storting* got together and formed their own *Venstreforening*. This did not mean that a national party had been organized, however, as the event should properly be considered the organization of a caucus. The national party was formed in late January 1884, when representatives for the local organizations met in Christiania (now **Oslo**), and Sverdrup was selected as its first leader. There was a schism in the party starting in 1888, when it split into the **Moderate Liberal Party** (*Moderate Venstre*) and the Pure Liberal Party (*Rene Venstre*). Sverdrup continued as the leader of the former, while **Johannes Steen** was the leading light in the latter.

In the late 1800s, *Venstre* wanted to extend the right to vote to all men, and this goal was achieved in 1898. In order to reduce the power of the ***embedsmann*** (public official) class, it successfully introduced **jury** trials in 1887. Somewhat in opposition to the State Church, it promoted full freedom of **religion**. The party also wanted to discontinue the union with **Sweden**, which had been in place since 1814, and this goal was reached in 1905. *Venstre* was also the party that spoke in favor of **women**'s rights, including the right to vote, which was granted in 1913. In general, in its earlier years *Venstre* represented the interests of the farmers, the cottagers (*husmenn*), day laborers and other workers, and the proponents of ***nynorsk*** (New Norwegian), the written form of Norwegian first championed by the writers **Ivar Aasen**, **Aasmund Olafsson Vinje**, and **Arne Garborg**. *Venstre* was thus the party of the poor and the downtrodden in their struggle against the powerful and the rich. The party was very successful and formed a number of governments, supplying the prime minister six times.

For all intents and purposes, Norway had a two-party system during the early years of *Venstre*. The formation and growth of the **Labor Party**, started in 1887, cut heavily into the support for *Venstre*, which received an absolute majority in the *Storting* for the last time in the 1915 parliamentary election. The Agrarian Party (*Bondepartiet*), later renamed the **Center Party**, was formed in 1920 and took away many rural voters. When the **Christian Democratic Party** was established in 1933, many low-church people for whom *Venstre* had been the natural home—low-church people relied more on lay preachers than on State Church ministers, whose **economic** and political interests coincided with those of the rest of the *embedsmann* class—voted Christian Democratic rather than Liberal. After the formation of these two parties, *Venstre* has had cabinet members only through its participation in coalition governments.

In the five parliamentary elections held in the 1950s and 1960s, *Venstre* averaged 9.7 percent of the popular vote and held an average of 15 seats in the *Storting*. A low point in its history came in 1972, however, when the struggle over Norwegian membership in the European Community (EC; *see* EUROPEAN ECONOMIC COMMUNITY [EEC])—later renamed the **European Union**—caused the party to split. The dissenters, favoring EC membership, formed a new party named the **New Left People's Party**, which was renamed *Det Liberale Folkeparti* (The Liberal People's Party) in 1980. Both the party leader, **Helge Seip**, and 9 of its 13 representatives in the *Storting* left *Venstre* at the split in 1972, and it got only 2 seats in the *Storting* in the 1973 election (the breakaway party received 1 seat). The two parties merged in 1988, but the damage to *Venstre* was largely done, and between 1985 and 1993, it held no seats in the *Storting*. **Lars Sponheim**, the colorful head of *Venstre* since 1996, became its lone member of parliament in 1993, and its representation increased to six in 1997. That number decreased to 2 in 2001—Sponheim and **Odd Einar Dørum**—but in 2005, *Venstre* recovered some of its pre-1972 position, as it got 5.9 percent of the popular vote and received 10 seats in the *Storting*.

Both socially liberal and centrist, the core values of the contemporary *Venstre* are civil liberties, **environmental** protection, and the interests of small business. The party wants Norwegian society to be less complex, more diverse, and more hospitable to a broader range of human self-realization. Its anticlerical heritage manifests itself in its desire to no longer have a Norwegian State Church. Its traditional distrust of big business shows up in its advocacy of legalized file sharing.

**LIE, TRYGVE (1896–1968).** Norwegian politician. Born in **Oslo** on 16 July 1896 as the son of a carpenter, Lie studied law at the University of Oslo, receiving his degree in 1919. He had joined the **Labor Party** six years earlier and quickly rose in the ranks, serving as its national secretary and as one of its representatives to the *Storting* (**Parliament**). In 1935, he was named minister of justice in the Labor government then formed by **Johan Nygaardsvold**, and he subsequently served in other cabinet posts, including that of minister of foreign affairs in the Norwegian exile government in Great Britain during **World War II**. He also held cabinet posts in the early 1960s.

The leader of the Norwegian delegation to both the **United Nations** (UN) conference in San Francisco in 1946 and to the general assembly of the UN in the same year, Lie was chosen as the first secretary general of the UN, serving until 1952. During the 1947–48 conflict in Palestine, he supported the founding of the state of Israel but failed to find a diplomatic solution to the Berlin blockade of 1948–49. His support for UN intervention in the conflict on the Korean peninsula in 1950 earned him the enmity of the Soviet Union.

**LITERATURE.** Norway's earliest literature consists of runic inscriptions made on stone during the **Viking** age as well as alliterative poetry that was mostly orally transmitted and is known in writing only from later Icelandic manuscripts. The Icelandic sagas of the 13th century also indicate that there was a Norwegian oral prose tradition that continued among the Norwegian settlers in Iceland. As Christianity arrived in Norway, missionary monks and priests brought with them both the writing technology and the alphabet that enabled large-scale creation of texts. During the High Middle Ages, there were writing traditions associated both with the royal court and the residences of **religious** leaders; for example, King **Sverre Sigurdsson** arranged to have a saga of his life composed. The finest literary text from medieval Norway is a handbook for kings called *Konungs skuggsjá* (the King's Mirror), which may have been composed around 1250, and that seems to have influenced the legislative work of **Magnus VI Lagabøte**. With the arrival of the **Black Death**, however, Norway lost so much of its population that the native literary tradition dwindled to almost nothing.

The medieval representatives of the church used Latin as a medium of writing, but this changed with the coming of the Lutheran **Reformation**. Lutheranism privileges the individual's relationship with God, and reading sacred scripture is a primary means by which that relationship can be developed. The New Testament was translated into **Danish** as early as in 1524, and the entire Bible was available in Danish by 1550. The Danish Bible translation was also used in Norway, which had entered into a union with Denmark in 1397. Many Lutheran ministers studied abroad and brought intellectual impulses with them when they returned home. Thus such general European movements as the Renaissance and humanism came to play a role in Norway as well, where there was a resurgence of interest in the literature of the Viking period as well as an outpouring of topographical descriptions. During the Baroque period, Norway had a great poet in **Petter Dass**, who wrote within a general European aesthetic. By the time of the Enlightenment figure Ludvig Holberg (1684–1754), there were established conduits of artistic and literary communication between Norway and the rest of Europe; however, the flow was generally northward rather than the opposite way. The influence of neoclassicism can be observed in Johan Herman Wessel's comedy *Kierlighed uden Strømper* (1772; Love without Stockings).

The northward migration of ideas is even more clearly visible during the period in literary and intellectual history that is referred to as romanticism. Such figures as Charles-Louis de Secondat Montesquieu (1689–1755), Jean-Jacques Rousseau (1712–78), and Albrecht von Haller (1708–77) laid the groundwork for the ideas and attitudes that inform this movement. Some of these ideas, further developed by the German philosophers Johann Gottlieb Fichte (1762–1814) and Friedrich Schelling (1775–1854), made it possible to regard the literary artist as a kind of prophet who communicated with the divine found in nature. Johann Gottfried von Herder (1744–1803) emphasized both the role of the nation and of language and its connection to this divine spirit, thus giving romanticism a national slant.

Although somewhat belatedly, a number of Norwegian writers were affected by the **national romanticism**'s emphasis on nature, the rural population, and the nation's glorious past. An early example is a story by **Maurits Hansen** (1794–1842) titled "Luren" (1819; The Shepherd's Horn), in which the narrator tells about a visit to a Norwegian farm family in the interior of the country. The farmer, named Thor, is said to be a direct descendant of the ancient King **Harald Fairhair**, and special mention is made of his expressive dialect. A few years later, the poet **Johan Sebastian Welhaven** wrote exquisite nature poetry as well as folklore poems, while the self-taught linguist **Ivar Aasen** single-handedly created a separate written form of Norwegian called *nynorsk* (New Norwegian), based on the dialects spoken in western Norway. A number of both men and **women**, led by **Peter Christen Asbjørnsen** and **Jørgen Moe**, collected, edited, and published folktales, legend, and ballads. In the early part of his career, **Henrik Ibsen** wrote plays that used material from history and folklore, as did his later drama *Peer Gynt* (1867; tr. 1892), which satirizes the preoccupations of the national romantics.

The national romanticism was succeeded by realism, which also came from outside of Norway, particularly France. The term *realism* in literary studies denotes a literary style that tries to describe life as it is, without the idealization and subjectivity of the romantics. Here it also refers to Norwegian prose and drama written from around 1855 through the 1880s but particularly in the 1870s. **Bjørnstjerne Bjørnson** wrote peasant stories and novels with a contemporary setting, while **Camilla Collett**'s seminal novel *Amtmandens Døttre* (1854–55; tr. *The District Governor's Daughters*, 1992), inaugurated feminist literature in Norway. Influenced by the Danish critic Georg Brandes (1842–1927), who wanted modern literature to discuss current issues, Ibsen wrote a number of plays critical of contemporary culture. The novelist Jonas Lie (1833–1908) depicted family life, business affairs, and other current topics. Lie's colleague **Alexander L. Kielland** (1849–1906) was the master satirist of his generation.

Implicit in the realist literary program was the sense that advocacy of social causes was efficacious, but when realism turns toward naturalism, such optimism largely disappears. Influenced by the ideas of the French critic Charles-Augustin Sainte-Beuve (1804–69), the novelist Émile Zola (1840–1902), and natural science as practiced by Charles Darwin (1809–92), the naturalists adhered to the doctrine of determinism. Truth was to be found in nature rather than, as for the romantics, in some kind of transcendental reality, and the task of the naturalist writer was to imitate the scientist as far as possible. Stories were told in great detail, almost approaching that of a lab report, as in the works of Amalie Skram (1846–1905). Her male colleague **Arne Garborg** (1851–1924) similarly offers numerous details in his naturalist works, for example, the novel *Hjaa ho Mor* (1890; Living with Mama), which is partly based on the life of his wife Hulda. In other works, Garborg further explored contemporary sex roles. Around 1890, Norwegian literature turned to a greater concern with the individual and with human consciousness; the early works of **Knut Hamsun** are its best example of this type of writing.

Norwegian literature in the first half of the 20th century is marked by the influence of Karl Marx (1818–83) and Sigmund Freud (1856–1939), as well as by the experience of the two world wars. The change in social conditions brought about by **World War I** was chronicled in the novel *Lillelord* (1955; tr. 1982) by Johan Borgen (1902–79), the first volume of a trilogy that concludes during **World War II**. Wartime profiteering is the theme of the play *Vår ære og vår makt* (1935; tr. *Our Power and Our Glory*, 1971), by the poet and dramatist Nordahl Grieg (1902–43). Marxism and Freudianism left their mark on the novelists Aksel Sandemose (1899–1965) and Sigurd Hoel (1890–1960); the latter probed the causes of Nazism in his novel *Møte ved milepelen* (1947; tr. *Meeting at the Milestone*, 1951). The effects of World War II can be observed with particular poignancy in the work of novelist and playwright **Jens Bjørneboe** (1920–76), who wrote about medical experiments performed by Nazi doctors on concentration camp prisoners and Norway's treatment of Nazi wartime collaborators at the close of the war.

Postwar Norwegian literature reflects people's concern about the realities of the cold war and the tension between the superpowers. The novelists **Tor Obrestad** (1938– ), **Espen Haavardsholm** (1945– ), and **Dag Solstad** (1941– ) were influenced by Maoism in the 1960s and wrote with the hope of furthering the cause the Marxist-Leninist revolution. In the 1980s, they tried to come to terms with their youthful selves. Existential questions were likewise of interest, as in the work of the novelist Alfred Hauge (1915–86). Many writers have also shown an interest in metafiction, fabulation, and other aspects of literary postmodernism, foremost among them **Kjartan Fløgstad** (1944– ) and Jan Kjærstad (1953– ). Fløgstad has written a series of novels that use antirealist techniques to depict the process of industrialization in western Norway, starting with *Dalen Portland* (1977; tr. *Dollar Road*, 1989). Kjærstad's novel *Forføreren* (1993; tr. *The Seducer*, 2003) is the first volume in a trilogy about a television personality. *See also* HOEM, EDVARD (1949– ); RØLVAAG, OLE EDEVART (1876–1931); UNDSET, SIGRID (1882–1949); VINJE, AASMUND OLAFSSON (1818–70); WERGELAND, NICOLAI (1780–1848).

**LOCAL GOVERNMENT LAWS.** Passed by the ***Storting*** (**Parliament**) in 1837, the local government laws (*formannsskapslovene*) constitute a cornerstone in the development of Norwegian democracy. Under the **absolute monarchy** as well as for the first couple of decades after 1814, government on the local level had been the province of members of the ***embedsmann*** (public official) class. The local government laws, supported by the rural members of the *Storting* under the leadership of **Ole Gabriel Ueland**, provided that locally elected representatives should make local government decisions. This system of local governance established an important training ground for citizen legislators on all levels, including the national one, and enabled especially rural dwellers with little access to advanced **education** an opportunity to gain experience in democratic life.

**LOFTHUS, KRISTIAN JENSSØN (1750–97).** Farmer and rebel. The prime mover behind Norway's largest peasant rebellion during its union with **Denmark**, Lofthus was christened on 15 May 1750 and inherited his father's farm in the district of Vestre Moland near Lillesand. By personal experience, he knew how badly the merchants in cities like Arendal and Kristiansand exploited the farmers, who by law were forced to **trade** only with specific merchants to whom they were usually indebted. He was also aware that the various public officials in the area often charged the farmers higher fees than what they were entitled to for various services. In a long tradition of bringing such grievances to the attention of the king in Copenhagen, Lofthus traveled there in 1787 and met with the crown prince. Because he was asked to bring proof of his accusations, he went back home and started meeting with groups of farmers at a time, obtaining their signatures on letters of complaint. Such assemblies were illegal, so Lofthus was ultimately arrested in spite of the huge gatherings of farmers—at one time 800—that came to his assistance. Because the authorities were afraid of the consequences if he were to be found guilty of rebellion and punished, his case was postponed until 1792, when the anger among the farmers had subsided. Lofthus was sentenced to life imprisonment, kept in chains, and died at the fortress of Akershus in 1797.

**LØVLAND, JØRGEN GUNNARSSON (1848–1922).** Norwegian politician and newspaper editor. Born in Evje, Setesdal, Aust-Agder County, on 3 February 1848, Løvland was the son of a farmer and completed the basic course for teachers in 1865. After working as a teacher and newspaper editor in Kristiansand until 1885, he was elected a **Liberal Party** member of the *Storting* (**Parliament**) in 1886–88, 1892–97, and 1913–15. From 1898 to 1903, he was minister of public works under **Johannes Steen** and **Otto Albert Blehr** and was assigned to the portion of the government located in Stockholm from 1899 to 1900. In 1905, he was for a time the Norwegian prime minister in Stockholm under **Christian Michelsen**, and he also served as Michelsen's minister of foreign affairs from 1905 to 1907. He was prime minister and head of the Norwegian government from 1907 to 1908. Between 1915 and 1920, he served as minister of ecclesiastical affairs in **Gunnar Knudsen**'s second government. Løvland had a central position during the **dissolution of the union** between Norway and **Sweden** in 1905, when he was part of the delegation that negotiated the final settlement. While prime minister in 1907, he oversaw the signing of the treaty in which Norway's territorial integrity was guaranteed by Great Britain, France, Germany, and Russia. Løvland resigned in 1908 because he felt that a plurality of the members of the *Storting* did not have full confidence in him.

**LYKKE, IVAR (1872–1949).** Norwegian politician. Born in **Trondheim** on 9 January 1872 to the merchant Peder Tangen Lykke, Lykke studied business and joined his grandfather's grocery firm in 1892, assuming ownership of it in 1910. Active in local politics, he represented the **Conservative Party** on the Trondheim City Council from 1905 to 1936. He was elected a member of the *Storting* (**Parliament**) in 1916 and served as the president of the *Storting* at times during the

1920s, starting in 1919. Lykke was party leader for the Conservatives from 1923 to 1926 and served as prime minister from 1926 to 1928, while also being in charge of the Ministry of Foreign Affairs. This was a minority coalition government made up of the Conservative Party and the **Liberal Left Party**, which was positioned in between the Conservatives and the **Liberal Party** in the political landscape. This government emphasized cost cutting and was quite unpopular, especially among workers because it pushed through a series of laws that were designed to prevent strikes, one of which gave special protection to scabs. The Conservatives therefore lost 24 seats in the 1927 election. Lykke is fondly remembered for having suggested the name *Trondheim* during the battle that raged from 1928 to 1930 over what the city formerly known as Trondhjem was to be named. During the summer of 1940, he had the misfortune of being one of the representatives from the *Storting* that negotiated with the German occupiers and eventually requested of King **Haakon VII** that he should abdicate the throne. After **World War II** was over, he was heavily criticized for his actions during the negotiations.

**LYNG, JOHN DANIEL FÜRSTENBERG (1905–78).** Norwegian politician. Born in **Trondheim** on 22 August 1905, Lyng studied law and held a number of important administrative appointments. During **World War II**, he spent time first in Stockholm and then in London, where he was associated with the Ministry of Justice of the Norwegian exile government. Having first affiliated with the **Liberal Left Party**, he joined the **Conservative Party** in 1945, was elected to the *Storting* (**Parliament**) several times, and served as the leader of his party's caucus from 1958 to 1965. A natural coalition builder, he became the prime minister in the Center–Right coalition that replaced **Einar Gerhardsen**'s third government in 1963, following a no-confidence vote in which the coalition parties were joined by the two representatives of the **Socialist People's Party**. Lyng's government lasted for only about four weeks, after which it was succeeded by Gerhardsen's fourth government, but it showed that the nonsocialist parties in the *Storting* were capable of setting their individual differences aside and working together as a viable nonsocialist alternative. Lyng's government, Norway's first nonsocialist government after World War II, thus prepared the ground for the coalition government headed by **Per**

**Borten** that took over in 1965. Lyng served as minister of foreign affairs in this government from 1965 to 1970.

# – M –

**MAGNUS VI LAGABØTE (1238–80).** Norwegian king and lawgiver. Born on 1 May 1238, Magnus was the son of King Haakon IV Haakonsson (1204–63) and great-grandson of **Sverre Sigurdsson**. He was named king in 1257, ruling with his father, who on his deathbed certified that Magnus was his only living son, and Magnus was crowned in 1263. Magnus was politically astute and focused both on diplomatic activity and consolidating his domestic power, entering into an agreement with the Scots by which the Isle of Man and the Hebrides were sold to Scotland while the Orkneys and Shetland were confirmed as Norwegian possessions. In 1269, he made a pact with England that guaranteed mutual free **trade**. In Norwegian history, Magnus is remembered mostly for his legal reforms. Like other European countries, Norway had a legal system that emphasized regional differences within the country. Each of the major regional *ting* (assemblies), Eidsivating, Frostating, and Gulating, had its own code of law. At first, Magnus worked to have each of these codes revised and improved, but in 1274, all three assemblies voted to accept a common code proposed by the king. A corresponding code for the cities appeared in 1276.

**MICHELSEN, CHRISTIAN (1857–1925).** Norwegian statesman. Peter Christian Hersleb Kjerschow Michelsen was born in **Bergen** on 15 March 1857 and was educated as a lawyer, a profession that he practiced while acquiring a significant merchant fleet. Involved in local politics, he became the mayor of Bergen and joined the **Liberal Party**. Elected to the *Storting* (**Parliament**) in 1892, he soon became central to the debate about establishing a Norwegian consular service separate from that of **Sweden** and became the head of the committee that studied this issue. His consular service bill was passed by the *Storting* 10 June 1892, but King Oscar II refused to sign it, which precipitated a crisis that had the potential for leading to war between the two countries.

Withdrawing from active national political life for a while, Michelsen wanted to create a centrist alternative to both the Liberal Party and the **Conservative Party**. Called the **United Party** and appearing at the parliamentary elections in 1903, it consisted of moderate members of the Liberal Party and the Conservative Party and was opposed to both the socially radical wing of the Liberal Party and the socialism represented by the **Labor Party**, which had been formed in 1887. Persuaded to stand for election as a United Party candidate in 1903, Michelsen won and soon became a member of the government headed by **Francis Hagerup**.

Michelsen precipitated Hagerup's fall as prime minister by resigning in early 1905, after which he became the head of the new government. Through his levelheadedness, sound political instincts, gregariousness, and skills as a negotiator, Michelsen was then able to successfully shepherd Norway through the final stages of the **dissolution of the union with Sweden**. When the consular service bill was again passed by the *Storting* on 18 May 1905 and presented to King Oscar II for his signature on 27 May 1905, the king declined to sign it, and the entire cabinet resigned on the spot. The king refused to accept their resignation because he knew that he would be unable to put together a new cabinet. When almost two weeks passed and no new cabinet was formed, Michelsen strategically claimed that King Oscar II was no longer functioning as king of Norway and that the union with Sweden was therefore automatically dissolved.

Michelsen's sound political instincts also manifested themselves in his attitude toward the form of government Norway should have after the dissolution of the union. While personally a believer in a republican form of government, Michelsen knew that a **constitutional monarchy** would be more easily accepted by both the Norwegian people and the European powers. The choice to call on Prince Carl of **Denmark**, who was married to the English princess Maud, was a brilliant strategic move, as it helped secure Norway's position in the international community.

Tired of partisan squabbling, Michelsen resigned as prime minister on 23 October 1907. In 1909, he was the prime mover behind a new political party called the **Liberal Left Party**, which consisted of the right wing of the Liberal Party, cooperated closely with the Conservative Party, and was a significant force in Norwegian political life in the 1910s and 1920s. He left a large portion of his substantial fortune to a foundation that was to promote cooperation and harmony between peoples and cultures through scientific and intellectual inquiry.

**MINING.** Paleolithic Norwegians mined greenschist rock (greenstone) at Bømlo in western Norway, and their Iron Age successors produced bog iron, but mining is not known from historical sources until around 1500. By the first half of the 17th century, actual mining was taking place, with the Kongsberg silver mine established by King **Christian IV** as the most outstanding example. There were also copper mines, first and foremost at Røros and elsewhere in Sør-Trøndelag County; the Røros mines have been memorialized in the novels of **Johan Falkberget**. A total of about 20 ironworks were also in operation.

The central government was heavily involved in the mining activities, particularly in the Kongsberg silver mine, which provided the metal needed for coins. Copper was also valuable with increasing prices and contributed to what was considered the country's real wealth in the age of mercantilism. Most of the people working in the mines had to be brought in from abroad, particularly from Germany, and the language of mining in Norway became mostly German. All of the mining operations needed firewood and charcoal, and in some cases, the king ordered the farmers within a certain area to deliver these commodities to the mines, however they were to receive payment. The iron works, which were usually owned by individuals and located mostly in eastern Norway, provided many work opportunities for those living close by. After the union with **Denmark** had come to an end in 1814 and with it the privileges given to the ironworks by the king, the works simply could not compete for long with cheaper iron from England, where coke rather than charcoal was used in its production. Times were, however, good for the copper works, and the Kongsberg silver mine became a great asset in the late 1830s. While mining was still a significant part of Norway's **economy** throughout the rest of the 1800s, it was clearly declining in importance.

There was a significant breakthrough in Norwegian mining during the years after 1900, however. An open-pit iron mine was started at Bjørnevatn close to Kirkenes in eastern Finnmark County in 1907, and Kirkenes became the mine's **shipping** port. There was also a major iron mine in the Dunderland Valley in the vicinity of Mo i Rana, Nordland County. Pyrites, including copper and zinc, were mined at Sulitjelma in Nordland County starting in 1888 and exported to Germany, which became a major bone of contention with Great Britain during **World War I**. The mines at Sulitjelma were Norway's second-largest industrial concern. Norway also has a molybdenum mine located at Sirdal in the southwestern part of the country; it was the only mine of its kind in Europe. Other minerals and ores continue to be mined as well, for example, nickel and titanium.

**MODERATE LIBERAL PARTY.** Founded in 1888, *Moderate Venstre* was Norway's third political party. The most important issues on its agenda were **religion**, morality, and temperance, and the party had a distinct low-church flavor. For a while, **Lars Oftedal** was its central figure. While similar to the **Conservative Party** in outlook, the Moderate Liberal Party was in favor of increased Norwegian autonomy within the union with **Sweden**. As the Conservatives became increasingly in favor of autonomy, too, the Moderate Liberals collaborated with them, and they were part of the **United Party** in 1903. The Moderate Liberal Party combined with the Conservative Party in 1906, and some have regarded it as a precursor to the **Christian Democratic Party**.

**MODERATE VENSTRE.** *See* MODERATE LIBERAL PARTY.

**MOE, JØRGEN ENGEBRETSEN (1813–82).** Norwegian folklorist, poet, and clergyman. Born on 22 April 1813 in Hole in the area of Ringerike north of **Oslo**, Moe early became a close friend of **Peter Christen Asbjørnsen**, with whom he edited and published two collections of popular tales, *Norske Folkeeventyr* (Norwegian Folktales) in 1843 and 1852. For generations of Norwegians, these cultural treasures have simply been known as "Asbjørnsen and Moe." Moe studied theology and served as a minister in the Norwegian State Church in Drammen and Christiania (now Oslo), ending his career as a bishop in Kristiansand. He also published a collection of mostly **religious** poetry titled *Digte* (1849; Poems), as well as a book for children that has become a Norwegian classic of its kind, *I Brønden og i*

*Tjærnet* (1851; In the Well and the Pond). Moe's *Samlede Skrifter* (Collected Works) was published in two volumes in 1877.

**MONRAD, MARCUS JACOB (1816–97).** Norwegian philosopher and critic. Born on 19 January 1816 at Nøtterøy, Vestfold County, Monrad grew up in rural Telemark as the son of a Lutheran minister, attended Latin school in the town of Skien, and studied theology at the university in Christiania (now **Oslo**). After study and travel in Germany and Italy, he was given a position in philosophy at his alma mater, where he became a professor in 1851. The most significant representative of right Hegelianism in Norwegian academic life, Monrad is known for his book *Tankeretninger i den nyere Tid* (1874; Intellectual Currents in the Recent Age), as well as works on ethics, aesthetics, and the philosophy of **religion**. He was also a prolific **literary** critic and frequent participant in the public debate. While in his youth he strongly supported the nationalist position taken by **Henrik Wergeland**, he later became very conservative and defended the values of aesthetic idealism against the exponents of realism, naturalism, and early modernism.

**MOWINCKEL, JOHAN LUDWIG (1870–1943).** Norwegian politician. Born in **Bergen** on 22 October 1870, Mowinckel studied **languages** and business in Germany, England, and France before becoming a major shipowner in his native city. The leader of the **Liberal Party** in Bergen, he was elected to the city council in 1899 and served as mayor in 1902–6 and 1911–13. He was a member of the *Storting* (**Parliament**) in 1906–9, 1912–18, and after 1921. He served as the president of the *Storting* from 1916 to 1918 but could not serve in the government because he was not a member of the Lutheran State Church. The point in the **constitution** that prohibited him from serving was changed in 1919, and Mowinckel became minister of foreign affairs under **Otto Albert Blehr** in 1922, serving until 1923. He served as prime minister from 1924 to 1926 while also serving as the head of the Foreign Ministry and again had both positions from 1933 to 1935, when a crisis agreement between the **Labor Party** and the Agrarian Party (*see* CENTER PARTY) allowed **Johan Nygaardsvold** to form a Labor government.

During his first government, Mowinckel proposed holding the referendum that ended Norway's liquor prohibition. While he was a classic principled liberalist in **economic** matters and preferred that the government should not intervene in the economy, even during a time of crisis, Nygaardsvold's reformist and pragmatic policies were supported by the voters. Mowinckel was, however, a capable businessman and administrator who negotiated several **trade** agreements and reorganized the Norwegian Foreign Service. In the late 1920s, he presided over the **League of Nations**.

**MUNCH, EDVARD (1863–1944).** Norwegian painter. Born to Christian Munch on 12 December 1863 in Løten, Hedmark County, Munch grew up in Christiania (now **Oslo**) and became acquainted with death at an early age. In 1868, his mother died from tuberculosis, and in 1877, his lost his older sister, Johanne Sophie, to the same disease. The Munch household was marked by **religious** austerity as well as by the loss of loved ones, as Munch's father, who died in 1889, drummed into his children a very dark **pietistic** variety of Christianity that emphasized the ubiquity of sin and the certainty of its punishment. When Munch started painting, he first chose the naturalist style of his teacher, Christian Krohg, but later, his subject matter became symbolistic, and his canvases and lithographs acquired the stylization and simplicity of postimpressionism. Munch's earliest major work was a series collectively titled *Livsfrisen* (the Frieze of Life) which was finished around 1900. Many of Munch's works are known and recognized all over the world. Foremost among these is *Skrik* (1893, Scream) and *Madonna* (five versions painted in 1894 and 1895). Munch died childless and willed a large quantity of his artistic works to the city of Oslo, where they are available to the public at the Munch Museum.

**MUNCH, PETER ANDREAS (1810–63).** Norwegian historian and nation builder. Born to the State Church minister Edvard Storm Munch on 15 December 1810, Munch grew up at Gjerpen and attended Latin school in Skien, where **Anton Martin Schweigaard** was one of his fellow students. He earned a law degree at the university in Christiania (now **Oslo**) in 1834 but wanted to make history his life's work. He became a lecturer in 1837 and professor of history at the university in Christiania in 1841. Given access to the archives at the Vatican, he produced an eight-volume history of Norway. Thoroughly familiar with the **language**, **literature**, and culture of medieval Norway, he encouraged **Ivar Aasen**'s dialectological research. Munch's work was of great importance to 19th-century nation building in Norway.

## – N –

**NANSEN, FRIDTJOF WEDEL-JARLSBERG (1861–1930).** Norwegian scientist, explorer, and diplomat. Nansen was born in Vestre Aker near Christiania (now **Oslo**) on 10 October 1861 to Baldur Frithjof Nansen, a lawyer. Although interested in natural science as early as secondary school, he wanted to become a navy officer. His father persuaded him to study zoology, however, which he did at the Royal Frederik's University (now the University of Oslo). He also studied medicine and worked as a curator at the **Bergen** Museum. Working on the neurology of worms, he made significant contributions to the understanding of neurons and synapses, earning a doctorate in 1886. He became a professor of zoology at the university in Oslo starting in 1887 (from 1908 as professor of oceanography), serving until his death.

Between 15 August and 29 September 1888, Nansen and five other men traveled on skis across the interior ice field of Greenland. His book about the experience, *Paa ski over Grønland* (1890; tr. *The First Crossing of Greenland*, 1890), is a classic in Norwegian **literature** of adventure. Soon after this expedition, Nansen had a ship specially constructed for travel in polar regions, *Fram*. In the summer of 1893, he traveled eastward from the town of Vardø in the extreme northeast of Norway and along the Northeast Passage until *Fram* got stuck in the ice in late September. The expedition drifted westward for the next three years. After the second winter, Nansen and his shipmate Hjalmar Johansen left *Fram* in order to reach the North Pole on skis and with the aid of a team of sled dogs. Having gotten farther north than any other human beings (84 degrees, 4 minutes, northern latitude), they tried to return to *Fram* but had to build a shack and winter on Franz Joseph's Land, living on blubber and polar bear meat. The next summer, they ran into a British expedition and secured passage back to Norway, arriving in Vardø on 13 July 1896. *Fram* and the rest of its crew made it back home soon afterward.

Nansen also had a significant diplomatic career. During the **dissolution of the union with Sweden** in 1905, he was initially in favor of a republican form of government but was persuaded to support the proposal that the **Danish** prince Carl should be offered Norway's throne. Prince Carl became king under the name of **Haakon VII**, and Nansen became one of his close friends. This was very much in Norway's interest in part because the new Queen Maud belonged to the British royal house, and Norway needed to secure Britain's support in order to secure its territorial integrity. This was facilitated by Nansen's service as Norway's ambassador to Great Britain from 1906 to 1908.

Toward the conclusion of **World War I**, Nansen was working with the Allies to get them to allow necessary supplies of food to be brought through their blockade of the Central Powers, and after the war, he became involved in the work of the **League of Nations**, helping to bring prisoners of war back home. As the League's high commissioner for refugees, he originated the so-called Nansen passports, travel documents for stateless individuals that became widely recognized. During the famine in Russia in 1921–22, he administered help to millions of people. This and other humanitarian work garnered Nansen the **Nobel Peace Prize** in 1922.

**NÆSS, ARNE DEKKE EIDE (1912– ).** Norwegian philosopher and **environmental** activist. Born in **Oslo** on 27 January 1912, Næss is Norway's best-known philosopher and was appointed professor at the University of Oslo at the age of 27. Through his widely used textbooks in logic and the history of philosophy used in a mandatory course, he powerfully affected the thinking and style of argumentation of generations of Norwegian students. Næss was influenced by the logical empiricism of the Vienna Circle in the 1930s and strongly supported the idea that scientific inquiry, as opposed to metaphysical speculation, is the only path to true knowledge. Also touched by the thought of the British philosopher Bertrand Russell (1872–1970), Næss may be regarded as Norway's first exponent of analytic philosophy. He is perhaps best known, however, for his concept "deep ecology," including the views that all species have a right to continue their existence and that human beings should be considered on a par with other living things. An accomplished mountaineer, Næss has been associated with the movement of environmentalism both in Norway and elsewhere. In 1970, he was among those arrested for using civil disobedience in the Mardøla protest, when a group of environmentalists tried to stop the building of a **hydroelectric power** plant in western Norway.

**NATIONAL ROMANTICISM.** Many Norwegian writers, artists, and scholars were greatly influenced by the ideas of the German thinker Johann Gottfried von Herder (1744–1803), who emphasized the role of the nation and its **language**, as well as its connection to the divine spirit that could be found in nature. Norway came into its own as a country with its own **constitution** in 1814, albeit in a union with **Sweden**. In the area of culture, the national breakthrough took place around 1840, when there was a concerted effort to collect folktales, legends, and ballads that were deemed expressions of the true spirit of the people. The people were seen as descendents of the Norwegians who lived during the **Viking** period, and they were intimately linked to Norway's nature. Many educated city dwellers, whose personal acquaintance with rural life was perhaps less than ample, had a considerable emotional investment in this nationalist mythology.

Among the writers who were influenced by the ideas of the national romanticism are **Johan Sebastian Welhaven**, who wrote both exquisite nature lyrics and folklore poetry; **Ivar Aasen**, who constructed a new form of written Norwegian built on the most archaic dialects he could find and resuscitated ancient **Scandinavian** meter in many of his poems; **Bjørnsterne Bjørnson**, whose prose style, especially in his peasant tales, was heavily influenced by the style of the ancient sagas; **Henrik Ibsen**, many of whose early plays dealt with historical and folkloristic topics; and **Aasmund Olafsson Vinje**, who gave suppleness and soul to a slightly different version of the written language that Aasen had created. Aasen was a great scholar as well as a passable creative writer, whose work on the lexicography and grammar of the dialects of western Norway is a major contribution. Among the many individuals who collected folklore texts are two whose names have been known by generations of Norwegians, **Peter Christen Asbjørnsen** and **Jørgen Moe**, who together gave Norway an edition of its folktales and legends that are simply referred to as "Asbjørnsen and Moe" and that constitute one of Norway's greatest cultural treasures. Similar treasures are found among the many ballads, some of them thought to go back to medieval times, that were collected and edited by **Magnus Brostrup Landstad**. Norway's greatest ballad, **"Draumkvedet"** (the Dream Ballad), is a visionary poem of great **religious** and ethical significance as well as a work of superior **literary** value.

Many painters and composers were also powerfully affected by the ideas of the national romanticism. **J. C. Dahl**, **Hans Gude**, and **Adolph Tidemand** were inspired by both Norwegian nature and rural life. The work of **Edvard Grieg** and **Ole Bull** was strongly affected by Norwegian folk music. *See also* ART; HANSEN, MAURITS CHRISTOPHER (1794–1842); STURLUSON, SNORRI (1178–1241); WELHAVEN, JOHAN SEBASTIAN CAMMERMEYER (1807–73).

**NEW LEFT PEOPLE'S PARTY.** The *Folkepartiet Nye Venstre*, which was renamed *Det Liberale Folkepartiet* (The Liberal People's Party) in 1980, was formed in a split from the **Liberal Party** in 1972 in a dispute over Norwegian membership in the European Community (EC; *see* EUROPEAN ECONOMIC COMMUNITY [EEC]). The dissenters, favoring EC membership, included the party leader, **Helge Seip**, and 9 of the Liberal Party's 13 representatives in the *Storting* (**Parliament**). In the 1973 parliamentary election, *Folkepartiet Nye Venstre* received one seat but has since not had parliamentary representation. It was discontinued as it merged with *Venstre* in 1988. In 1992, some of the old members of *Det Liberale Folkepartiet* brought the party back to life and were joined by some disaffected members of the **Progress Party**. The new iteration of *Det Liberale Folkepartiet* is extremely libertarian, particularly in **economic** matters, and garnered a total of 213 votes in the 2005 parliamentary election.

**NOBEL PEACE PRIZE.** The most prestigious award in the world, the Nobel Peace Prize was instituted as one of five prizes through the will of the Swedish inventor and industrialist Alfred Nobel

(1833–96). It is awarded at the **Oslo** City Hall on 10 December of each year, the anniversary of Nobel's death, and a special concert, the Nobel Peace Prize Concert, is held the following day and attended by a large number of dignitaries. The recipient of the prize is selected by the five-member Norwegian Nobel Committee, appointed by the Norwegian *Storting* (**Parliament**). The only Norwegian recipient is **Fridtjof Nansen** (1922).

**NORDIC COUNCIL.** Formed in 1952, the *Nordisk Råd* consists of representatives from the **parliaments** of the Nordic countries. **Denmark**, Finland, Norway, and **Sweden** have 20 members each; Iceland is represented by 7 members; and the Faeroes and Greenland, which have home rule under Denmark, have 2 members each. The Nordic Council is headquartered in Copenhagen, has an annual plenary session, and arranges meetings devoted to specific subjects throughout the year. A forum for cooperation among the parliaments of the Nordic states, the Nordic Council has no legislative power of its own, so the individual parliaments must act so as to implement its recommendations. During the early years of its existence, the Nordic Council was intended to bring about a high level of Nordic integration, but these hopes were not realized. Many of its intended functions are now carried out within the framework of the **European Union**. Five Norwegians have served as secretaries general: Emil Vindsetmoe (1971–73), **Helge Seip** (1973–77), Gudmund Saxrud (1977–82), Jostein Osens (1990–94), and Frida Nokken (1999–2007). *See also* EUROPEAN INTEGRATION.

**NORDLI, ODVAR (1927– ).** Norwegian politician. Born in Tangen, Hedmark County, on 3 November 1927, Nordli was educated as a certified public accountant and spent many years as an auditor. Active in **Labor Party** politics, he had several significant leadership positions and was elected a member of the *Storting* (**Parliament**) in 1961, serving until 1985. While he was considered for the post of chair of the Labor Party, he lost this appointment to **Reiulf Steen** and was instead chosen to serve as the Labor candidate for prime minister. In 1976, he formed a minority government that was in power until 1981, when **Gro Harlem Brundtland** took over as prime minister, serving for approximately nine months. Nordli served as *fylkesmann* (chief administrator) of Hedmark County from his resignation as prime minister until his retirement in 1993.

Nordli was the first Norwegian prime minister to preside over significant income from the **oil** fields along the coast of Norway and had to deal with how to best make use of this bonanza without wrecking the Norwegian **economy**. His administration was also marked by one of the most significant political controversies in recent Norwegian history, the resistance to the plan to build a **hydroelectric** dam across the salmon-rich Alta River in traditional **Sámi** reindeer-herding territory in Finnmark County. For a time, Nordli successfully calmed these troubled waters by initiating a review of the decision made by the *Storting*. Although the dam was eventually built after its opponents lost their case before Norway's Supreme Court, the controversy united Norwegian **environmentalists** and placed the question of Sámi rights on the public agenda.

*NORGES KOMMUNISTISKE PARTI. See* NORWAY'S COMMUNIST PARTY.

*NORGES SOCIALDEMOKRATISKE ARBEIDERPATI. See* NORWAY'S SOCIAL-DEMOCRATIC LABOR PARTY.

**NORTH ATLANTIC TREATY ORGANIZATION (NATO).** At the conclusion of **World War II**, it was clear to the Norwegian government that maintaining the prewar policy of neutrality was no longer a realistic possibility. Norway's strategic position was such that there was simply no hope of remaining outside a major European conflict, so some kind of defensive alliance was clearly necessary. One option was a Nordic alliance, and in 1948 and early 1949, this possibility was discussed by **Denmark**, Norway, and **Sweden**. Sweden had managed to remain outside of both **World War I** and World War II and had a significant domestic armaments **industry**, so it did not feel a strong need for an alliance that involved countries outside of **Scandinavia**. Norway had no armaments industry of its own and therefore was dependent on being able to purchase weaponry on the world market, which, in practical terms, meant either from Great Britain or the **United States**, so it felt that it needed security guarantees far beyond those required by Sweden. Norway believed that a Nordic alliance simply had to have some kind of tie to Great Britain and the United States, while Sweden did not want to see a pretense of Nordic neutrality while Scandinavia had in reality already sided with a western alliance. The differences between the Norwegian and the Swedish perspectives were thus simply too great to make a Nordic alliance a realistic option.

In the meantime, the cold war was becoming a reality and, with it, the need for a strong western defense. The Communists had taken power in Czechoslovakia in 1948, and Russia broke off all land-based connections between West Germany and Berlin. The Norwegian **Labor** government headed by **Einar Gerhardsen** long debated whether to seek an alliance with Britain and the United States, while the nonsocialist parties were strongly in favor of one. As the groundwork for NATO was being laid by the United States and Britain, it was clear that Norway would be invited to participate if the Norwegian government so wished. The Labor Party finally concluded that there was no better option, and on 29 March 1949, the *Storting* (**Parliament**) voted that Norway would participate. The treaty was signed in Washington, D.C., on 4 April 1949, and the Norwegian minister of foreign affairs, **Halvard Lange**, was present to sign it on Norway's behalf. NATO's basic premise was that an attack on any member would be considered an attack on all of them.

Norway early made it clear, however, that no foreign military bases would be established on Norwegian soil in peacetime, meaning if Norway had not been attacked or was not threatened by an imminent attack. It is likely that this declaration was necessary to keep the Labor Party from splitting apart because of its internal disagreements over NATO. The United States expressed no concern about Norway's seeming reluctance, however, possibly because Washington realized that it would have been unwise to establish an American outpost so close to Soviet territory, as it would surely have been regarded as a major provocation.

With the fall of the Soviet Union and the end of the cold war in 1991, NATO's original goal was gone, and there was a need for a redefinition of the organization's purpose. NATO still exists primarily in order to defend member states, but it may now intervene in a conflict even though a member country has not been directly attacked.

Furthermore, it may do so whether there is **United Nations** (UN) authorization for the action or not. For example, in 1999, NATO intervened in the war between Serbs and Kosovo-Albanians without UN authorization, while its intervention in Bosnia in 1995 had been authorized by the UN. NATO also leads the International Security Assistance Force in Afghanistan; the mandate of this force is underwritten by the UN Security Council, and Norwegian troops are part of the force. By 2007, NATO's original 12 members had been expanded to 27, including a number of former East Bloc countries.

**NORWAY'S COMMUNIST PARTY.** *Norges Kommunistiske Parti* (NKP) was formed in 1923, when the **Labor Party** decided to withdraw from the Communist International (Comintern). Labor had joined the Comintern in 1919, and its moderate wing had become concerned about the required fealty to Vladimir Ilyich Lenin's Moscow theses, which presented Soviet communism's expectations of what it, in effect, viewed as its daughter parties. Initially, NKP had a strong position in Norwegian political life, with 13 of Labor's existing representatives in the *Storting* (**Parliament**) leaving the mother party and joining the NKP. The support dwindled throughout the 1920s and 1930s, and the party had no parliamentary representation from 1930 to the end of **World War II**. The NKP's resistance to the occupiers during the war was strong, however, and the 1945 parliamentary election gave it 11.9 percent of the popular vote and 11 seats in the *Storting*.

The Labor Party was quite hostile toward the NKP, and its support again dwindled. Some of its political positions were doctrinaire and unpopular—for example, it opposed the Marshall Plan—and internal strife, followed by the exclusion of centrally placed members, took its toll. Its opposition to Norwegian membership in the European Community (*see* EUROPEAN ECONOMIC COMMUNITY [EEC]) in 1972 was popular with the voters, however, and when a leftist coalition was organized in preparation for the 1973 parliamentary election, the NKP's leader from 1965 to 1975, Reidar T. Larsen, was one of the 16 persons elected on the coalition ticket. Otherwise, the NKP has had no parliamentary representation since 1957, and its representation in local government is minimal.

**NORWAY'S SOCIAL-DEMOCRATIC LABOR PARTY.** *Norges Socialdemokratiske Arbeiderparti* (NSA) was started in 1921 by members of the **Labor Party** who were concerned about the radical developments in the mother party during and after **World War I**. When the party accepted the Moscow theses and joined the Communist International (Comintern), thus essentially making itself a tool of Soviet communism, the split was unavoidable. The result was that in the 1921 election, the Labor Party lost 10 percent of the popular vote, compared with the previous election, while the NSA gained 9 percent. The two parties were combined in 1927, however, after the Labor Party had largely moved to the position of the NSA and had withdrawn from the Comintern, and the extreme left wing splintered off by forming **Norway's Communist Party** in 1923.

**NYGAARDSVOLD, JOHAN (1879–1952).** Norwegian politician. Born the son of a tenant farmer in Hommelvik near **Trondheim** on 6 September 1879, Nygaardsvold started working in a lumber mill while yet in his childhood. In 1902, he immigrated to Canada and worked there and in the western **United States** as an agitator for the International Workers of the World. Back in Norway in 1907, he was a member of the **Labor Party**, serving as one of its representatives in the *Storting* (**Parliament**) from 1916 to 1949. He first served as minister of **agriculture** in the short-lived Labor Party government formed by **Christopher Hornsrud** in 1928, and in 1935, he established the second Labor Party government in Norwegian history. Although technically a minority government, it had the support of the Agrarian Party (*see* CENTER PARTY) and thus enjoyed great stability similar to that of a government based on a parliamentary majority. Including its years in exile in London during **World War II**, when it gradually took on the characteristics of a unity government, this government lasted until 1945.

Nygaardsvold's chief task in the 1930s was to find ways of mitigating the effects of the Great Depression, and he was sufficiently successful that European Fascism received little support among the common people in Norway. Less attention was paid to Norwegian defense, however, and it has been argued that Nygaardsvold bears some responsibility for the lack of readiness of the Norwegian military forces when Germany attacked Norway on 9 April 1940.

*NYNORSK.* Usually referred to as New Norwegian in English, *nynorsk* is a written form of Norwegian that since 1885 has had the same legal status as the more commonly used form, *bokmål* (book **language**). *Nynorsk* was originally created by **Ivar Aasen** as *Landsmaal* (country language) and was first cultivated as a **literary** language by him as well as by **Aasmund Olafsson Vinje** and **Arne Garborg**. Although less than 15 percent of the Norwegian population uses it as its primary written language, some of the foremost Norwegian writers, including **Kjartan Fløgstad**, **Edvard Hoem**, and **Tor Obrestad**, have used it as their written medium during the second half of the 20th century.

– O –

**OBRESTAD, TOR (1938– ).** Norwegian novelist, poet, and short-story writer. Born on 12 February 1938 in Hå close to the city of **Stavanger**, Obrestad writes in *nynorsk* (New Norwegian). After publishing several collections of poetry and prose, he turned to the ideology of Marxism-Leninism associated with the **Socialist Youth Federation**. Obrestad's revolutionary fervor is on display in his documentary novel *Sauda! Streik!* (1972; Sauda! Strike!), which tells the story of a strike in the **industrial** community in western Norway that **Kjartan Fløgstad** has memorialized as Lovra. Other volumes in praise of revolution are the poetry collections *Sauda og Shanghai* (1973; Sauda and Shanghai) and *Stå saman* (1974; Stand Together). Like many other writers of his generation, Obrestad became less strident in the 1980s and has written many other volumes of poetry and prose, as well as biographies of such canonical Norwegian writers as **Arne Garborg** and **Alexander Kielland**, as well as the politician Einar Førde (1943–2004). *See also* LITERATURE.

*ODELSTING.* The *Storting*, the Norwegian **parliament**, is largely a unicameral body, but for purposes of considering legislative matters, it is divided into two compartments. The *Odelsting* (literally, an assembly of those who possess allodial rights to farmland) functions as a type of lower house in that it consists of three fourths of the members of the *Storting*, the parliamentary representatives who have not been elected by their colleagues to sit in the *Lagting* (literally, an assembly that considers laws) shortly after a new *Storting* has been chosen by the voters. The *Odelsting* receives bills from the government or legislative proposals from its members, which, after they have been debated and passed, are then submitted to the *Lagting* for further consideration. The *Odelsting* is also the body that considers whether to carry out impeachment proceedings or not. The *Odelsting* was abolished by the *Storting* on 20 February 2007, and this **constitutional** change will take place after the 2009 parliamentary elections.

**OFTEDAL, LARS (1838–1900).** Norwegian politician, newspaperman, and evangelist. Born in **Stavanger** on 27 December 1838, Oftedal studied theology and was ordained a minister in the Norwegian State Church. He was an exceptionally gifted evangelist who started his career by traveling around and holding meetings under the auspices of the Inner Mission. His message was simple. People should not only believe passively in Christianity but actively strive for repentance and sanctification. Similarly to **Hans Nilsen Hauge** before him and Ole Hallesby in the 1950s, Oftedal managed to paint the tortures of hell in such vivid colors that the minds of his listeners were deeply affected. His speech was simple, and his outward appearance was not much different from that of the ordinary man, so people felt like he was truly one of them and understood their concerns.

Oftedal was also an organizational genius who built chapels and schools, as well as homes for widows, orphans, fallen **women**, and the children of fallen women. He helped people with money and found them places to live. While appointed to a parish in Stavanger, he founded his paper *Vestlands-Posten* (West Norway Post), which lasted from 1878 to 1916 and was published three times a week. It expressed the views of the farmers who belonged to the **Liberal Party** and had a significant impact on the region's level of political awareness. Oftedal was also a Liberal Party representative to the *Storting* (**Parliament**) in two periods, 1883–85 and 1889–91. He was one of those who led the opposition to giving the writer **Alexander Kielland** governmental support, for to Oftedal, Kielland was a **freethinker** and a dangerous person. He resigned his position in the church in 1891, when he announced that he had been living in an immoral relationship with a woman. He kept building his network of **religious** and charitable institutions, however, and founded the paper *Stavanger Aftenblad* (Stavanger Evening Post), which became one of Norway's foremost regional papers. Both Kielland and **Knut Hamsun** have provided **literary** portraits of Oftedal.

**OIL AND NATURAL GAS.** Exploratory drilling started in the Norwegian part of the North Sea in 1966, but it was not until late 1969 that the first significant discovery was made. In 1971, the first quantity of oil was shipped to **Stavanger**, and by 1980, the production of oil and gas amounted to 50 million metric tons per year. By 1990, it had increased to 120 million tons, of which 90 million tons was oil.

In 1963, the *Storting* (**Parliament**) had passed a law that made natural resources located on the Norwegian continental shelf state property, and the oil companies that wanted to conduct explorations in Norwegian territorial waters had to be licensed to do so by the government. Licenses were issued in three rounds between 1965 and 1975 and only south of the 62nd parallel. There has been considerable pressure on the Norwegian authorities to allow exploration north of this line as well, and significant finds have been made as far north as the Barents Sea.

The development of the oil **industry** was a boon to Norway's **economy**. By 1975, enough oil was being pumped to supply Norway's own needs, and since then, Norway has become one of the world's greatest exporters of oil and gas. While the oil was transported to shore by ship in the early years, gas is transported from the North Sea to the Netherlands in underwater pipe lines, and oil is similarly brought ashore in Great Britain. Oil and gas from northern finds are piped to shore in Norway.

While many of the earliest workers in the Norwegian oil industry were Americans and other foreigners, Norwegian nationals gradually took over the work and built up significant expertise. Even as early as 1980, the oil industry employed twice the number of those involved in **fishing**. Most of the workers came from southwestern Norway and were former industrial laborers, seamen, fishermen, and farmers.

The industry was plagued by accidents, particularly in the early years, when the American leaders on the drilling rigs showed a general disregard for security measures. The sinking of a single platform in 1980 claimed 123 lives, 3 helicopter accidents killed a total of 34 people, diving accidents killed another 14, and 8 people lost their lives in 2 major fires. These accidents led to the institution of strict safety measures that gradually changed the earlier culture onboard the platforms.

**OLAV V (1903–91).** King of Norway. Born in England to the later King **Haakon VII** and Queen Maud on 2 July 1903, Olav was given the name Alexander Edward Christian Frederik and was, as his father, a **Danish** prince. When his father became the king of Norway in 1905, he received the name Olav.

As crown prince, Olav attended public school in **Oslo**, receiving his matriculation certificate in 1921. He spent the next three years at the Norwegian War College, after which he studied **economics** and law in Oxford. He was also a superb athlete and competed in ski jumping and sailing, winning a gold medal in the 1928 summer Olympics. In 1929, he married his cousin, Princess Märtha Sofia Lovisa Dagmar Thyra of **Sweden**, and they became the parents of a son and two daughters. In 1991, the son succeeded his father as King Harald V. Crown Princess Märtha died in 1954.

King Olav, who inherited the throne from his father in 1957, was very popular and was referred to as *folkekongen* (the people's king) because he was so close to his people. For example, during the 1973 **oil** crisis, when weekend driving was prohibited in Norway, the king took the streetcar in order to go skiing, just like everybody else. He remained physically active, enjoying skiing and sailing until late in his life. Fifteen years after his death, he was voted the Norwegian of the century in a vote that drew 400,000 participants.

**ORGANIZATION FOR ECONOMIC COOPERATION AND DEVELOPMENT (OECD).** The OECD was formed in 1961 as a successor organization to the **Organization for European Economic Cooperation** (OEEC), when non-European countries were admitted. Its purpose is to promote free **trade**, to foster the development of strong market **economies** in its member countries, and to help improve the efficiency of the economies of both **industrialized** and developing nations. While its instruments are nonbinding, the organization covers all economic, **environmental**, and social issues; collects data; issues forecasts; and provides performance evaluations. Norway was a member of the OEEC from the time of its founding and remains a member of the OECD. *See also* EUROPEAN INTEGRATION.

**ORGANIZATION FOR EUROPEAN ECONOMIC COOPERATION (OEEC).** The OEEC was formed in 1948 for the purpose of administering aid from the **United States** and Canada under the Marshall Plan. It was succeeded by the **Organization for Economic Cooperation and Development** in 1961. Norway has been a member since the beginning. *See also* EUROPEAN INTEGRATION.

**OSLO.** Oslo, in the past also known as Christiania and Kristiania, is generally thought to have been founded approximately in 1000 CE, although **Snorri Sturluson** claims that it was about 50 years later. Recent archeological discoveries indicate that he may have been correct, but Oslo celebrated its millennial jubilee in 2000. The name *Oslo* is of Old Norse origin and may signify a level meadow located in close proximity to an elevated ridge. Oslo is the name that was used in medieval times, but after a city fire in 1624 destroyed Oslo, King **Christian IV** had it moved to the opposite side of the bay Bjørvika, close to the Akershus Fortress, and renamed it Christiania (since 1877, the spelling *Kristiania* was generally used, but the change in the name was never made legally). The old site of the city was still known as Oslo and remained outside of the new city limits until 1859. In 1925, the name of the city was officially changed by the city council to Oslo, and the medieval part of town was henceforth referred to as Old Town (Gamlebyen). Oslo's nickname is *Tigerstaden* (City of Tigres), first used in writing by **Bjørnstjerne Bjørnson** and very popular in mystery stories set in Christiania/Oslo written from the late 1800s to the middle of the 20th century.

Oslo is located at the end of the Oslo fjord and sits in a bowl surrounded by hills and lakes. The climate is chilly, especially in the fall and winter, when cold air and fog have a tendency to collect in the bowl (*Oslo-gryta*). During the coldest months, January and February, the average maximum temperature is slightly below minus 1 degree Celsius, while the average minimum temperature is below minus 5 degrees Celsius. The average maximum temperature during the summer is around 20 degrees Celsius. Oslo gets a fair amount of snow during the winter months, which is a boon to skiers, especially because there are some excellent cross-country skiing areas close to town; these areas are even accessible by streetcar. The average annual precipitation is 75 centimeters.

An important center of **trade**, **education**, health care, and public administration, Oslo has a bit more than 550,000 inhabitants, while as many more live within the surrounding area. Oslo is both a county and a municipality (*kommune*) and is governed by a city council (*Bystyret*) with 59 members headed by a mayor with largely ceremonial functions. However, the form of government is **parliamentary**, so there is also a small executive body called *Byrådet*, whose leader corresponds to a prime minister in a parliamentary democracy. For the purpose of local administration, Oslo is also divided into 15 areas that have their own local councils responsible for such functions as health care delivery and other social services.

Oslo has been Norway's capital since 1299, and the *Storting* (Parliament) and government offices are located there. The city also hosts a number of military installations; large hospitals, including the research-oriented *Rikshospitalet* (National Hospital); and educational institutions, including the University of Oslo, which was founded in 1811. It is also the center of private business and trade in Norway, although most **industrial** production has now been discontinued. It is a very expensive place to live, by one account, 32 percent more expensive than New York City.

Archeological evidence indicates that there was a significant population in the Oslo area as early as the Stone Age, and there is also archeological evidence dating to the **Viking** period. The first king who spent much time in Oslo was Sigurd Jorsalfare (1090–1130). With an important harbor and as an early center of trade, Oslo became the seat of the Roman Catholic bishop for eastern Norway, who was associated with the Saint Hallvard Cathedral. Other churches and several cloisters were also built, as well as fortified residences for both the king and the bishop. When the **Black Death** swept across the country in 1349, Oslo lost a lot of its population and declined to the point that only one church was still in operation. The city remained relatively insignificant during the early centuries of the union with **Denmark** and especially after the

**Reformation**, when it was merely a provincial town. It experienced 14 major fires, and in 1567, it was burned down while invaded by Swedish troops during the Seven Years War.

After the 1624 fire and subsequent move to the vicinity of the Akershus Fortress, Christiania developed a number of suburbs outside the city walls. The city grew only slowly, however, until the union with Denmark came to an end in 1814, and Christiania regained its status as Norway's capital. Several important public buildings were erected, for example, the university buildings in the city center, completed in 1852, and the royal residence, *Slottet*, completed in 1849. The Parliament (*Stortingsbygningen*) was finished in 1866—earlier sessions of the *Storting* were held in *Gamle Festsal* (Old Celebration Hall) at the university—and the National Theater was not finished until 1899.

Starting in the 1840s, the development of the city's industry led to a large increase in the population but also to a division between the west side, where people lived in single-family homes and nice apartment buildings, and the east side, where workers who needed to be close to their jobs were crowded together into tenements. The **economic** expansion in the 1880s and the 1890s further increased both population and building construction. The increased size meant that new means of transportation had to be developed, and horse-drawn streetcars were used starting in 1875. The surface light rail system was electrified in 1894. Long-distance transportation was handled by ship and train.

**Knut Hamsun** depicts life in Christiania in the late 1880s in his novel *Sult* (1890; tr. *Hunger*, 1899) as that of a city that is on its way to becoming a modern European metropolis, and by 1900, that process had largely been completed. The city had monumental **architecture**, a large and effective network of streetcar lines, electricity, and the beginnings of a modern sewer system. It had 250,000 inhabitants, and in 1905, it again became the seat of a complete state administration, including a royal family. A large-scale financial reversal in 1899 led to a serious downturn in construction and other economic activity, and little expansion took place prior to **World War I**. Most of the new apartments were built with public financing. The interwar period was characterized by reduced economic activity across the board, and it was not until 1946 that large-scale annexation took place, and the city again began to expand. During the post–**World War II** era, many large apartment houses were built away from the city center. Oslo also changed from being an industrial city to being a center for administration and various services. Starting around 1970, there was a large influx of immigrants from Asian and African countries, and this trend shows no signs of slowing down.

Tourists find Oslo a very interesting town to visit. The Frogner Park **Vigeland** sculptures have achieved world renown, and there are a number of **art** galleries and museums, including the Viking Ship Museum and the Kon-Tiki Museum, which houses crafts used by the explorer **Thor Heyerdahl**. The Fram Museum memorializes the explorations of **Fridtjof Nansen** and **Roald Amundsen**. There are also museums devoted to the work of **Henrik Ibsen** and **Edvard Munch**.

## – P –

**PARLIAMENTARISM.** In the Norwegian context, *parliamentarism* means that the cabinet ministers are obligated to appear before the *Storting* (Parliament) to answer questions and to justify their actions and that no cabinet may remain in power against the wishes of a parliamentary majority. The year 1884 is usually thought of as the time when parliamentarism was established in Norwegian political life, and the process by which this change in Norway's government structure came about is strongly linked to the name of **Johan Sverdrup**, one of Norway's great statesmen and the father of its **Liberal Party**. The story of these events is one of the most gripping chapters in Norwegian political history.

A man with great charisma and considerable leadership ability, Sverdrup became a member of the *Storting* in 1851. He quickly became one of the leaders of those who opposed the king, and his conservative cabinet, which worked to further the interests of a ruling class of government officials, included State Church ministers, university professors, large landowners, and wealthy businessmen. The opposition consisted primarily of farmers, lawyers, intellectuals, tradesmen, and fishermen, along with **religious** people who relied mostly on the ministry of lay preachers for their spiritual needs rather than solely on the state's version of Christianity as promulgated by its clergy. Some members of the opposition were **freethinkers** as well; they questioned the traditional view of authority as located in God and his servants on earth, first among whom were the king and his appointees, and believed that human beings were themselves responsible for creating their sense of life's meaning.

The *Storting* had by law convened only every three years, which meant that most of the work associated with the actual governance of the country was done by the members of the king's cabinet. The *Storting* was thus truly a citizen legislature, and there was little opportunity for its members to develop into a class of professional politicians. The cabinet ministers were not truly professional politicians either, but they were largely drawn from the class of the ***embedsmann***, or public officials, whose profession it was to govern the country as representatives of both the church and the state. This was a class of people who felt that they were more or less born to rule and that they were superior to most other members of society. While Norway had no nobility, certain families supplied a large number of the *embedsmann*, and this group of people had a clear sense of entitlement as well as class allegiance. Religion, law, and custom all supported this view, which was thus considered proper and just.

The **constitution** of 1814 provided for a political system where there was a division of power between the legislative, executive, and judicial branches of the government. In practice, the king's cabinet, the state administration, and the judiciary, including the Supreme Court, were firmly in the hands of the conservatives, while the influence of the opposition was limited to the arena provided by the periodic meetings of the *Storting*, which, however, had the power to authorize expenditures. The farmers who were members of the *Storting*, under such leaders as **Ole Gabriel Ueland** and especially **Søren Jaabæk**, tended to focus their resistance to the government of the *embedsmann* on limiting government expenditures, thus keeping the tax burden—which rested heavily on the farmers—as low as possible.

The political struggle in Norway between 1814 and 1884 was thus primarily between the king and his administration on the one hand and the opposition, which mostly worked through the *Storting*, on the other. As long as the supporters of the administration controlled the

*Storting*, it made sense to the conservatives that cabinet ministers should be able to appear before this body, as this would facilitate communication between parliament and cabinet. The cabinet's supporters in the *Storting* also realized that such an arrangement would strengthen the administration, which would be able to participate in debates and thus put persuasive pressure on the people's elected representatives (it is important to note here that the distinction between members of the *Storting* and the cabinet ministers is that the former were elected while the latter were not). Sverdrup was originally against giving the members of the cabinet access to the *Storting*, for he realized that this would shift the balance of power between the parliament and the cabinet in favor of the latter. Such a change would also violate the constitutional principle that there should be a division of power between the three branches of government.

Once the *Storting* was largely in the hands of the opposition, however, Sverdrup's opinion changed, for he realized that it would be easier to hold the cabinet responsible for its actions if its members could be summoned to appear before the *Storting* to answer questions and to hear expressions of lack of confidence. Another constitutional change had recently increased the power of the people's elected representatives, for in 1869, King Carl XV signed the law that provided for annual *Storting* sessions. While the cabinet wanted to engage in some political maneuvering—its desire was that the cabinet should be given the right to dissolve the *Storting*, thus forcing new elections to be held, in exchange for consenting to annual *Storting* sessions—this threat to Norway's emerging democracy was warded off. In 1870, the *Storting* voted to bring the cabinet ministers into parliamentary deliberations in order to promote their willingness to act according to the will of the people. On the advice of his cabinet, King Carl XV refused to sign the bill into law, arguing that too little time had passed since the 1869 change to annual *Storting* sessions and that one should avoid too rapid constitutional changes. In 1872, Sverdrup formulated the goal that drove his political activity for the next 12 years: All political power in Norway was to be located in the *Storting*, which would turn Norway into a truly modern democracy unfettered by the lingering traditions of the **absolute monarchy**.

Norway's constitution specifies that bills become law when passed by the *Storting* and signed by the king, or if they are passed three times by the *Storting* and if parliamentary elections are held between each of these votes, regardless of whether they are signed by the king. This is referred to as *utsettende veto* (veto of postponement), as opposed to absolute veto, which means that the king could prevent a bill from ever becoming law by vetoing it every time it was passed. When King Carl XV was succeeded by Oscar II as king of Norway and **Sweden** in 1872, he modified his cabinet structure somewhat, adding a second prime minister located in Christiania (now **Oslo**) to the one whose office was in Stockholm, Sweden. This necessitated a slight modification of the text of constitutional amendment passed in 1870, which, however, passed the *Storting* handily in 1873, after which King Oscar II refused to sign it. The same thing happened in 1876 and 1879, which meant that the bill had now met the criteria for becoming law regardless of the king's veto.

The bill was, however, in effect a constitutional amendment, and the administration, under the leadership of Prime Minister **Frederik Stang**, argued that the veto of postponement only applied to ordinary bills, not amendments to the constitution, where the king had an absolute veto. This conservative argument could be made only because the constitution was silent regarding the matter. Sverdrup and his supporters maintained that this silence indicated that no veto was allowed in the case of constitutional amendments or at least that there was to be no distinction between amendments and regular bills as far as the king's right to veto was concerned. The class-based argument made by the *embedsmann* would essentially disable the democratic process by allowing a minority of the voters to hold constitutional amendments hostage.

In 1879, when the amendment had been passed three times, the majority of the *Storting* was in a very difficult situation. If King Oscar II's veto were allowed to stand unchallenged, that would in essence mean that the *Storting* had accepted as law the idea that the king had an absolute veto in matters relating to the constitution. Challenging the veto would bring about a constitutional crisis, as it would seriously abrogate the principle of division of power, a cornerstone of Enlightenment thought that had been cherished by the framers of the Norwegian constitution of 1814. To those of a conservative bent, this and other Enlightenment ideas were expressions of decency and order, while Sverdrup's progressive thought—which from the perspective of future generations seems as obviously fair and just as the ideas of the Enlightenment surely seemed to the Norwegian conservative mind of 1879 — were an example of the tyranny of the majority and a refusal to play by existing rules.

Committed to what he felt was the true spirit of the Norwegian constitution, Sverdrup therefore proposed that the *Storting* should formally declare that the bill that was essentially a constitutional amendment passed in 1873, 1876, and 1879 was thus the law of the land. His proposal passed on 9 June 1880, after three days of debate, with 74 votes in favor and 40 against. Stang, exhausted and disgusted with the turn of events, followed the wish of King Oscar II and resigned as prime minister, after which the king appointed **Christian Selmer** in his place. The cabinet refused to accept the vote of 9 June 1880 as valid, and the question was now what Sverdrup and his people could do to bring them into compliance with the popular will. The constitution allowed for impeachment (*riksrett* or "national court" in Norwegian), and specified that the decision to impeach was to be made by the *Odelsting*, a body consisting of three fourths of the members of the *Storting*, while the panel of judges deciding the case was to be comprised of the members of the *Lagting*, a body made up of one fourth of the members of the *Storting*, together with the justices on the Supreme Court. In order to mount a successful impeachment, Sverdrup would therefore need a sufficiently large *Storting* majority that he could pack the *Lagting* and still have a comfortable majority in the *Odelsting*, for it was taken for granted that the Supreme Court justices would side with the cabinet ministers being impeached.

Sverdrup did not feel that his parliamentary majority in 1880 was sufficient to impeach the cabinet, and his situation was complicated by the fact that there were not yet any formally organized political parties in Norway. He therefore moved to make the 1882 parliamentary elections a referendum on the vote on 9 June 1880 and the need for impeachment. Norway was in political turmoil, as religious leaders and other conservatives equated Sverdrup's policies with religious apostasy, political tyranny, and the abandonment of all traditional values. Liberal political associations were formed across the country, and there were rumors that the king was preparing for a coup d'état. These rumors were well founded, for King Oscar II and his prime minister, Selmer, were planning to not adhere to a possible negative decision of the impeachment panel but to allow the cabinet to continue in power with the support of the military. Some conservatives also formed gun clubs, training to defend themselves if necessary. This led to the establishment of a large number of liberal gun clubs that could form the basis for a militia in support of Sverdrup and the majority of the *Storting*. The **Liberal Party** was formally organized in early 1884, and Sverdrup was elected chair.

The 1882, *Storting* elections were a huge success for Sverdrup, who got the large majority that he needed to successfully impeach the cabinet. The main question was what kind of punishment the ministers were to receive. Were they simply to lose their posts or should they also be declared to be without honor and unfit for public service? Sverdrup argued for the latter, but when the decision was made, one minister at a time beginning with Selmer on 27 February 1884, the sanction was simply loss of position. Sverdrup had nevertheless won on all fronts, and after a briefly serving government headed by Christian Schweigaard, which Sverdrup threatened to also impeach, King Oscar II had to resign himself to naming Sverdrup, the leader of the detested new Liberal Party, prime minister. This happened on 26 June 1884, and the new cabinet met with the *Storting* for the first time on 2 July 1884.

It took some time before the consequences of the events of 1884 were fully understood and accepted. Sverdrup proved unwilling to abide by the political rules that he had helped establish and remained in power in spite of flagging parliamentary support. In 1889, he resigned after a vote of no confidence had been proposed by the **Conservative Party** but before the vote was actually taken. Even though 1884 is usually considered the year of parliamentarism's breakthrough in Norwegian political life, it is perhaps best to consider it an unwritten rule that has been mostly and tacitly obeyed since that time. Parliamentarism was, however, included in a package of constitutional reforms that were voted in by the *Storting* on 20 February 2007.

**PETERSEN, JAN (1946– ).** Norwegian politician. Born in **Oslo** on 11 June 1946, Petersen earned a law degree at the University of Oslo in 1973 and spent several years in a leadership position in the Norwegian

Agency for Development Cooperation. He served as mayor of the Oppegård municipality from 1975 to 1981, when he was elected a member of the *Storting* (**Parliament**), representing the **Conservative Party**, and was the head of the Conservative Party's parliamentary caucus from 1994 to 2001. He became the minister of foreign affairs in Prime Minister **Kjell Magne Bondevik**'s second government, serving from 2001 to 2005. During his tenure, the Ministry of Foreign Affairs was heavily criticized for its slow response to the aftermath of the 2004 Indian Ocean earthquake and tsunami.

**PIETISM IN NORWAY.** Derived from the Latin word for *piety*, *pietism* denotes an emphasis on personal righteous living as opposed to proper beliefs. Originating in Germany in the second half of the 17th century, it was a reaction to the ravages of the **religious** wars. It stresses the individual's relationship with God and deemphasizes the church as a custodian of salvation. Simultaneously, however, it upholds the idea of the fellowship of the believers, but this fellowship tends to be democratic rather than authoritarian.

Starting with the ascension of Christian VI (1699–1746) to the throne of **Denmark** and Norway in 1730, pietism had a strong position in the public life of the two countries; for example, Ludvig Holberg suspended his writing of comedies for many years. A second wave of pietism swept across Norway starting in 1796, when **Hans Nilsen Hauge** had the religious experience that set the tone for his life. The Haugeans, as his followers were called, became very influential, both politically and **economically**. Pietism often allied itself with those who opposed the use of alcoholic beverages, and in western Norway, there has been an association between pietists and users of *nynorsk* (New Norwegian), the written **language** first created by **Ivar Aasen**. Some aspects of pietism can be observed in the charismatic movement in Norwegian 20th-century religion.

**PROGRESS PARTY.** *Fremskrittspartiet* (FrP) was established in 1973 as *Anders Langes Parti til sterk nedsettelse av skatter, avgifter og offentlige inngrep* (Anders Lange's Party for Strong Reduction of Taxes, Fees, and Public Involvement), which was known simply as Anders Lange's Party. **Carl I. Hagen** led a splinter group named *Reformpartiet* (Reform Party) in 1974; however, the two factions united in 1975. The party adopted its current name in 1977. In 1985, it got two representatives in the *Storting* (**Parliament**) and used them to help provide a vote of no confidence against **Kåre Willoch**'s coalition government in 1986.

Hagen became the head of the Progress Party in 1978, but it was only in 1987 that he chanced on the issue that was to propel him and his party to stardom on the Norwegian political firmament. The issue was immigration from non-European countries, and Hagen diligently fanned the flame of xenophobia, suggesting that Muslim immigrants were threatening Norway's Christian **religious** foundation. While the support for the party has fluctuated a great deal, Hagen made it a force to be reckoned with, and it came through the 2005 parliamentary election as Norway's second-largest party, only behind Labor. Typically, Progress Party advances have taken place in tandem with **Conservative Party** decline, and there is reason to believe that the two parties compete, in part, for the same group of voters. Hagen retired as party head in 2006 and was succeeded by **Siv Jensen**.

# – Q –

**QUISLING, VIDKUN ABRAHAM LAURITZ JONSSØN (1887–1945).** Norwegian politician and military officer. Born on 18 July 1887 in Fyresdal, Telemark County, to the clergyman Jon Lauritz Quisling, Quisling attended Latin school in Drammen and the War College of the Norwegian army (*Krigsskolen*), from which he graduated in 1911 as its top student of all time, later rising to the rank of major. In the 1920s, he assisted **Fridtjof Nansen** in his efforts to save millions of starving people in the Soviet Union, after which he served as minister of defense in the Agrarian Party (*see* CENTER PARTY) governments of **Peder Kolstad** (1931–32) and **Jens Hundseid** (1932–33). On 13 May 1933, he was one of two organizers of the Norwegian National Socialist Party (*Nasjonal Samling* [NS]), of which he became the leader (*fører*; modeled after the German *Führer*, the title used by Adolf Hitler). While initially garnering some support, NS lost most of it as it became increasingly pro-Germany and anti-Semitic.

When Germany brought Norway into **World War II** by its attack on the morning of 9 April 1940, Quisling attempted a coup d'état, which he announced on the radio that day, arguing that the Norwegian government headed by Prime Minister **Johan Nygaardsvold** had abdicated its responsibilities. He also unsuccessfully ordered the Norwegian armed forces to stop their resistance to the invasion. Quisling had the support of Hitler, with whom he had met on 18 December 1839. The civilian leadership of the German invasion did not support Quisling's coup, however, instead trying to establish an appearance of political legitimacy by acknowledging the authority of an administrative council established by the Norwegian Supreme Court under the leadership of **Paal Berg**.

When **Josef Terboven** was named commissioner for Norway by Hitler on 24 April 1940, there was a protracted power struggle between him and Quisling, although Terboven named him the political leader of a new provisional government on 25 September 1940. On 1 February 1942, Terboven accepted a change that made Quisling *Ministerpräsident*, or prime minister, in a permanent government that consisted mostly of members of the NS, which was the only legal political party in Norway at the time. Quisling served in this role until his arrest on 9 May 1945 and governed with considerable independence, even though Terboven retained control. Most of Quisling's actions were completely in line with German policy, although he had hoped to have Norwegian national sovereignty transferred from the occupants to his government, but this did not happen.

Quisling was found guilty of treason, sentenced to death, and executed by firing squad on 24 October 1945.

## – R –

**RED.** *Rødt* is a political party formed in 2007 by an alliance between the former **Workers' Communist Party** (AKP) and the **Red Electoral Alliance**. Red considers itself a revolutionary, democratic, and socialist party. Its youth organization is Red Youth, formerly the youth organization of both the **Socialist People's Party** and the AKP.

**RED ELECTORAL ALLIANCE.** The *Rød Valgallianse* (RV) was combined with the **Workers' Communist Party** in 2007, with **Red** being the name of the new party. RV had a single representative in the

*Storting* (**Parliament**) between 1993 and 1997 and also had some influence in local politics. A revolutionary, democratic, and socialistic party, RV was particularly concerned about the dominance of Microsoft products in the high-tech **industry** and actively promoted the operating system Linux as a democratic alternative to those provided by Microsoft.

**REFORM ASSOCIATION.** Established by **Johan Sverdrup** and **Ole Gabriel Ueland** in 1859, the Reform Association (*Reformforeningen*), in which rural representatives could work together with liberal city members of the *Storting* (**Parliament**), was not a political party but helped pave the way for the development of parties in the 1880s. It is the first significant attempt at developing a caucuslike forum for cooperation among like-minded members of the *Storting*. Some of the most important issues of common interest that the Reform Association promoted were Norwegian equality with **Sweden** within the union, annual sessions of the *Storting*, a **jury law** that would allow lay judges in criminal cases, and improvement of the local government system. Sverdrup had hoped that the members of the Reform Association would commit to vote according to the will of the group's majority, but this kind of party spirit was too much for many members, and the group was short-lived. Many points on its agenda resulted in pathbreaking legislation, however. For example, annual sessions of the *Storting* were held starting in 1869, and the jury law was passed in 1887. Furthermore, the **dissolution of the union with Sweden** was achieved in 1905.

**REFORMATION.** When the Roman Catholic Church was raising funds for the construction of St. Peter's Basilica in Rome early in the 16th century, one of its tools was the sale of indulgences, certificates of sin cancellation that assured their purchasers that they would not have to spend time after death in purgatory, there to be cleansed of the sins they had committed subsequent to purchasing the indulgences. The German Roman Catholic monk Martin Luther objected to this practice, and in 1517, he formulated his objections in 95 written theses, or statements, that he affixed to the door of the castle church in Wittenberg, Germany. This event marks the beginning of the Lutheran Reformation in northern Europe. The tremendous changes brought about by the Reformation were not just caused by the thinking of a single individual, however. The church had managed to not only consolidate its power as an institution that existed separately from the worldly state but even to claim power over the various heads of state in Europe according to the basic principles of **feudalism**. Along with the church's victory over the state, there was a general relaxation of spiritual discipline, and many people felt that the church needed to reform itself from within.

As Luther's original demand for an internal self-reformation of the church went unheeded, the heads of state in northern Europe, including **Denmark** and Norway, saw an opportunity for temporal and political advancement. In Norway, ownership of and income from some of the monasteries were soon turned over to men appointed by the king, although with the proviso that they had an obligation to support the resident monks and nuns. In 1536, the Lutheran Reformation started in earnest, as the Danish council of the realm and a meeting of the estates determined that bishops were to be imprisoned and their offices abolished. Roman Catholic bishops were replaced with government appointees, so-called superintendents; farmland and other properties of the church were transferred to the crown; and the liturgy and other practices of the church were changed. Objects of value were taken from individual churches, and icons were destroyed.

While outwardly the Reformation could be imposed by force (e.g., through the power of King **Christian III**), it took two or three generations before the mentality of the people was changed significantly. Most of the Catholic priests were allowed to continue in their positions and were only gradually replaced by trained Lutheran clergymen. While the organizational superstructure of the church had changed, on the parish level, things went on much as before. Gradually, however, married priests with families replaced the celibate Catholic ones. Sermons were preached in Danish, a **language** that Norwegian farmers could mostly understand, rather than in Latin. The idea that forgiveness of sin comes through a specific ecclesiastical process was replaced by a sense that personal faith was the crucial element of **religious** life.

The Reformation undoubtedly led to a reduced sense of social and spiritual stability and a general slackening of moral life. There were fewer priests than before, and as family men, the new ones had personal and **economic** responsibilities that demanded much of their attention. The greatest cultural advance associated with the Reformation, however, was no doubt that it led to an increase in the ability to read. Lutherans are taught to read the scriptures, so the New Testament was translated into Danish in 1524, while the entire Bible was available by 1550. Other religious and secular books soon became available, and thus the Reformation led to the kind of widespread literacy that is a foundation for the development of a true democracy.

**RELIGION.** Judging from petroglyphs found throughout the country, Paleolithic Norway may have had a simple religion in which various forces of nature, including human and animal fertility, were worshiped. While some conclusions can be drawn from archeological finds and information provided by such writers as Tacitus and Ibn Fadlan, the best sources of **Viking**-age religion do not appear until the 13th century, when **Snorri Sturluson** composed his *Prose Edda*. At that time, Norway had been at least nominally a Christian country for more than 200 years. Snorri's work and other written sources from the same time period make it clear, however, that Viking Norway knew a large number of gods as well as other supernatural beings and that there were established local and regional cults where these deities were worshipped. Norwegian farmers were particularly fond of Thor, who, as the lord of thunder and lightening, also had power over the weather. Odin was the god of war and poetry, while Frey and his sister Freya were the most important fertility deities.

The coming of Christianity brought not only a belief system that had been known for centuries throughout Europe prior to its arrival in Norway but also a strong central church organization and a **literary** tradition that is one of Christianity's major contributions to Norwegian life. Many of the old religious ideas persisted, however. The white Christ was seen as a warrior king whose enemies were both the devil and evil in general, while the early Norwegian conception of the devil shows that he had taken on some of Odin's characteristics. Some of the roles played by Freya in pre-Christian times were transferred to the Virgin Mary, for example, assistance in childbirth. While Christianity became Norway's official religion soon after the death of **Saint Olaf** in 1030, it took considerable time before the popular belief system caught up with the doctrines of the church. As that process advanced, people gradually gained a sense of stability in their lives, as they qualified for the salvation of their souls by taking part in the rituals and other practices of the church.

While the power of the state, embodied in that of the king, had clearly played an important role when Norway made the transition from paganism to Christianity, the **Reformation** in Norway was largely accomplished through royal fiat. As King **Christian III** in 1536 looted the wealth of the church in order to pay off his mercenaries, there was little concern with the religious feelings of common men and **women**. Because the former Roman Catholic priests were in most cases allowed to keep their positions, however, the spiritual dislocation was probably less than what might have been the case under a harsher policy toward the priests. Lutheran theology only gradually replaced Roman Catholic teachings in the services and practices of the new State Church, and it took even longer before popular religious conceptions were significantly affected. Gradually, Roman Catholic doctrine was relegated to the category of the superstitious and could be used only clandestinely, as, for example, in the chants and charms used by wise women and other popular healers.

Still, by the end of Norway's union with **Denmark**, there is no question that Norway had truly become a Lutheran country. This is, for example, demonstrated by the paragraph in the 1814 **constitution** that prohibited Jesuits from entering the realm. The danger to the Lutheran State Church was no longer residual Roman Catholic belief but the possibility that common men might take the word of God into their own hands, thus diminishing the power of the professional clergy. This had happened in 1797, when **Hans Nilsen Hauge** set out to spread his **pietistic** gospel of sin, redemption, and the individual's need to develop a close personal relationship with the deity. In spite of the persecutions and imprisonments to which he was subjected, his movement gained such force that it became literally unstoppable. Hauge did not advise his followers to leave the State Church, but other religious enthusiasts did, becoming dissenters from the true faith. Among them were Norwegian prisoners of war who had been befriended by English Quakers while in captivity during the Napoleonic wars and brought the faith with them when they returned home. Norwegian Quakers were given permission to organize themselves in 1818 but were still legally obligated to be christened, confirmed, married, and buried according to the rituals of the State Church. This situation created obvious problems, and individual exceptions were made.

However, the question of religious freedom was debated by the *Storting* (**Parliament**) throughout the 1830s. The year 1842 saw the repeal of the law called *Konventikkelplakaten* (Conventicle Notice) that regulated religious assemblies and stated that no meeting could be held without the express permission of the local State Church minister. In 1845, the *Storting* passed the Dissenter Act, according to which all Christian churches and groups, not just the Lutheran State Church, had the right to free exercise of religion. On the other hand, it was leading State Church theologians who would serve as expert witnesses when the courts had to determine which groups were Christians and which were not.

Hauge's activity as a lay preacher was connected with the rationalist spirit that held sway in the State Church around 1800 and caused its leaders to be very critical of popular pietism. Later Lutheran theologians, on the other hand, worked to make pietism a characteristic of the church itself. This is, to some extent, the case with ministers like **Lars Oftedal** and even more so with **Gisle Johnson**, the professor of theology who in 1855 organized the *Christiania Indremissionsforening* (Christiania Society for the Inner Mission) and founded *Den norske Lutherstiftelse* (The Norwegian Luther Foundation) in 1868. In 1891, the latter changed its name to *Det norske lutherske Indremisjonsselskap* (The Norwegian Lutheran Society for Inner Mission), commonly just known as the Inner Mission, and was enormously influential all over Norway, sending its emissaries to hold meetings in even the most out-of-the-way and hard-to-reach communities. The spirit cultivated by the Inner Mission was put on display in 1907, when the appointment of a liberal theologian to a professorship at the Royal Frederik's University (now the University of **Oslo**) School of Theology precipitated the organization of a conservative **educational** institution, *Det teologiske Menighetsfakultetet* (MF; The Norwegian School of Theology; literally, the School of Theology of the Congregations), which became a guardian of both Lutheran orthodoxy and the spirit of pietism. A similar degree of commitment informed the many Norwegian missionary activities in foreign lands. *Det Norske*

*Misjonsselskap* (The Norwegian Mission Society) had been started as early as 1842, *Den Norske Santalmisjon* (The Norwegian Santal Mission) was formed in 1867, and *Det Norske Kinamissionsforbund* (The Norwegian China Mission League) in 1891. These organizations operated within the bounds of Lutheran theology.

The increasing secularization of Norwegian society throughout the 20th century led to both less public support for the State Church and an increase in the number of and support for dissenter groups. *Den Evangelisk Lutherske Frikirke* (The Evangelical Lutheran Free Church), a Lutheran church where each congregation is led by a pastor and governed by a council of elders, had been formed in 1877 because of dissatisfaction with the control and practices of the State Church. The first Norwegian Baptist congregation had been organized in 1860, while the first Norwegian congregation of the Seventh-Day Adventists was formed in Christiania (now Oslo) in 1879. The Pentecostal movement established itself in Norway in 1907, and gradually other charismatic groups came into being, including *Det Norske Misjonsforbund* (The Norwegian Mission League), which does not require its members to leave the State Church. The Salvation Army began its work in Norway in 1888. These groups did their work partly in cooperation with the State Church but mostly in opposition to it. As much of the religious energy in Norway went to the dissenter organizations rather than to the State Church itself, attendance at Sunday services declined even though nonattending members would still come to it for christenings, confirmations, marriages, and funerals. There was also an increasing number of agnostics and atheists in the country, and some of them organized themselves in such associations as the *Human-Etisk Forbund* (League of Secular Humanists), which got its start in 1956, and *Det norske Hedningesamfunn* (The Norwegian Society of Heathens), formed in 1974.

In the 1960s, there were two major changes to the legislation governing the exercise of religion in Norway. Complete freedom of religion for all, and not just Christians, was constitutionally guaranteed in 1964, and state financial support of all registered churches and *livssynssamfunn* (philosophy of life societies) was established in 1969. This leveling of the playing field has led to increased pluralism and tolerance in religious matters, especially as other world religions, including Islam, have made themselves increasingly visible in Norwegian society. Secularization and religious pluralism seem to get along well in Norway. *See also* FREETHINKER.

**RINNAN, HENRY OLIVER (1915–47).** Norwegian war criminal. Born in Levanger, Nord-Trøndelag County, on 14 May 1915, he became a German agent soon after the invasion on 9 April 1940. Having established a group, the so-called *Rinnanbanden* (Rinnan Gang), he infiltrated Norwegian resistance activities and turned the names of the participants over to the Germans. Later, he got authority to carry out his own questioning of suspected resistance workers, several hundred of which were tortured, while as many as 80 were killed. Rinnan was arrested while trying to flee to **Sweden** shortly after the German capitulation. Sentenced to death for his murders during the war, he was executed by firing squad on 1 February 1947.

***RØD VALGALLIANSE.*** *See* RED ELECTORAL ALLIANCE.

***RØDT.*** *See* RED.

**RØISELAND, BENT (1902–81).** Norwegian politician. Born in Holme, Vest-Agder County, on 11 October 1902, Røiseland was the first farmer to become the head of the **Liberal Party** and Norway's first politician to become a media celebrity. He served as a member of the *Storting* (**Parliament**) between 1945 and 1973 and was the leader of the Liberals from 1952 to 1964. He was a spiritual heir to the low-church movement and was deeply committed to matters of **religion**, particularly the Inner Mission, as well as to abstinence from alcohol and the use of *nynorsk* (New Norwegian). Very popular even among those who did not share his political views, he was a candidate for prime minister in 1965, when the **Conservative Party**, the **Christian Democratic Party**, the **Center Party**, and the Liberal Party agreed to form a coalition government. While the Conservatives had approximately twice as many seats in the *Storting* as any of the other three parties, the other three agreed that the prime minister should not come from the Conservatives. When they could not agree which of the three parties should supply him, however—the two prime candidates were Røiseland and **Per Borten**—the Conservatives threw their support behind Borten, whom they considered more reliably conservative than Røiseland. Røiseland was one of the members of the Liberal Party who broke away and formed the **New Left People's Party** in 1972.

**RØLVAAG, OLE EDEVART (1876–1931).** Norwegian novelist. Born on 22 April 1876 in Dønna, Nordland County, Rølvaag lived in the **United States** while writing novels in Norwegian. His work thus belongs to both Norwegian and American **literature** and is studied and taught in both countries and in their respective **languages**. While growing up, he worked as a fisherman for many years before immigrating to South Dakota. After attending Augustana Academy and St. Olaf College, he did graduate work at the University of **Oslo** and then returned to St. Olaf as a teacher of Norwegian.

As an immigrant himself, Rølvaag was in a unique position to both understand and interpret the experience of his fellow Norwegians in America, and several novels written between 1912 and 1921 offer insights into both their material and emotional struggles. His masterpiece, however, was written on the occasion of the centenary of organized **emigration** from Norway to America, commemorated in 1925. Titled *I de dage* (1925, tr. *In Those Days*), it was followed by *Riket grundlægges* (1925, tr. *The Kingdom Is Founded*); the two volumes were translated by Lincoln Colcord and published as *Giants in the Earth: A Saga of the Prairie* (1927). Two additional volumes in the series, *Peder Seier* (1928; tr. *Peder Victorious*, 1929) and *Den signede dag* (1931; tr. *Their Fathers' God*, 1931) were completed before the author's untimely death from heart disease.

Rølvaag also wrote short stories as well as a book of essays that argued for cultural preservation, *Omkring fædrearven* (1922; tr. *Concerning Our Heritage*, 1998).

– S –

**SAINT OLAF (995–1030).** Norwegian king, later canonized. Also known as King Olaf II Haraldsson of Norway, Olaf was born to Harald Grenske, the great-grandchild of **Harald Fairhair**. After several years' absence in England, he returned to Norway in 1015 to claim the throne, supported by several local kings in the area to the north of

**Oslo**. In 1016, he defeated Earl Svein, who was based in Trøndelag and was the ruler in a large part of the country, in the battle of Nesjar in the Oslo fjord. He later successfully gained control both of the coast and some of the interior valleys, ruling the entire land of Norway in a more real sense than any of his predecessors and Christianizing the inhabitants by force. He also asserted his dominion in the islands to the west and carried out a successful raid against **Denmark**. In 1028, he had to flee Norway for Russia, however, as the Norwegian chieftains, whose power he had curtailed, came to the support of the Danish king Knut the Great. When Olaf returned a year later, crossing the border from **Sweden** and marching down through Verdalen in the area of Trøndelag, he was met by a large army of peasants. According to the sagas written by **Snorri Sturluson**, a battle between Olaf's 3,600 men and the 7,000-men-strong peasant army took place at Stiklestad, and Olaf died from wounds received there. His body was secretly buried in Nidaros (now **Trondheim**), and when it was exhumed a year later, it was apparent that both his hair and his fingernails had grown. Soon miracles associated with his remains were reported, and he was beatified a year after his death, becoming Norway's eternal king, the *Rex Perpetuum Norvegiae*, as well as **Scandinavia**'s most important saint. He thus became both a central symbol of Norwegian national unity and the belated victor in his campaign in favor of Christianity.

**SÁMI.** The Sámi people have traditionally lived in the interior of Norway, **Sweden**, Finland, and Russia, as well as next to the fjords of northern Norway. They have typically made a living from reindeer herding, hunting, **fishing**, and (in the case of the fjord Sámi) small-scale **agriculture**. The Norwegian Sámi population is usually divided into two groups, the northern Sámi, who have inhabited all of northern Norway, and the southern Sámi, whose territory historically stretched from Trøndelag to Hedmark. There are two additional groups, a very small number of Skolte-Sámi people living in the community of Neiden at the end of the Varanger fjord in eastern Finnmark, and a Lule-Sámi population in Tysfjord, Nordland County.

Modern genetic research has indicated that the ancestors of the Sámi hail from the Iberian peninsula, not from Siberia as was earlier believed, and that they are more closely related to other Europeans than to any other population group. Their core cultural area was long claimed simultaneously by Norway, Sweden, and Russia, and the Sámi were at times taxed by all three states. As the national borders were established, Norway's Sámi population was put under great pressure to give up its **language**, **religion**, and unique way of life. While **Thomas von Westen**, the great Christian missionary to the Sámi, believed that they should be taught the true religion in their own language, his successors did not, and Christianity was used as a tool to make the Sámi Norwegian. As Norway's **educational** system developed, Sámi children were compelled to attend schools at which they were taught in a language they could not understand. It was only as late as 1959 that the law was changed so as to permit Sámi children to be taught in their native tongue.

The Norwegian government's policy vis-à-vis the Sámi has changed significantly during the post–**World War II** era. The Sámi are now recognized as an aboriginal people, an elected Sámi assembly has been established, and their traditional rights to the land they have inhabited for thousands of years has begun to become codified. When the *Storting* (**Parliament**) passed the Finnmark Act in 2005, property rights to land and water in Finnmark County was legally transferred back to the Sámi people. This act is of far more than symbolic significance, even though today more Sámi people live in **Oslo** than in Finnmark.

*SAMLINGSPARTIET. See* UNITED PARTY.

**SCANDINAVIANISM.** Prominent around the middle of the 19th century, the movement of Scandinavianism emphasized the similarities in **language**, culture, and origin among **Denmark**, Norway, and **Sweden**. Some of its roots can be traced back to the ideas of the **national romanticism**, when the movement's proponents wanted to strengthen the ties that already bound the three countries to each other. For example, there were some that hoped that Denmark would join the already-existing union between Norway and Sweden and that this expanded union would increase the security of the three countries vis-à-vis Germany and Russia. This hope had much currency during the years of conflict between Denmark and Prussia, but Denmark's defeat in 1864, after a war in which Denmark received no assistance from the governments of Norway and Sweden, brought it to an end. Norway's **dissolution of the union with Sweden** in 1905 also created bitter feelings. Intellectuals and students were generally among the more ardent proponents of Scandinavianism; these included, for example, **Bjørnstjerne Bjørnson**, **Henrik Ibsen**, and **Marcus Jacob Monrad**.

**SCHWEIGAARD, ANTON MARTIN (1808–70).** Norwegian politician and legal scholar. Born in Kragerø on 11 April 1808, Schweigaard became an orphan at the age of 10 and as a youth worked in a variety of jobs. His great academic ability soon became evident, however, and he attended the Latin school in Skien, from which he graduated with the highest marks ever given in Norway. A member of **Johan Sebastian Welhaven**'s circle in the 1830s, he argued in favor of maintaining strong cultural connections with **Denmark**, which he regarded as Norway's gateway to European culture. After earning a law degree at the university in Christiania (now **Oslo**) in 1832, he studied abroad for two years, became a lecturer and later professor of law at the university, and wrote on political **economy** and jurisprudence. A strong believer in economic liberalism and capitalism, he nevertheless believed that the state must actively regulate the economy for the betterment of society as a whole. Through these ideas, he had a great impact on the development of Norwegian economic and social life.

Schweigaard was elected a member of the *Storting* (**Parliament**) in 1842, serving until 1869. Conservative by nature, he believed that the *embedsmann* (public official) class needed to take the lead in society in cooperation with the middle class and that these leaders had a paternalistic responsibility vis-à-vis the farmers and the rest of the population. An optimist, he believed in social, economic, and technological progress through wise management and the appropriate deployment of resources but also that social discipline was necessary to promote the common good. He took a middle position in the struggle between free **trade** and protectionism, holding that free trade should in principle be maintained but that pragmatic exceptions must be made. For example, the state was to receive a monopoly in the areas of telegraph and mail, while Norway's first railroad, opened in 1854, was a joint public–private venture.

At the time of his death on 1 February 1870, Schweigaard enjoyed perhaps greater respect and admiration than any of his Norwegian contemporaries. Shortly thereafter, the poet and journalist **Aasmund Olafsson Vinje** wrote a lengthy essay in which, in the context of a survey of the cultural struggle in Norway from 1830 to 1870, he summed up Schweigaard's contribution. Vinje's judgment was that Schweigaard had not been sufficiently idealistic. This may very well be true, at least from Vinje's point of view, but one of Schweigaard's main contributions to Norwegian intellectual development in the 19th century was surely his ability to move beyond idealism to a pragmatism that presages the political choices made by Norway in the 20th century.

**SEIP, HELGE LUNDE (1919–2004).** Norwegian politician and newspaper editor. Born in Surnadal, Møre and Romsdal County, on 5 March 1919, Seip was educated at the University of **Oslo**, receiving a degree in **economics** in 1941 and a law degree in 1942. After holding government positions in the Department of **Trade** and the Central Bureau of Statistics, he became political editor in the Oslo daily *Dagbladet* (Daily Paper), which was affiliated with the **Liberal Party**, in 1954 and served as its editor-in-chief from 1958 to 1965. He represented Oslo in the *Storting* (**Parliament**) on the Liberal Party ticket in 1954–61 and 1965–73. Between 1970 and 1973, he also chaired the Liberal Party parliamentary caucus. From 1965 to 1970, he served as minister of local government in the coalition government headed by **Per Borten**, in which the **Conservatives**, **Christian Democrats**, and Liberals participated along with Borten's own **Center Party**. Both as an editor and as a politician, Seip was a spokesperson for the culturally radical wing of the Liberal Party, which has traditionally had its center of gravity in the capital city and in eastern Norway. The west coast wing, which traces its roots to low-church movements, opposition to the use of alcohol, and a historical commitment to the use of *nynorsk* (New Norwegian), at times found Seip exasperating.

When Norwegian participation in the European Community (EC; *see* EUROPEAN ECONOMIC COMMUNITY [EEC]) became a major issue in 1972, Seip came out in favor of full membership. As party chair from 1970 to 1972, he bucked the majority of his own party, which vehemently opposed joining. At an extraordinary party convention held at Røros in 1972, Seip led a group of prominent Liberal Party members who broke with the party and formed the *Folkepartiet nye venstre* (**New Left People's Party**), later known as *Det Liberale Folkepartiet* (The Liberal People's Party), that supported Norwegian EC membership. This split, which actually went deeper than just the EC issue, as there was disagreement about whether the Liberal Party should have participated in the coalition government, proved a disastrous event for both parties. The mother party quickly lost most of its influence in Norwegian national politics—for example, the party went without a single representative in the *Storting* for a period of eight years—and the daughter party never gained any influence, eventually joining forces with the Liberals again in 1988.

Seip was, however, a very colorful figure who later served as a much appreciated TV election commentator. He worked for the **Nordic Council** from 1973 to 1977, served as editor-in-chief for the newspaper *Norges Handels-og Sjøfartstidende* (Norwegian Commerce and **Shipping** News) from 1977 to 1980, and was the founding director of *Datatilsynet* (the Data Inspectorate), which guards people's right to privacy in the digital age.

**SELMER, CHRISTIAN AUGUST (1816–89).** Norwegian politician. Born in Fredrikshald, Østfold County, on 16 November 1816, Selmer served as a **Conservative Party** member of the *Storting* (**Parliament**) from 1871 to 1874 and as a cabinet minister from 1874 to 1880, heading the Department of Defense and the Department of Justice. When **Frederik Stang** resigned as prime minister in 1880, King Oscar II selected Selmer to take his place. Selmer was a competent administrator but lacked the flexibility and breadth of vision necessary for him to successfully deal with the political challenges of the early 1880s. **Johan Sverdrup**, the leader of the opposition in the *Storting*, was preparing to impeach the cabinet, thus laying the groundwork for the introduction of parliamentarism in Norwegian political life. Selmer, like his predecessor Stang, stubbornly refused to yield to the wishes of a substantial popular and parliamentary majority. He and the rest of his government were impeached and convicted, beginning with Selmer himself on 27 February 1884.

*SENTERPARTIET. See* CENTER PARTY.

**SHIPPING.** Norway has been a seafaring nation at least since **Viking** times, and the coastal population has been thoroughly familiar with boats of various sizes used for **fishing** and transportation. The Vikings even had a particular type of vessel, the *knarr*, that was wider and deeper than the longship and that was thus very well suited to activities involving **trade** and transport.

Norway's lengthy decline after the arrival of the **Black Death** manifested itself in its shipping traditions as well as in all other areas of national life. In the early 1600s, most trade involving Norway was carried on foreign ships. The city of **Bergen** had an oceangoing fleet, but it was not until 1670 that a national fleet can be seen, and it consisted of only approximately 240 ships. By 1696, the fleet had quadrupled in size, and most of the new ships had been built in Norway. There soon was a decline, however, as trade conditions worsened, followed by another upswing between 1750 and 1800. Another significant change took place at this time, too, for Norwegian ships no longer carried goods only from and to Norway but between third-party countries as well.

The shipping fleet grew rapidly starting in the 1820, and by 1878, it was the third-largest in the world. Especially the British repeal of the Navigation Acts in 1849 led to golden times for Norway's merchant fleet, and so did the steady growth in world trade and the gradual spread of free competition. Norwegian ships were usually owned by several individuals together, and a single individual might have an interest in many different ships. Most of the ships continued to be sailing vessels, except for those based in Bergen; the Bergen fleet was largely converted to steam by the end of the 1870s.

At the beginning of the 20th century, the general conversion to steamships was speeding up, and an increasing number of ships were owned by limited-liability companies rather than held by groups of individuals owning a ship together. The large shipping firm was a far more efficient business model, and long-term charter agreements made the shipping business increasingly stable. The ability to safely predict future earnings was also one of the reasons Norwegian shipowners were able to rapidly make the transition from steamships to motor ships in the 1920s and 1930s.

The Norwegian merchant fleet was a significant asset to the Allies during **World War II**, as it was the most modern in the world and particularly strong in the area of **oil** tankers. After the war, there was a large increase in container ships as well as larger and more efficient tankers that required smaller crews. By the end of the 1950s, Norwegian ships increasingly hired foreign crew members, however the officers tended to remain Norwegian. This development continued during the second half of the 20th century.

As of 2001, the Norwegian shipping fleet consisted of 1,631 registered ships, totaling 23.59 million gross tons, which was 4.3 percent of the gross tonnage of the world fleet. Approximately 800 of the ships were dry cargo vessels, almost 400 were passenger ships and ferries, and 339 were tankers. The offshore oil **industry** employed 151 ships. In 1999, 46 million passengers traveled by ship in Norway, and almost 200 car ferries were in operation. *Hurtigruten* (literally, "the fast connection") has world renown and operates along the coast between Bergen and Kirkenes. Originally a transport lifeline for the coastal population, it now serves mostly tourists. Other cruise ships are frequent visitors to Norwegian waters. While many ships are owned and operated by local companies, such Norwegian shipowners as Sigval Bergesen, Fred. Olsen, and Wilhelm Wilhelmsen founded large companies of worldwide importance. Color Line and Fred. Olsen Cruise Lines are two well-known Norwegian cruise-ship operators.

**SIGURDSSON, SVERRE (c. 1151–1202).** Norwegian king. Sverre Sigurdsson was born and grew up in the home of a foster-father, Bishop Roe, in the Faeroe Islands. When he was in his mid-20s, his mother, Gunnhild, told him that he was the illegitimate son of Sigurd Munn, one of a number of kings claiming the throne and ruling Norway for a while during the turbulent years of the civil wars between 1130 and 1240. Modern historians consider it highly improbable that this claim was accurate, but there is no doubt that Sverre himself believed in it and that it motivated his actions in the years to come. He contacted a leaderless, rag-tag band of rebels referred to as *birkebeinere* (birch bark legs)—actually, they were tax resisters—whom he led in a number of victorious actions. Their opponent was King Magnus Erlingsson (1156–84), the son of Erling Skakke, and his wife, Kristin, who was the daughter of King Sigurd Jorsalfare (1090–1130). Magnus had the support of the church, by which he had been crowned, because the church tried to establish the rule that a king's oldest son born in wedlock was his legitimate successor. The church wanted to delegitimatize all offspring of concubines as lawful pretenders to the throne, and Sverre was precisely the type of person the clergy wanted to avoid.

Sverre managed to get himself accepted as king at the Øreting in Nidaros (now **Trondheim**) in 1177, which meant that he had a legitimate claim to rule all of Norway. The church resisted his claim even after the death of King Magnus at the Battle of Fimreite in 1184, when Sverre won a decisive victory and no other serious pretenders to the throne were left. In 1194, two bishops, Nikolas and Eirik, managed to get the pope to excommunicate Sverre, and two years later they formed a group that continued the fight against him. They, too, were beaten, and after Sverre's death, they had to make peace with the *birkebeinere* party. It may be said that Sverre's appearance on the scene of Norwegian national politics prolonged the civil war period, but because a lot of members of the inherited aristocracy were killed fighting against him, he can also be credited with promoting the egalitarian spirit in Norway.

**SOCIALIST LEFT PARTY.** The *Sosialistisk Venstreparti* (SV) was formed in 1975 after an alliance consisting of the **Socialist People's Party**, **Norway's Communist Party** (NKP), the Democratic Socialists, and a number of independent socialists gained 16 seats in the *Storting* (**Parliament**) in 1973. This alliance was named the *Sosialistisk Valgforbund* (Socialist Electoral League). During negotiations held in 1975 and aimed at uniting the partners into a single party, however, the NKP broke away and left those remaining to form the SV. The SV is in favor of socialism, **environmental** protection, and solidarity with the world's poor. It wants to repeal Norwegian membership in the **North Atlantic Treaty Organization** and increase state ownership of means of production. Representatives of the SV have been accused of making irresponsible statements, for example, that the **United States** is a terrorist nation and that Israel is a Nazi state. During the parliamentary elections in 2005, the SV received 8.8 percent of the popular vote and 15 seats in the *Storting*. It also became a member of the coalition government headed by **Jens Stoltenberg**. Kristin Halvorsen has served as its leader since 1997.

**SOCIALIST PEOPLE'S PARTY.** The *Sosialistisk Folkeparti* (SF) was formed in 1961 by some members of the **Labor Party** who were unhappy with its foreign policy, particularly its supportive attitude toward the **North Atlantic Treaty Organization**. The 1961 **parliamentary** election gave the SF two representatives in the *Storting* (Parliament), **Finn Gustavsen** and Asbjørn Holm, both of whom were reelected in 1965. The SF used its power to bring down the minority Labor government in 1963, but four weeks later, they voted against the Center–Right coalition that replaced it. The **Socialist Youth Federation** was the party's more radical youth group.

**SOCIALIST YOUTH FEDERATION.** The *Sosialistisk Ungdomsforbund* (SUF), originally named *Sosialistisk Ungdomsfylking* (Socialist Youth Array), was the youth organization of the **Socialist People's Party**. In the middle of the 1960s, its members became increasingly enamored with revolutionary Marxism, being inspired by both Mao Zedong's China and Enver Hoxha's Albania, and the SUF broke away from the mother party in 1969. Shortly thereafter, the SUF changed its name to *Sosialistisk Ungdomsforbund (Marxist-leninistene)* (Socialist Youth Federation [Marxist-Leninist]; SUF [m-l]), some of whose members published the paper *Klassekampen* (Class Struggle). The SUF (m-l) was thus a precursor of the *Arbeidernes kommunistparti* (**Workers' Communist Party**). It changed its name to *Rød ungdom* (RU; Red Youth) in 1973.

**SOLBERG, ERNA (1961– ).** Norwegian politician. Born in **Bergen** on 24 February 1961, Solberg studied political science and **economics**, graduating from the University of Bergen in 1986. She served in a number of positions in student organizations, the youth organization of the **Conservative Party**, the **women**'s organization of the Conservatives, and the Conservative Party itself. She was a member of the Bergen City Council from 1983 to 1991, having spent four years before that as a substitute member, and was elected a member of the *Storting* (**Parliament**) in 1989. She served as vice chair of the Conservative Party from 2002 to 2004 and became party leader in 2004, succeeding **Jan Petersen**. She was appointed minister of local government and regional development in the government headed by **Kjell Magne Bondevik** in 2001, serving until 2005, when a red and green coalition, consisting of the **Labor Party**, the **Socialist Left Party**, and the **Center Party**, got into power. A strong-willed and combative person somewhat in the mold of the long-serving British prime minister Margaret Thatcher, Solberg earned the nickname "Jern-Erna" (Iron Erna).

**SOLSTAD, DAG (1941– ).** Norwegian novelist. Born on 16 July 1941 in the **whaling** town of Sandefjord, Solstad is recognized as one of the foremost Norwegian writers of his generation and a chronicler of life in the Norwegian welfare state. Having started out as an exponent of **literary** modernism, he soon turned to a kind of socialist realism that was intended to help bring about a Marxist revolution in Norway. When the revolution did not materialize, Solstad's writing style changed to a rather traditional psychological realism.

Around the time of the student revolt of 1968 and while a student at the University of **Oslo**, Solstad and some other young writers, including **Tor Obrestad** and **Espen Haavardsholm**, affiliated with the **Socialist Youth Federation**, which later became part of the **Workers' Communist Party**. This party served as Solstad's ideological home for the rest of the decade. Solstad's transition from late modernist to committed Marxist is described in his novel *Arild Asnes, 1970* (1971), at the end of which the first-person protagonist goes door to door to sell the socialist newspaper *Klassekampen* (Class Struggle). His next book, the novel *25. september-plassen* (1974; The 25th of September Square), named for the date of the European Community (*see* EUROPEAN ECONOMIC COMMUNITY [EEC]) referendum in 1972, explicates social democracy in postwar Norway from a thoroughgoing Marxist perspective and argues that the Norwegian working class was betrayed by the leaders of the **Labor Party** who collaborated with American capitalism and steered Norway toward membership in the **North Atlantic Treaty Organization**. A similar perspective governs a trilogy about working-class life in the late 1930s and during **World War II**, in which Solstad again wants to show that social democracy is incompatible with the true needs of the workers.

By 1980, it was becoming increasingly difficult to maintain any hope for a Marxist revolution in Norway, and Solstad began a process of self-examination carried out in several novels. He also wrote books without a strong ideological bias, in which he analyzed contemporary Norwegian life and society.

***SOSIALISTISK FOLKEPARTI.*** *See* SOCIALIST PEOPLE'S PARTY.

***SOSIALISTISK UNGDOMSFORBUND.*** *See* SOCIALIST YOUTH FEDERATION.

***SOSIALISTISK VENSTREPARTI.*** *See* SOCIALIST LEFT PARTY.

**SPONHEIM, LARS (1957– ).** Norwegian politician. Born in Halden, Østfold County, on 23 May 1957, Sponheim was educated as an agronomist and worked in that profession in Ulvik in western Norway. He also taught **agriculture** from 1984 to 1993. Sponheim was active in local politics and was the mayor of Ulvik from 1987 to 1991, after which he served in the county assembly. He was elected a member of the *Storting* (**Parliament**) in 1993, representing the **Liberal Party**, which at that time had been without parliamentary representation for eight years. In 1996, while still the single Liberal representative in the *Storting*, Sponheim was elected head of the Liberal Party against the opposition of a significant segment of its membership. He was reelected rather uneventfully until 2002, when he won only after a tough fight. He was again challenged in 2004, when Olaf Thommessen was the candidate of the opposition, but was reelected. He was reelected unanimously in 2006, after he had led the Liberals to a significant victory—the party received 5.9 percent of the popular vote and 10 representatives—in the 2005 parliamentary elections. In 1997, Sponheim became minister of **industry** and commerce in the coalition government headed by **Kjell Magne Bondevik**, serving until 2000. He next served as minister of agriculture in Bondevik's second government, serving from 2001 to 2005.

Sponheim has been a colorful presence in Norwegian public life. Relentlessly advocating for the Liberal Party's core values of civil liberties, **environmental** protection, and the interests of small business, Sponheim wants Norwegian society to be less complex, more diverse, and more hospitable to a broader range of human self-realization. He drew considerable ire, however, with a proposal—made while serving as the minister of agriculture—that Norwegians living close to the **Swedish** border should not buy agricultural products in Sweden, where prices are generally lower. Some people were also provoked when in 2007 he suggested that in the interest of lowering carbon emissions, people should voluntarily refrain from taking more than one vacation trip to southern climes per year.

**STANG, EMIL, SR. (1834–1912).** Norwegian politician. Born the son of **Frederik Stang** on 14 June 1834, Stang studied law at the university in Christiania (now **Oslo**). He was actively involved in the organization of the **Conservative Party** in 1884 and became its first head, serving in 1884–89, 1891–93, and 1896–99. He succeeded **Johan Sverdrup** as prime minister in 1889, serving until 1891, and again served as prime minister from 1893 to 1895. Stang was known for his realism and complete intellectual honesty and acted as a counterweight to those who wanted to pursue independence from **Sweden** at any cost. As the Conservative Party was making its transition from being mainly a party for the *embedsmann* (public official) class to a party that represented the interests of large landowners, factory owners, wholesale merchants, and other members of the upper middle class, Stang's wisdom and political savvy helped keep the Conservatives from experiencing the kinds of schisms that plagued the Liberals.

**STANG, FREDERIK (1808–84).** Norwegian politician. Born in Stokke, Vestfold County, on 4 March 1808, Stang began studying law at the university in Christiania (now **Oslo**) in 1824, receiving his degree in 1828 when he was but 20 years old. Two years later, he started teaching law at the university, specializing in **constitutional** law and publishing a highly regarded book about Norway's constitution in 1833. The year after that, he went into private practice and became known as a superb trial lawyer. Stang also was in favor of the idea that the cabinet ministers should meet with the *Storting* (**Parliament**) in order to offer reasons for their choices and actions. **Christian Magnus Falsen** had made a suggestion along this line as early as 1818, but the reform did not happen until 1884. From 1846 to

1856, Stang served as minister of the interior, and he was a driving force behind many practical reforms. The postal system, for example, was modernized, and the cost of sending a letter within Norway became the same regardless of distance. The infrastructure—roads, canals, and harbors—was improved, lighthouses were built, and Stang strongly supported the building of a railroad. He was named *førstestatsråd* (first minister) in 1861 and became the leader of the Norwegian government in Christiania (there was also a smaller Norwegian government in Stockholm). In 1873, the position of first minister was changed to prime minister, and Stang continued his service with this title until 1880.

**STAVANGER.** Stavanger is located on a peninsula at the northern end of the **agricultural** district of Jæren, Rogaland County, in southwestern Norway. It measures 72 square kilometers and consists of an area mostly on the mainland, with an additional 15 inhabited islands. It has a mild climate, with very little snow during the winter and an early spring, and its growing season is the longest in Norway. The terrain is relatively flat and low lying, and there are several lakes within the city limits.

Throughout most of its history, Stavanger has served as a market town for the farmers surrounding it and for people living along the fjord and on the islands northeast of town. Founded around 1125, it became the seat of the Roman Catholic bishopric of an area stretching from Haugesund to Eidanger. It received the privileges of a market town in 1425, but numerous city fires and some outbreaks of the plague kept it from flourishing. After a fire in 1684, a governmental decision was made to abandon the town, and some administrative offices were moved to Kristiansand farther south and east. In 1695, 15 percent of the population died in an epidemic of spotted typhoid. Five major city fires followed, the last one in 1860. At this time, the herring **fisheries** were exceptionally lucrative, however, and a large number of canneries were later established when the brisling fisheries developed. Stavanger sardines canned in olive oil were exported all over the world, and the city was a major **industrial** center into the 1950s. To some extent, shipbuilding replaced the old fish-based industry.

When exploratory **oil** drilling in the North Sea was conducted in the 1960s and significant discoveries of oil and natural gas were made, Stavanger was in the right geographical location to become Norway's oil city. Its excellent airport and existing industrial infrastructure, along with its proximity to the oil fields, made it the obvious choice both for the location of company headquarters and district offices and for supply and support bases. Norway's leading oil company, Statoil, has its headquarters in the Stavanger area, and the Norwegian Oil Directorate is headquartered there as well.

Stavanger is also the location of Norway's fifth university, the University of Stavanger, established on 1 January 2005 as the next step in the development of Stavanger University College. A highly internationalized and multicultural city, Stavanger has also been recognized for its efforts in cultural preservation, particularly of the *Gamle Stavanger* (Old Stavanger), which is the best-preserved collection of wooden structures in any city in northern Europe.

**STEEN, JOHANNES VILHELM CHRISTIAN (1827–1906).** Norwegian politician. Born in Christiania (now **Oslo**) on 22 July 1827, Steen studied at the university in Christiania, graduated in 1848, and became a teacher and headmaster at the grammar school in **Stavanger**. He was first elected to the *Storting* (**Parliament**) in 1859 and served as a member on and off until 1900. He was considered brilliant and an excellent speaker and supported **Johan Sverdrup** at first but later was too radical for Sverdrup's tastes. He served as prime minister twice, in 1891–93 and 1898–1902. Steen was the leader of the Pure Liberal Party (*Rene Venstre*), which in 1888 split off from Sverdrup's **Moderate Liberal Party** (*Moderate Venstre*). Steen was thus prominent in the events that led to the **dissolution of the union with Sweden**.

**STEEN, REIULF (1933– ).** Norwegian politician. Steen was born in Hurum, Buskerud County, on 16 August 1933 and entered politics early, when at the age of 14 he became the head of his local **Labor Party** organization. As a teenage factory worker and later as a journalist in the Labor-affiliated press, he had formative experiences that prepared him well for a career as a full-time politician, starting in 1958 and ending in 1992, when he became Norway's ambassador to Chile. After occupying a number of positions of trust in the Labor

Party, he became its head in 1975, serving until 1981, when **Gro Harlem Brundtland** took over. He was a member of the *Storting* **(Parliament)** from 1977 to 1992 and served in the government twice, once as minister of transport (1971–72) and once as minister of **trade** (1979–81).

Steen's sharp and incisive intellect made him a frequent participant in Norway's public debate. One of his many areas of expertise has been **educational** policy, to which a committee led by him contributed substantially by furnishing a report that formed the basis for a significant reform of secondary education in 1974. He has also been one of the best-known proponents of Norwegian membership in the **European Union** and has written a number of books on various political subjects, foremost among them *Ørnen har landet: Om Arbeiderpartiets strateger* (2003; The Eagle Has Landed: On the Strategists of the Labor Party). Having suffered from endogenous depression, Steen, who was past the age of 60 when his illness was finally diagnosed and treated, has with great courage used his status as a public figure to encourage awareness of this and other mental conditions.

**STOLTENBERG, JENS (1959– ).** Norwegian politician. The scion of a family known for its public service and the son of the former Minister of Foreign Affairs **Thorvald Stoltenberg**, Jens Stoltenberg was born on 16 March 1959 in **Oslo**. He had served in several responsible positions in the **Labor Party** as well as in the Labor Party Youth League before being elected a member of the *Storting* **(Parliament)** in 1993. Trained as an **economist**, Stoltenberg served as minister of **trade** and energy under **Gro Harlem Brundtland** from 1993 to 1996 and as minister of finance and customs under **Thorbjørn Jagland** from 1996 to 1997. He first served as prime minister in a Labor Party minority government from 2000 to 2001, and the controversial and seemingly illiberal policies of this government led to a bitter but successful battle with Jagland for the leadership of the Labor Party in 2002. After the parliamentary elections in 2005, when the Labor Party took 61 out of 169 seats, Stoltenberg formed his second government, a majority coalition in which the Labor Party joined forces with the **Socialist Left Party** and the **Center Party**. This red–green coalition was still in power in 2007.

**STOLTENBERG, THORVALD (1931– ).** Norwegian **Labor Party** politician and diplomat. Born in **Oslo** on 8 July 1931, Stoltenberg studied law at the University of Oslo before becoming employed by the Norwegian Ministry of Foreign Affairs in 1958. After a number of significant assignments at home and abroad, he became minister of defense in 1979, serving under Prime Minister **Odvar Nordli**. Nordli resigned in 1981, and Stoltenberg next served as minister of foreign affairs from 1987 to 1989 in **Gro Harlem Brundtland**'s second government. He served in the same position from 1990 to 1993 in Brundtland's third government. Stoltenberg's influence on Norway's foreign policy under Nordli and Brundtland cannot be overestimated. He had a strong commitment to alleviating the plight of refugees and personally assisted people fleeing Hungary in 1956. In 1990, he served as the **United Nations** high commissioner for refugees. He is a member of the Trilateral Commission as well as the president of the Norwegian Red Cross. His son, **Jens Stoltenberg**, followed him into politics and became the prime minister of Norway, first in 2000 and then again in 2005.

**STØRE, JONAS GAHR (1960– ).** Norwegian politician. Born in **Oslo** on 25 August 1960, Gahr Støre graduated from a prestigious college preparatory school and was educated as an officer for the Royal Norwegian Navy at the *Sjøkrigsskolen* (Naval Academy) in **Bergen**, completing his training in 1981. From 1981 to 1985, he studied political science, including political **economy** and history, at the elite *Institut d'études politiques de Paris*, after which he enrolled as a doctoral student at the London School of Economics. After a stint as a teaching fellow at the Harvard Law School, he became a researcher at the Norwegian School of Management (Bedriftsøkonomisk Institutt, BI) from 1986 to 1989. From 1989 to 1995, Gahr Støre was a special adviser at the office of the prime minister, mostly under **Gro Harlem Brundtland**, finally joining the **Labor Party** in 1995. From 1995 to 1998, he was director general (*ekspedisjonssjef*) for international affairs at the office of the prime minister, and from 1998 to 2000, he was Brundtland's chief of staff at her office and director general of the World Health Organization. After a period at a Norwegian think tank, he became the head of the Norwegian Red Cross, serving from 2003 to 2005, when he was selected minister of foreign affairs by Prime Minister **Jens Stoltenberg**.

***STORTING.*** The *Storting* (**Parliament**) is Norway's national assembly. When it was first established according to the **constitution** of 1814, it met every three years. Annual sessions were introduced in 1869, and until 1921, the number of members varied from 77 to 126. From 1921 to 1973, it had 150 members, and the number has since been gradually increased to 155, 157, 165, and 169 (in 2005). While largely a unicameral body, for purposes of legislation, it is divided into two chambers, the ***Lagting*** and the ***Odelsting***. However, according to a constitutional change that was adopted on 20 February 2007 and that will take effect on 1 October 2009, both the *Lagting* and the *Odelsting* will be discontinued. The second reading of legislative proposals currently done in the *Lagting* will be performed by the *Storting* as a whole subsequent to a first reading in which legislative proposals may be amended (if amendments are made during the second reading, a third reading will be necessary).

In addition to the legislative function of the *Storting*, it also approves the state budget and supervises the government, which according to the principles of parliamentarism serves at its pleasure. The 169 members of the *Storting* are elected every 4 years, and 150 of them serve as representatives of Norway's 19 counties, which are electoral districts in which the various parties are given proportional representation. The number of seats in the *Storting* allotted to each county depends on the geographical size and the population of the county and is adjusted every eight years. The remaining 19 seats are divided among all parties that receive 4 percent or more of the national popular vote and are allotted in such a manner that each party's percentage of the seats in the *Storting* is as close as possible to the percentage of the popular vote received by that party. Each county gets 1 of the 19 *utjevningsmandater* (equalization seats) in the *Storting*.

Much of the work of the *Storting* is done in 1 of its 13 standing committees, and each representative is a member of 1 committee. At the present time, the *Storting* is led by a president and a vice president. After the change in 2009, it will be led by a president, five vice presidents, and two secretaries.

**STRAY, SVENN THORKILD (1922– ).** Norwegian politician. Born on 11 February 1922 in Arendal, Stray studied law at the University of **Oslo**, earning a degree in 1946. He was active in the leadership of student organizations as well as in the youth organization of the **Conservative Party** and later in the party itself. He also served as a member of the Moss City Council from 1959 to 1979. After serving as a substitute, he was first elected a member of the *Storting* (**Parliament**) in 1958, serving until 1985. He was caucus leader for the **Conservatives** from 1965 to 1970. He was chosen minister of foreign affairs by Prime Minister **Per Borten** in 1970, serving until the following year, and again by Prime Minister **Kåre Willoch** in 1981, serving in both Willoch's Conservative government and in his coalition with the **Christian Democrats** and the **Center Party**. When Labor took over the government subsequent to the 1981 elections, Stray was succeeded by **Knut Frydenlund**. From 1971 to 1981, Stray was the leader of the *Europabevegelsen* (Europe Movement), which advocated for Norwegian membership in what later became the **European Union**.

**STURLUSON, SNORRI (1178–1241).** Icelandic historian. The greatest man of letters in medieval Iceland, Snorri was educated in a **literary** tradition that combined medieval European scholarship with native Icelandic learning and was well equipped to provide a reasonably critical history of the old **Scandinavian** kings. Having first compiled a history of the Norwegian king **Saint Olaf**, he added shorter histories, or sagas, that dealt with the preceding rulers back to mythological times. Sagas of the kings that succeeded Saint Olaf were also added until 1177, when the reign of King **Sverre Sigurdsson** began, for Sverre had already arranged for the history of his reign to be written during his lifetime. Snorri's great historical work came to be known as *Heimskringla*, after the first two words of his text, *kringla heimsins* (the round disc of the world). Snorri also composed a handbook for young poets that came to be known as *The Prose Edda* (also known as *The Younger Edda* and *Snorra-Edda*), in which he surveyed the ancient myths that had served as source material for the poetic imagery and diction of the court poets of the past. His historical work was well known in translation in Norway and strongly influenced Norwegian **national romanticism**.

**SUNDT, EILERT LUND (1817–75).** Norwegian sociologist. Born in Farsund in southwestern Norway on 8 August 1817, Sundt earned a degree in theology at the university in Christiania (now **Oslo**) in 1846 but turned to the study of the common people instead of becoming a minister. His first book, *Beretning om Fante-eller Landstrygerfolket i Norge* (An Account of the Gypsies or Traveling People of Norway), was published in 1850. Sundt was particularly interested in the historical factors, manners, and customs that helped shape the individual human being. Early on, he viewed people's mode of existence from a moral and Christian point of view, but gradually, he turned away from moralistic explanations and adopted a more rational view of causation. Between 1851 and 1869, he received grants from the *Storting* (**Parliament**) in order to study the conditions under which Norway's common people lived. He examined cleanliness, illegitimacy, public health, the use of alcohol, and other subjects. When studying the instances of illegitimate births, for example, he used statistical methodology and compared parts of the country, reserving his greatest sense of dismay for the northern end of Gudbrandsdalen, Norway's central interior valley, where two thirds of all children were born out of wedlock. When studying the lack of hygiene, he emphasized the connections between the constraints placed on people by their daily work and other circumstances, refusing to see filth as a manifestation of an inferior sense of morality, which at the time was the common perception by the members of the *embedsmann* (public official) class. The lack of latrines in most farming areas, for example, was seen as a counterpart to the way animal manure was handled on the farms. Sundt also realized that many young men did little to get rid of scabies because this condition was grounds for exemption from military service. He also disagreed with the standard medical opinion of his time that leprosy resulted from a lack of proper hygiene, and this view was later vindicated by the research of the medical doctor **Armauer Hansen**.

**SVERDRUP, JOHAN (1816–92).** Norwegian politician. Born on 30 July 1816 in Sem, close to Tønsberg, as the son of the **agricultural** innovator Jakob Sverdrup, Sverdrup studied law at the university in Christiania (now **Oslo**) and received his degree in 1841. After working as a lawyer, he was a member of the *Storting* (**Parliament**), representing the towns of Larvik and Sandefjord from 1851 to 1858, while from 1858 to 1885, he represented Akershus County. A man with great charisma and considerable leadership ability, he quickly made his mark politically, enjoying a series of substantial political victories. These victories include the 1859 establishment of the *Reformforeningen* (**Reform Association**), an organization of progressive members of the *Storting*; the change to annual sessions of the *Storting* in 1869; and above all, the events associated with the introduction of parliamentarism in Norwegian political life. Sverdrup's achievements came at a considerable cost, however.

Sverdrup is Norway's first example of a professional politician who was not primarily an ***embedsmann***, a public official who served the king, often with little consideration for the interests of the people who were governed. Because members of the *Storting* were not well compensated for their work, his attention to political matters took a terrible toll on his finances, and his health suffered because of overwork and worries. He was unable to make payment on his financial obligations and was threatened with foreclosure. His financial situation was so bad, in fact, that his friends, many of them fellow members of the *Storting*, issued a public plea for donations. His health was at times extremely poor; he was plagued by both a persistent and painful winter cough and rheumatism. On 9 June 1880, the evening of one of his most decisive parliamentary victories, when the *Storting* took the crucial vote that cemented his greatest achievement, he was so ill that he could barely sign the minutes of the meeting. He was a sick and worn-out old man when he was finally appointed prime minister by King Oscar II on 26 June 1884 after a bitter political struggle that ended in the impeachment of the previous conservative cabinet and led to the organization of Norway's first political party, the **Liberals**, in 1884.

Sverdrup was, however, less successful as a prime minister than he had been as the leader of the opposition. Not nearly as radical and forward thinking as some of his adherents had assumed, he disappointed many intellectuals when his government refused to grant **Alexander Kielland** a writer's stipend. The Liberal Party was split between a smaller but very vocal faction that opposed most of his proposals and a larger but less influential segment consisting of **religious** people and teetotalers. Leaning for support on his old opponents in the **Conservative Party**, which had been founded in 1884, his cabinet hung on to its political life in spite of the lack of support from many Liberals. However, in 1889, it was voted out of power by a combination of Conservatives and disaffected members of his own party.

There is no question, however, that Sverdrup left an important political legacy. He has been credited with the formation of political parties as a force in Norwegian political life, and he made considerable contributions to the development of Norwegian parliamentarism, whose father he is often thought to be.

**SWEDEN.** As Norway's closest neighbor to the east, Sweden has played a major role in Norwegian history from medieval times to the present. In 1319, a common Swedish-Norwegian kingship was established under Magnus VII Eiriksson (1316–74), and in 1397, a union among **Denmark**, Norway, and Sweden was established in **Kalmar**. Sweden had effectively left this union as of 1521, leaving Norway united with Denmark. The following centuries saw a series of wars between Sweden and Denmark-Norway. The Seven Years War raged between 1563 and 1570 and led to considerable destruction in Norway, including the burning of **Oslo**. The Kalmar War lasted from 1611 to 1613 but did not involve direct hostilities in Norway. From 1643 to 1645, there was a war between Norway and Sweden that is usually referred to as the Hannibal Affair; it resulted in the loss of Jemtland and Herjedalen to Sweden through the Treaty of Brømsebro in 1645. The Three Years War was fought between 1657 and 1660 and resulted in Norway's loss of **Båhuslen** to Sweden. The Gyldenløve Affair was fought against Sweden from 1675 to 1679, and the **Great Northern War** took place from 1711 to 1720. Denmark-Norway and Sweden were on the opposite sides during the Napoleonic wars, and there were direct hostilities between Norway and Sweden in 1808. In 1814, the European Great Powers transferred Norway from Denmark to Sweden at the **Treaty of Kiel**, and there was a brief war later that year as the rather recalcitrant Norwegians were compelled to accept a union with Sweden.

During the decades that followed, Sweden's **agriculture** grew rapidly, and its population expanded. A large number of Swedes immigrated to the **United States**, however, and the process of

**industrialization** did not take off until approximately 1870, when people started migrating from the countryside to the cities.

The relationship between Norway and Sweden was at times tense during the 1880s and 1890s, but disagreements between the two countries were settled with political and diplomatic weapons, culminating in the **dissolution of the union with Sweden** in 1905. Through a series of political maneuvers that left Swedish political leaders, including King Oscar II, with a great deal of bitterness, **Christian Michelsen** managed to break the union, while the Swedes managed to resist the temptation to resort to force. During the following decades, most of the bitterness dissipated.

Sweden had become a modern industrial democracy by the time of **World War I**, when it managed to stay neutral. It also maintained its neutrality during **World War II**, becoming a haven for Norwegian refugees. While in no position to resist Germany by force, Sweden used its neutrality to carry out significant diplomatic and humanitarian efforts that saved many lives.

With an intact industrial base, Sweden developed rapidly during the postwar years, creating a strong welfare state and an affluent society. Strictly neutral during the cold war, it joined the **European Union** on 1 January 1995. Sweden remains an important trading partner for Norway and a favorite destination for a large number of Norwegian tourists.

**SYSE, JAN PEDER (1930–97).** Norwegian politician. Born in Nøtterøy, Vestfold County, on 25 November 1930, Syse studied law at the University of **Oslo**. Firmly anchored in conservative thought but of an equally strong moderate bent, he was a prominent student leader and later held leadership positions in both the **Conservative Party** and its youth organization, rising to the position of party chair in 1988. From 1963 to 1971, he was a member of the Oslo City Council. He was first elected to the *Storting* (**Parliament**) in 1973, having earlier acted as a substitute representative. From 1983 to 1985, he was the minister of **industry** in the government headed by **Kåre Willoch** but left this position in order to become the caucus leader for the Conservative Party. After the parliamentary elections in 1989, Syse formed a minority coalition government consisting of the Conservative Party, the **Christian Democrats**, and the **Center**

**Party**. Negotiating this coalition was a considerable feat, and much of the credit for its existence should be given to Syse, a very likable man whose personal qualities of moderation, fairness, and humor were greatly appreciated. The struggle over possible Norwegian membership in the **European Union** caused the Center Party to leave the government in 1990, and Syse resigned as prime minister. In addition to his involvement in Norwegian political life, Syse was also deeply committed to cooperation within the **Scandinavian** and Baltic areas, serving the **Nordic Council** in various capacities, including as its chair in 1993. He served in the *Storting* until his death two weeks before the end of his term in 1997.

– T –

**TERBOVEN, JOSEF ANTONIUS HEINRICH (1898–1945).** German commissioner in Norway during **World War II**. Born in Essen, Germany, on 23 May 1898, Terboven served as a military officer during **World War I**, after which he studied political science and law. Joining the Nazi Party in 1923, he quickly rose through the ranks and became known for his ruthlessness. Named commissioner for Norway by Adolf Hitler on 24 April 1940, Terboven became one of the most hated men in Norway during the war. He reluctantly acted in some degree of concert with **Vidkun Quisling**, who after an abortive coup d'état on 9 April 1940, the day of the German invasion, later became the country's political leader under Terboven's control. Terboven used the secret police (Gestapo) to ferret out, torture, and execute resistance workers; he also carried out acts of extremely cruel reprisal against Norwegian civilians. On 8 May 1945, the day of the formal German capitulation in Norway, Terboven committed suicide by blowing himself up with a large quantity of dynamite.

**THRANE, MARCUS MØLLER (1817–90).** Norwegian **Labor** leader. Born on 14 October 1817 in Christiania (now **Oslo**) to David Thrane, a merchant and managing director of the Bank of Norway, Thrane obtained his matriculation certificate in 1840, after which he briefly studied theology. He married and lived in several places before settling in Drammen in 1848, where he edited a newspaper, but was fired because of his radical opinions. Influenced by the ideas of the French February revolution, he invited the workers in Drammen to attend a meeting that resulted in the formation of a trade union. The movement spread, other unions were formed, and Thrane started the newspaper *Arbeiderforeningenes Blad* (Paper of the Trade Unions), in which he vehemently attacked both the **embedsmann** (public official) class and the rural members of the **Storting (Parliament)**.

A petition to the king, signed by 13,000 persons, laid out the program of the trade unions. They wanted universal voting rights, a requirement of both rich and poor to do military service, removal of protective tariffs (thus making food less expensive), better elementary schools, and stronger restrictions on the sale of liquor. Arable but as yet uncultivated land was to be expropriated by the government and made available at low cost to the cottagers, who were **economically** dependent on the owners of larger farms. Because there was no response to the petition from the king, it was forwarded to the *Storting*, which declined to put it on its agenda. A convention of representatives from the various trade unions was held in Christiania, and the revolutionary rhetoric used at this convention made the authorities uneasy. Some union members had also behaved disorderly, and this was enough to get Thrane and other leaders arrested. He and many others were found guilty of crimes against the state, and Thrane was sentenced to four year in prison. After his release in 1858, Thrane worked for a while as a photographer but immigrated to the **United States** in 1862.

**TIDEMAND, ADOLPH (1814–76).** Norwegian painter. Born in Mandal on 14 August 1814 as the son of customs inspector and member of **parliament** Christen Tidemand, Tidemand studied **art** in Copenhagen from 1832 to 1837, after which he traveled to Düsseldorf, Germany, remaining a student at the art academy there until 1841. He traveled widely in Norway and painted a number of works with motifs from rural Norwegian life. These works exhibited the sentimentality of the **national romanticism**. Together with his colleague **Hans Gude**, he collaborated on several paintings—Gude painted the landscapes and Tidemand the figures—*Brudeferden i Hardanger* (1849; The Bridal Journey in Hardanger) being the best known of these. Another well-known painting is *Haugianerne* (1852; the Haugeans), which depicts a group of the followers of **Hans Nilsen Hauge**. Tidemand also taught at the art academy in Düsseldorf.

**TORDENSKJOLD, PETER WESSEL (1691–1720).** Norwegian naval hero. Born in **Trondheim** to Jan Wessel on 28 October 1691, Peter Wessel distinguished himself by his service to the **Dano**-Norwegian king Frederik IV (1671–1730) during the Great Nordic War (1700–1721). An audacious adventurer, he rose through the ranks in the Dano-Norwegian navy, ending up as vice admiral. His most daring exploit took place at the Battle of Dynekilen on the west coast of **Sweden** on 8 July 1716. With a small flotilla, Tordenskjold captured or destroyed the Swedish fleet, with a total of 76 casualties to his own force. Also a hot-headed young man, Tordenskjold died in a duel that he was tricked into fighting without a proper weapon.

**TORP, OSCAR (1893–1958).** Norwegian politician. Born in Skjeberg near Sarpsborg, Østfold County, on 8 June 1893, Torp was trained as a smith and an electrician. He led the **Labor Party** in Sarpsborg from 1918 to 1923 and was national Labor Party chair from 1923 to 1945. He was elected a member of the *Storting* (**Parliament**) in 1936 and held cabinet posts under **Johan Nygaardsvold** and in **Einar Gerhardsen**'s first government. After leading the Labor Party caucus in the *Storting* from 1948 to 1951, he traded places with Gerhardsen and became Norway's prime minister until 1955. Torp's career was characterized by an exceptional ability to engage people in fruitful cooperation in order to reach common goals.

**TRADE.** Norwegians have engaged in trade at least as far back as the Migration period, and trade was an important aspect of **Viking** times. During the Middle Ages, Norway was dependent on imported grain and salt, which were paid for with stockfish and furs. The history of the Norwegian **shipping** fleet is a reflection of not only the country's seafaring traditions but also of its need for imported commodities.

According to the *CIA World Factbook*, the value of Norwegian exported goods in 2006 amounted to $122.6 billion, and the exports consisted mainly of **oil and natural gas** as well as other petroleum products, machinery, equipment, metals and chemicals (especially those refined through the use of **hydroelectric power**), ships, and products of the **fishing** and aquaculture **industries**. The value of Norwegian imported goods, on the other hand, totaled just $59.9 billion, and the imports consisted mainly of chemicals, machinery, metals, and food. Norway also imports a significant amount of electric power. The trade surplus is the result of the sale of oil and natural gas, which makes up for a major imbalance in the trade of traditional goods. But Norway's sensitivity to the international market price of oil and natural gas also means that the trade surplus tends to fluctuate with the oil price.

In part, the trade imbalance in traditional goods has been a function of the increased success of the Norwegian **economy**. As the gross domestic product has risen, the demand for imported goods has increased. Because the Norwegian economy depends strongly on the service sector, in which 74 percent of the Norwegian workforce was employed in 2006, many imports are ultimately paid for with oil money.

Norway's most important export partners in 2006 were the United Kingdom (26.6 percent), Germany (12.2 percent), the Netherlands (10.4 percent), France (8.2 percent), **Sweden** (6.5 percent), and the **United States** (5.9 percent). Imported goods came from Sweden (15.0 percent), Germany (13.5 percent), **Denmark** (6.9 percent), the United Kingdom (6.4 percent), China (5.7 percent), the United States (5.3 percent), and the Netherlands (4.1 percent). Norway has a long history of promoting free trade and is a member of the **European Economic Area** (EEA), thereby contributing considerably to the budget of the **European Union**, which it has chosen not to join but to whose inner market it has access through the EEA. *See also* EUROPEAN INTEGRATION.

**TRANMÆL, MARTIN OLSEN (1879–1967).** Norwegian politician and **Labor** leader. Born on 27 June 1879 in Melhus, Sør-Trøndelag County, Tranmæl was the son of a farmer, worked in construction, and actively participated in the Labor Party. He became a journalist in the worker paper *Ny Tid* (New Time) in **Trondheim** starting in 1899 and became the editor in 1906, serving until 1918. Under his leadership, the paper became an effective tool for socialist agitation. Tranmæl also rose quickly in the party ranks. In 1911, he supported a group of trade union activists who formed the Labor Party's Union Opposition, arguing that the party needed to use revolution to reach its socialist goals. This group wanted to nationalize Norway's **economy** and managed to take control of the Labor Party at its 1918 convention. Tranmæl was not the party's formal leader, but he was possibly its most powerful member. Partly at his instigation, the party accepted Vladimir Ilyich Lenin's 21 Moscow theses and joined the Communist International (Comintern) based in Moscow, thus essentially making itself a tool of international Soviet communism. By 1923, Tranmæl had second thoughts about this decision, and the Labor Party left the Comintern.

Through these actions, Tranmæl became partly responsible for two schisms within the Labor Party. The first one took place in 1921, when **Norway's Social-Democratic Labor Party** split off (it returned to the mother party in 1927) because of the Comintern membership, and the second one in 1923, when **Norway's Communist Party**, which consisted of people loyal to the goals of the Comintern, was formed. In the 1930s, Tranmæl, who in 1921 had become the editor of the *Social-Demokraten* (Social Democrat), Norway's most important Labor Party newspaper, supported the reformist goals of the party. He spent **World War II** in exile in Stockholm, working for Norway's National Trade Union Association, and after the war, he was one of Labor's supporters of Norwegian membership in the **North Atlantic Treaty Organization**. In 1949, he retired as editor of the *Arbeiderbladet* (Worker's Paper), the successor of *Social-Demokraten*.

**TREATY OF KIEL.** An accord between **Sweden** and **Denmark** dated 14 January 1814. The Danish king Frederik VI had been supporting France during the Napoleonic wars and was on the losing side. As Karl Johan, formerly **Jean-Baptiste Bernadotte**, and the adopted crown prince of Sweden threatened to invade Denmark, the Danish king ceded Norway to Sweden. However, the ancient Norwegian possessions of Greenland, Iceland, and the Faeroe Islands were excluded. Once informed of the Treaty of Kiel, Frederik VI's son **Christian Frederik**, who was viceroy in Norway, became the point man in a Norwegian effort to establish a **constitution** as a means of full political independence. This effort was successful, and even though a union between Norway and Sweden was established, the Treaty of Kiel was never truly put into force.

**TROMSØ.** The largest city in northern Norway, Tromsø is located close to 70 degrees northern latitude on the landward side of the island Tromsøya (Troms Island). The municipality, which has approximately 64,000 inhabitants, consists of several islands as well as a chunk of the mainland connected to Tromsøya by the majestic 1,016-meters-long Tromsøbrua (Tromsø Bridge). The climate is surprisingly mild for a place located so far to the north, as it is moderated by a branch of the Gulf Stream. The summer is cool but light, with a period of more than three months without any darkness. During the winter, on the other hand, there are a few days on either side of the winter solstice when there is no appreciable daylight.

Judging by the archeological record, people lived in the area as early as 9,000 years ago, and there is some evidence of the presence of ethnic Norwegians during the Iron Age. King Haakon IV Haakonsson (1204–63) had a church built there in 1252. Nothing remains of it, but a turf rampart that is still in existence may have been built around the same time. Medieval Tromsø was just a place where people gathered to attend church, although some minor **trade** may have also taken place there. When the **Bergen** trade monopoly came to an end in 1789, however, three cities in northern Norway were given charters, and Tromsø was one of them. The city slowly grew from about 80 inhabitants in 1789, as trade along the coast all the way to Russia developed and **fish** became the basis for significant **economic** activity. In the 1820s, Tromsø also became an important base for hunting in the Arctic, and three decades later, it was the leading outfitter in Norway for this very profitable work. By the end of the 1900s, Tromsø had become *Ishavsbyen* (Arctic City), the world's most important gateway to the north. Men with experience working and living in cold climates were to be found there, and it is no wonder that Tromsø was used as a base during **Roald Amundsen**'s attempted rescue of Umberto Nobile.

The king and the government stayed in Tromsø for three weeks during the military campaign in Norway in the beginning of **World War II** until they left for Great Britain on 7 June 1940. Tromsø saw little serious action during the war but hosted numerous refugees of the German scorched-earth tactics used in Finnmark in 1944. The city languished during the first part of the postwar era, but growth took off again in the 1960s. In 1964, Tromsø municipality was combined with several of its neighbors for a combined population of approximately 32,000, which had doubled four decades later, giving Tromsø the highest rate of growth of all Norwegian cities. Tromsø Airport, located at Langnes, was opened in 1964, and the University of Tromsø was established by law in 1968 and opened in 1972; it and other **educational** institutions bring 10,000 students to the town.

During recent years, **industry** has been of little significance in Tromsø, and the biggest employers are the regional hospital and the university. The city has a number of museums, some of them related to its Arctic location. Tromsø also has a large number of restaurants, nightclubs, and bars, with a combined capacity of approximately 20,000 guests, making it a lively town indeed.

**TRONDHEIM.** Trondheim is Norway's third-largest city with approximately 160,000 inhabitants, although that number reaches about 250,000 if the surrounding area is included. The only Norwegian city to have experienced near-riot conditions because of a change in its name, it was known as Nidaros (the mouth of the river Nid) and Kaupangen (the Marketplace) in **Viking** times, when it was supposed to have been established by King Olav Tryggvason (c. 960–1000) in 997 CE. The population in the sheltered area at the end of the Trondheim fjord where the city now stands, however, goes back to the Stone Age, according to archeological evidence, and there was already a population center in place when Olav Tryggvason chose the place for his residence. During the union between **Denmark** and Norway, the name of the city was spelled *Trondhjem*, and it was during an ill-fated attempt by the Norwegian *Storting* (**Parliament**) in 1930–31 to reintroduce the name Nidaros that the natives became exercised to the point that a compromise, Trondheim, was the result.

Trondheim's sheltered location gives it a relatively mild climate, tempered by the Gulf Stream off the coast. It can be very cold when the wind blows from the east during the winter, however. *Byåsen* (City Ridge) provides an excellent cross-country skiing area. The **agricultural** areas close to the city have traditionally provided Trondheim with its commercial basis, and it also has a history of rendering different types of services to the maritime **industry**. The home of several **educational** institutions, including Norway's second-largest university, the Norwegian University of Science and Technology, Trondheim's local **economy** also benefits from these institutions as well as from the spin-offs that occur when new technology is commercialized.

Trondheim was the capital of Norway until 1070 and experienced rapid growth during the first decades of its existence. It was the center for the cult of **Saint Olaf**, and the construction of the first church on his grave site was started in approximately 1070. In 1152, the city became the seat of Norway's archbishop, whose residence was built adjacent to the Olaf Church, where Nidaros Cathedral is now located. Many other churches and several cloisters were also built. The city was plagued by periodic fires, however, and at the time of the **Reformation** in 1536–37, Trondheim lost much of its earlier luster. In 1658, Trondheim, together with its surrounding area, was briefly part of **Sweden**.

The increase in **trade** in the early modern period was a significant benefit to Trondheim, but the city was again devastated by fires in 1599, 1651, and 1681. After the fire in 1681, the city was given wider streets and rectangular blocks, but there was another major fire in 1708. Wooden structures were still built, however, and more fires followed, until 1845, when people were compelled to use brick and stone in building construction. At this time, many suburbs were annexed, the harbor was improved, and Trondheim was connected with Christiania (now **Oslo**) by rail in 1877. The population grew rapidly around 1900, and industrial zones were established. Trondheim was occupied by the Germans as of 9 April 1940, and the invaders held it until 8 May 1945.

During the post–**World War II** era, Trondheim has developed into a modern city with an emphasis on the service economy as well as education and high technology. Its modern airport at Værnes, less than an hour's drive away, offers frequent flights to other major Norwegian cities, with connections to Europe and the rest of the world. Tourists find the natives open and friendly, there are many interesting museums and historical places to visit, and the long summer evenings — with little or no darkness at night for a period of about two months — make Trondheim one of the most intriguing cities anywhere.

– U –

**UELAND, OLE GABRIEL (1799–1870).** Norwegian politician. Ueland was born into very limited **economic** circumstances on 28 October 1799 in the Dalane district in southwestern Norway. He married the daughter of the farmer at Ueland in the community Heskestad, however, and owned and operated this farm starting in 1825. Before his marriage, he worked as an itinerant schoolmaster from 1817 to 1825 and then as a schoolmaster and sexton in Heskestad from 1827 to 1852. He was the local sheriff (*lensmann*) from 1852 to 1856 and was involved in local politics as well, serving as mayor in 1837–51 and 1856–59. He was elected to the *Storting* (**Parliament**) in 1833, serving until 1869.

The year 1833 was an auspicious start of a parliamentary career, for elected for the first time that year were a large number of representatives with rural backgrounds and an improved outlook for farmers, while the representation of the *embedsmann* (public official) class declined proportionally. Ueland was a man with great intelligence and sound political instincts, and he quickly became a leader among the farmers elected to the *Storting*. Like **Søren Jaabæk** a few years later, he was a liberalist who wanted to get rid of government restrictions on **trade** and choice of occupation, and he strongly supported legislation concerning occupations (1839) and commerce (1842) that furthered this end. He wished to reduce the tax burden on the rural people by encouraging steep reductions in public expenditures, and he wanted to offer the people living in farming communities greater opportunities for political self-development. He also wanted people to take increased responsibility in **religious** matters. A religious man, he admired the work of **Hans Nilsen Hauge**. While Ueland was not formally a Haugean and did not disparage the work of the ministers of the State Church, he wanted common people to participate in the governance of the local parishes. With his own background and service record, he was a sterling example of the kind of commitment to and participation in public life that he was hoping to make increasingly common.

Ueland therefore strongly backed the **local government laws** (*formannsskapslovene*) that were passed in 1837. Members of the *embedsmann* class had previously been in charge of local governance, but after 1837, delegates to local governing councils were selected through local elections. The *formannsskapslover* provided a local political training ground that made Norway's modern democracy possible. Ueland is also credited with helping establish the first forum for organized cooperation among members of the *Storting*, the so-called *Reformforeningen* (**Reform Association**), which **Johan Sverdrup** and Ueland organized in 1859. An association in which rural representatives could work with liberal city members of the *Storting*, it was not a political party but helped pave the way for the development of parties in the 1880s.

While Ueland is remembered mostly for his contributions to Norway's democratic development, his instincts were not always on the side of democracy. He resisted the **constitutional** change that allowed Jews access to Norway, and he wanted to keep legislation that restricted the freedom of worship for religious dissenters. He was against prison reform but wanted to get rid of debtor's prison and make it harder for creditors to collect debts. Conservative by temperament, he looked out for the interests of his own constituents, thus contributing mightily to the modernization of Norwegian life and society.

**UNDSET, SIGRID (1882–1949).** Norwegian novelist. Born on 20 May 1882 in Kalundborg, **Denmark**, to the Norwegian archeologist Ingvald Martin Undset, Sigrid Undset is the third Norwegian writer to be awarded the Nobel Prize (after **Bjørnstjerne Bjørnson** and **Knut Hamsun**). Her worldwide reputation rests on her trilogy *Kristin Lavransdatter* (1920–22), which has been translated into more than 70 languages. Undset early on developed a love for the Middle Ages, but on the advice of the editor that rejected her first work of fiction, a story with a medieval setting, she at first published works that were set in her own time. Great examples of the neorealism of the early 20th century, these books deal both with social issues and the existential situation of their protagonists, particularly their love relationships.

Throughout her long career, Undset published a large number of novels with both medieval and modern settings. While the tenor of her works is significantly at variance with the feminism of her age, Undset wrote with great insight into the female psyche. She discussed her views on the relationship between the sexes in a collection of articles titled *Et kvindesynspunkt* (1919; A **Woman's** Point of View). Her interest in **religion** came to the fore after her own conversion to Roman Catholicism. During **World War II**, she lived in the **United States** as an unofficial cultural ambassador for Norway. While she published no more works of fiction, she wrote articles, speeches, memoirs, and biographies of saints. *See also* LITERATURE.

**UNION WITH SWEDEN IN 1814.** From an early 21st century perspective, the union that Norway entered into with **Sweden** in 1814 appears as a necessary step toward Norway's democratic development in the 20th century. At the time when the union was introduced, however, many Norwegians viewed it as the disappointing conclusion of a valiant struggle for complete self-determination.

The Napoleonic wars overshadow all other events in early-19th-century European history. The **Scandinavian** countries, which had maintained neutrality during the conflicts of the late 18th century, could no longer hold on to that policy. Sweden sided with England in 1805, and after England's 1807 attack on Copenhagen, when **Denmark** lost its fleet, Denmark and Norway were on the side of Napoleon Bonaparte's France. Denmark was also motivated by its fear of a land invasion from the south. This fateful Danish foreign policy decision drove a wedge between Norway and Denmark, however, for Norway's true interests have traditionally been tied to those of England, which has largely controlled the high seas on which Norwegian **trade** and **shipping** have been dependent. The year 1807 marked the beginning of a very difficult period of time for Norway. Its coast subjected to a merciless British blockade, the people of Norway starved. In addition, eastern Norway was attacked overland by Sweden, and this attack abated only as the Swedish troops had to be turned toward Russia, which was allied with France and used the opportunity to wrest Finland away from Sweden.

As Russian troops threatened Sweden itself, some Swedish officers arranged to have their king, Gustaf IV Adolf, murdered, replacing him with the childless Karl XIII. The Norwegian military commander, **Christian August** of the house Augustenborg, was adopted by Karl XIII as his heir, changing his name to Karl August. The new crown prince died in 1810, however, which created an opening for one of Napoleon's most controversial marshals, **Jean-Baptiste Bernadotte**, to be elected as Sweden's heir-apparent and adopted by Karl XIII under the name Karl Johan. A brilliant strategist, Karl Johan realized that he needed to side with England and Russia—a peace accord that gave Russia Finland had been signed with the latter in 1809—against his former emperor. When Napoleon attacked Russia in 1812, Karl Johan made a treaty with the Russian czar that promised him Norway in exchange for his support of the war against Napoleon. Great Britain also agreed that Sweden should be given Norway once it had been taken away from Denmark.

In the summer of 1813, a Swedish army went to north Germany to join the fight against Napoleon and helped force his army to retreat back to France. Then Karl Johan made an unexpected move, as he marched northward against the southern part of Jutland, the peninsula through which Denmark is connected with continental Europe. In the **Treaty of Kiel** signed by the Danish king Frederik VI on 14 January 1814, Norway was ceded to Sweden. Frederik VI informed his son, Crown Prince **Christian Frederik**, immediately, and the news reached him in Christiania (now **Oslo**), Norway, on 24 January 1814.

Christian Frederik had a somewhat romantic disposition and immediately offered to step in as king of a wholly independent Norway, united with neither Denmark nor Sweden. This proposal was in line with nationalistic sentiments present in Norway and partly a result of the country's suffering due to the miscalculations and direct blunders in Denmark's foreign policy. Christian Frederik was quickly brought to understand, however, that to the Norwegians, the Treaty of Kiel meant that Norwegian sovereignty had been transferred to the people of Norway and that it did not rest with him. On 19 February 1814, a proclamation signed by Christian Frederik was sent to Norwegian parishes with instructions that it be read from the pulpit. The members of all the congregations were to take an oath that they would defend Norway's independence, and representatives to a **constitutional** convention were to be selected. Christian Fredrik also sent his close friend **Carsten Anker** to London, there to persuade the British government to support Norway's bid for independence. His mission was largely unsuccessful, but at least it brought the Norwegian popular desire for independence to the attention of the British.

As of 10 April 1814, 112 representatives from various parts of the country were gathered for the constitutional convention at Eidsvoll, a short distance north of Oslo. These men divided themselves into two factions. One side fervently believed that Norway might indeed succeed in winning its independence and that it should be defended with arms if necessary. The other side was of a more realistic bent and acknowledged the reality of the politics of the European Great Powers. The convention voted to limit its work to writing a constitution and electing a king of Norway, and a constitutional committee was established on 12 April. Its draft was complete on 2 May, and the constitution was officially accepted and signed on 17 May 1814. Christian Frederik was also elected to the throne.

Not without reason, the Great Powers suspected that Christian Frederik's activities in Norway were taking place at the instigation of his father, who would someday yield the Danish throne to Norway's new king, and that father and son had as their common purpose to circumvent the Treaty of Kiel. When representatives of the European powers traveled to Denmark, though, they understood that this was not the sole reason for the drive toward independence. A British government representative sent to Norway came to the same conclusion and realized that the constitution was the outgrowth of a genuinely popular movement. The purpose of all these emissaries was to see to it that the union between Norway and Sweden was made into a reality, but they had little concern about exactly what kind of a union it was going to be. Christian Frederik sacrificed his personal ambitions in favor of negotiating the best possible terms for Norway, arguing that whatever was done had to be done in accordance with the new Norwegian constitution and that the *Storting* (**Parliament**) needed time to meet and participate in the negotiations with Sweden. By effectively giving up its demand for complete independence, Norway showed that it was willing to yield to the demand of the Great Powers and left the next step in the process up to Karl Johan.

When Karl Johan chose to go to war against Norway and was met with more resistance than what he had probably expected, he chose to negotiate, and this was a choice that pleased the Great Powers, as there was no desire for further military conflict that might spread to parts of the continent. An agreement was signed in Moss, Norway, on

14 August 1814, and peace was restored between the two countries. When the *Storting* met in session starting 7 October 1814, the revisions to the constitution made necessary by the union with Sweden were begun and finalized by 4 November, and the Swedish king Karl XIII was elected to Norway's throne. These constitutional revisions make it reasonable to think of the November constitution as a different constitution than the one signed on 17 May, but the changes were far from radical and generally weakened the position of the king in favor of that of the *Storting*. In 1815, the procedures governing the relationship between Norway and Sweden were enshrined in the Union Law, which regulated joint affairs of the two countries for the next 90 years.

**UNITED NATIONS (UN).** The purposes of the UN include promoting international peace and security, as well as the friendship among nations; cooperating in finding solutions to international problems; and promoting international law and the respect for human rights. It is a successor organization to the **League of Nations** as well as to the organized group of Allies that signed the UN declaration on 1 January 1942. The declaration was, in turn, descended from the Atlantic Charter signed by Great Britain and the **United States** on 12 August 1941, which expressed the principles they were to follow during **World War II** as well as their ideas about what the world would look like after the war. The Atlantic Charter was later ratified by a number of states, including the Norwegian exile government in London, which signed the UN declaration as well.

The UN charter was signed on 26 June 1945, and Norway was one of the original 50 signatories. Norway attempted to remain neutral during the first three years after the end of World War II, and the Norwegian minister of foreign affairs, **Trygve Lie**, was chosen to serve as the UN's first secretary general in January 1946. When Norway joined the **North Atlantic Treaty Organization** in 1949, the attempt at being neutral was abandoned, and Norway actively supported the United States and Great Britain. Over the years, Norway has been a staunch supporter of the mission of the UN as well as of the organization itself. Norway has also actively participated in UN peacekeeping forces, providing a total of 39,841 troops to 30 different missions, including the UN Emergency Force I in Gaza from 1956 to

1957, with the loss of 9 troops, and from 1978 to 1998 the UN Interim Force in Lebanon (UNIFIL), with the loss of 21 troops. *See also* EUROPEAN INTEGRATION.

**UNITED PARTY.** Formed in 1903 by **Christian Michelsen**, **Bjørnstjerne Bjørnson**, and **Wollert Konow**, the *Samlingspartiet* (United Party) was designed to be an alternative for those who had traditionally voted with the **Liberal Party** but who were uncomfortable with the ideas of its left wing. The United Party also appealed to conservative voters and cooperated closely with the **Conservative Party**. Together, in the 1903 **parliamentary** election, the United Party and the **Conservatives** jointly won 63 seats in the *Storting* (Parliament), while the Liberal Party won 49. Because the focus of the United Party was negotiations rather than military conflict with Sweden during the **dissolution of the union** between the two countries, it was rather short lived and was succeeded by the **Liberal Left Party** (*Frisinnede Venstre*) a few years later.

**UNITED STATES OF AMERICA.** On the whole, Norway has had a cooperative and productive relationship with the United States, politically, **economically**, and culturally. Between 1825 and 1915, approximately 750,000 Norwegians immigrated to the United States, and their descendants and other interested individuals maintain a number of cultural and fraternal associations. Many of these groups provide scholarships that allow American students to study in Norway, and many do. For example, when the International Summer School at the University of **Oslo** started in 1947, it was largely aimed at American students. Many Norwegian students also study in the United States, often at institutions that have links to Norway, for example, **Saint Olaf** College in Northfield, Minnesota, and Pacific Lutheran University in Tacoma, Washington, both of which were founded by Norwegian immigrants.

The United States is Norway's most important **trade** partner outside of Europe, receiving 7 percent of Norwegian exports annually. Approximately half of this is **oil and natural gas**, but the United States also buys Norwegian metals and seafoods. Norway is not, of course, as important to U.S. exports as the United States is to Norway, but the trade is roughly in balance. Norway imports American cars and computer equipment. The United States also provides approximately one fourth of the foreign investment in Norway, much of it in the oil and gas sector. The United States has a Mutual Recognition Agreement with Norway in the areas of telecommunications and marine equipment, as well as other trade pacts.

Norway has historically been one of the staunchest allies of the United States. Although neutral, Norway did much to support the Allies during **World War I**, and during **World War II**, Norway relied heavily on the United States. After the war, the Marshall Plan was a boon to Norwegian reconstruction. Since Norway became a charter member of the **North Atlantic Treaty Organization** in 1949, Norwegian and U.S. troops have trained together and worked together in the cause of peace.

Norwegians tend to be very interested in and informed about U.S. social and political issues but often prefer Democratic administrations to Republican ones. Many have a particularly strong sense of admiration for President Franklin Delano Roosevelt (1882–1945), who with his wife, Eleanor, showed much kindness toward Crown Princess Märtha, the wife of the later King **Olav V**, when she lived in exile in Washington, D.C., with her children during World War II. Roosevelt had spoken with admiration about the Norwegian resistance to the Germans on 13 April 1940, and on 16 September 1942, he delivered his famous "Look to Norway" speech, which became a source of inspiration to Norwegian freedom fighters.

Like the rest of the world, Norway has also been strongly influenced by American popular culture. American country singers have been very popular; for example, Jim Reeves (1923–64) was the first American artist to have a golden record in Norway, where he gave a famous concert shortly before his death. American cinema, particularly westerns, has played a major role as popular entertainment, and translated American western and detective fiction has sold very well. On account of the political and cultural connections between the two countries, the United States remains an important destination for Norwegian tourists. *See also* EMIGRATION FROM NORWAY TO AMERICA.

# – V –

**VÅRVIK, DAGFINN (1924– ).** Norwegian politician. Born on a farm at Leinstrand, Sør-Trøndelag County, on 8 June 1924, Vårvik was educated as an **economist** and began his political career as the secretary of the **Center Party**'s **parliamentary** caucus. He was the political editor of the *Nationen* (Nation), the major daily newspaper of the Center Party, when he became the minister of finance in the short-lived government headed by **John Lyng** in 1963. From 1965 to 1971, he was the minister of wages and prices under Prime Minister **Per Borten**, and from 1972 to 1973, he was the minister of foreign affairs in the government headed by **Lars Korvald**. He was head of the Center Party from 1973 to 1977, after which he became the editor-in-chief of *Nationen*.

**VENSTRE.** *See* LIBERAL PARTY.

**VIGELAND, GUSTAV (1869–1943).** Norwegian sculptor. Born in the town of Mandal, Vest-Agder County, on 11 April 1869, Vigeland was a gifted and highly prolific sculptor. He was educated primarily in the capital city of Christiania (now **Oslo**), where he learned the **art** of wood carving, and later studied in Berlin, Copenhagen, Florence, and Paris. Engaged to work on the restoration of the Nidaros Cathedral in **Trondheim**, he also created famous portrait busts of such leading Norwegian cultural figures as **Camilla Collett**, **Henrik Ibsen**, and Nils Henrik Abel. Vigeland's best-known work, however, consists in the monumental sculptures found at the Frogner Park in Oslo. Strongly vitalist in tenor, many of these works deal with the relationship between the male and female elements of existence as well as the continuity of the human family. An all-time favorite is the *Sinnataggen* (Spitfire), a sculpture of a foot-stomping, angry little boy.

**VIKINGS.** The term *Viking* may refer both to the inhabitants of **Scandinavia** during the time from approximately 793 CE to 1066 CE and more specifically to those Scandinavians who traveled abroad primarily in search of adventure and plunder. The origin of the term is unclear, but it may be etymologically related to the word *vik*, meaning "an inlet or a bay." The Vikings are famous for their ferocity and courage, as well as for their shallow-drafted longships, which afforded them easy maneuverability in coastal waters and estuaries.

Norwegian Vikings traveled mostly north and west, reaching the Faeroe Islands, Iceland, Greenland, and North America, but also the Orkneys, the Shetland Islands, the Hebrides, and the Isle of Man. They also operated in the Five Burroughs area around the city of York in England, as well as in Scotland and Ireland, where there was a durable Viking kingdom centered in Dublin. The Viking raids subsided as Christianity penetrated Scandinavia, including Norway, and was victorious soon after 1030 CE.

**VINJE, AASMUND OLAFSSON (1818–70).** Norwegian writer. Born on 6 April 1818 to Olav Aasmundsen in Vinje, Telemark County, Vinje adhered to many of the ideas of the **national romanticism**. He felt particularly strongly that Norway, independent from **Denmark** since 1814 and in a union with **Sweden** during his entire lifetime, should develop a written **language** based on popular dialects rather than the Danish-inspired written norm that had developed in the course of the 400-year-long union with Denmark. Vinje did not share **Ivar Aasen**'s love of archaic grammar and vocabulary, however, and instead based his form of *Landsmaal* (later renamed *nynorsk* or New Norwegian) on the dialect of his native district. Although educated in Dano-Norwegian, Vinje used his own form of *Landsmaal* when in 1858 he started his own newspaper, the *Dølen* (Dalesman), in which he commented on the social, political, and cultural issues of his day. He was the first person to extensively use the new alternative to Dano-Norwegian in prose. Along with Aasen and **Arne Garborg**, Vinje is regarded as one of the founders of the *nynorsk* written form of Norwegian. A substantial essayist and gifted poet, he is remembered particularly for a number of poems that were given musical settings by **Edvard Grieg**.

**VOLLEBÆK, KNUT (1946– ).** Norwegian politician. Born in **Oslo** on 11 February 1946, Vollebæk is the son of a State Church minister and provost and belongs to the **Christian Democratic Party**. After completing secondary school, he studied **economics** and received his degree in 1972. Having spent a year studying political science at the University of California, he joined the Norwegian Foreign Service in 1973. His many diplomatic assignments include service as Norway's ambassador to the **United States** since 2001. He was asked by Prime Minister **Kjell Magne Bondevik** to serve as minister of foreign affairs in the coalition government consisting of the Christian Democrats, the **Center Party**, and the **Liberal Party** that was in power from 1997 to 2000.

**VON WESTEN, THOMAS (1682–1727).** Norwegian missionary to the **Sámi** people. Born in **Trondheim**, von Westen studied theology at the University of Copenhagen starting in 1697. While a State Church minister at Veøy, Romsdal, he led a group of ministers that worked toward beginning missionary work among the Sámi people of northern Norway. The mission organization was established with the support of King Frederik IV in 1714, and von Westen became its leader in 1716. After studying the Sámi **language**, he made three significant missionary journeys among the Sámi between 1716 and 1723, teaching them Christianity and recording information about their traditional beliefs. Both a church and a school were established at Mo i Rana, a center for the Sámi population in the district of Helgeland, and many other schools as well. A school for missionaries was organized in Trondheim. Von Westen believed that the language of the Sámi people should be respected, but he viewed their belief system as merely a collection of superstitions.

## – W –

**WEDEL JARLSBERG, JOHAN CASPAR HERMAN (1779–1840).** Norwegian politician and nobleman. Born in Montpelier, France, as the son of Anton Fredrik Wedel Jarlsberg on 21 September 1779, Wedel Jarlsberg studied law and political science at the University of Copenhagen, receiving a law degree in 1801. Like his father, he was the Count of Jarlsberg near Tønsberg. He understood that Norway's interests during the Napoleonic wars were very different from those of **Denmark** because Norway was particularly dependent on a good relationship with England. Arguing for a Norwegian union with **Sweden** as early as 1809, he regarded **Christian August** of Oldenborg, the popular Danish military commander in Norway who was elected crown prince of Sweden in 1809, as a future king of Norway as well as Sweden. When the **constitutional** convention was held at Eidsvoll in 1814, Wedel Jarlsberg was the leader of the group that was pushing for a **union with Sweden**. In 1822, he became Norway's minister of finance.

He was elected a member of the *Storting* (**Parliament**) in 1824, serving until 1830, and was repeatedly elected president of the

*Storting*. He was the first Norwegian to represent the Swedish king as *stattholder* (vice regent) in Norway, serving from 1836 to 1840, as he was highly trusted and enjoyed great respect. While he was ineligible for the title of *visekonge* (viceroy), which could only be given to the crown prince or his son, Wedel Jarlsberg served as *stattholder* with the formal authority of a *visekonge*.

**WELHAVEN, JOHAN SEBASTIAN CAMMERMEYER (1807–73).** Norwegian poet and critic. Born in **Bergen** to Johan Ernst Welhaven on 22 December 1807, Welhaven is one of Norway's most significant poets of the **national romantic** era. While he was supposed to study theology at the university in Christiania (now **Oslo**), he spent much of his time reading aesthetics and **literature** instead, paying particular attention of the activities of his **Danish** second cousin, the critic Johan Ludvig Heiberg (1791–1860). In 1830, he became well known for his attack on the work of **Henrik Wergeland** (1808–45), whose poetry he found undisciplined and formless. A cycle of sonnets, *Norges Dæmring* (1834; Norway's Dawn), argued in favor of maintaining Norway's cultural ties with Denmark, which Wergeland's followers wanted to deemphasize in favor of a focus on the culture of the Norwegian rural population. His poetry is centered on both personal memories and, especially in the latter half of his career, the cultural memory of his people as expressed in popular tales and legends. Many of his folklore poems are also among Norway's finest examples of nature poetry.

Appointed lecturer in philosophy at the University of Oslo in 1840, Welhaven became a professor in 1843, after which he married a Danish woman, Josephine Bidoulac, in 1845. While not having much impact on his academic subject, he was a popular lecturer and also made significant contributions to the budding literary historiography of the time.

**WERGELAND, HENRIK ARNOLD (1808–45).** Norwegian poet, dramatist, and essayist. Born in Kristiansand to **Nicolai Wergeland** on 17 June 1808, Wergeland is recognized as Norway's greatest poet. His father was a significant political and cultural leader, and his sister was the early Norwegian feminist writer **Camilla Collett** (1813–95). A writer of tremendous talent, Wergeland was politically progressive and spearheaded the drive to publicly observe Norway's **Constitution** Day on 17 May. After earning a theology degree in 1829, his undisciplined personal life disqualified him from receiving an appointment as a pastor, and he was plagued by financial problems. He nevertheless stood at the center of Norway's public discourse for most of his short life.

Those who opposed Wergeland in the cultural debate of the day interpreted his focus on liberty in both **art** and politics as a lack of personal restraint. While Wergeland claimed complete freedom for his own genius, his enemies saw his effusive style as evidence of both bad taste and lack of responsibility. The debate between Wergeland's friends and his opponents became particularly bitter both because it took place within a relatively young nation (the Norwegian constitution dates only to 1814) and because Christiania (now **Oslo**) was a rather small town where events, however minor, could be quickly blown out of proportion.

At issue were the related questions of whether political power in Norway should rest with the upper middle class, consisting mostly of *embedsmenn* (public officials), large landowners, and merchants, or if it should be shared with farmers and other previously disenfranchised groups. A related issue was the cultural question of whether the new nation should emphasize the creative potential of the indigenous population, particularly the farmers, or foster continuity with the **literary** culture of **Denmark**, the political union with which had been severed in 1814. A subissue of the latter was the extent to which Norway should accept the political leadership of **Sweden** in the recently established **union** with that country. In all these matters, Wergeland and other progressives were bitterly opposed by the traditionalists.

Wergeland's youthful poetry celebrates Norway's potential for social and political change and led to a bitter feud with his contemporary and rival poet, **Johan Sebastian Welhaven**, who prized the classical qualities of balance, organization, and adherence to established form. When Welhaven attacked Henrik Wergeland for violating the dictates of reason, his father, Nicolai Wergeland, came to his aid, and a bitter and long-lasting feud ensued. Wergeland's political radicalism joins his disdain for conventional poetics in his major work, a world-historical poem titled *Skabelsen, Mennesket og Messias* (1830; Creation, Man, and the Messiah), which both offers a ringing defense for the ideas of the Enlightenment and establishes a cosmic context for human life.

Among Wergeland's other works are great quantities of **educational** materials written for the common people, many of them published in his paper *For Arbeidsklassen* (1840–45; For the Working Class), and the imaginative and lyrical *Jan van Huysums Blomsterstykke* (1840; tr. *Jan van Huysum's Flower Piece*, 1960), a great poetic cycle about the nature of art and the connection between art and life. His concern with justice was expressed in a campaign to have the Norwegian constitution amended so as to allow Jews entrance into Norway. When the **parliament** debated this issue in 1842 and 1844, he published two collections of poetry designed to influence public opinion, *Jøden* (1842; The Jew) and *Jødinden* (1844; The Jewess).

**WERGELAND, NICOLAI (1780–1848).** Norwegian theologian and cultural leader. Born in Hosanger, Hordaland County, on 9 November 1780, Wergeland's family hailed from the farm Verkeland in the district of Sogn in western Norway. After earning a theology degree with superb marks, Wergeland worked as a teacher, assistant minister, parish priest, and ecclesiastical provost. He first made his mark on Norwegian cultural life with the book *Mnemosyne* (1811), in which he argued persuasively in favor of establishing a separate Norwegian university (until that point, the University of Copenhagen had served the needs of both **Denmark** and Norway). Wergeland was a leading figure in the **constitutional** convention held in 1814, but after the establishment of the constitution and the ensuing **union with Sweden**, his collaborative attitude toward the Swedes kept him from becoming a representative in the newly established Norwegian **parliament**, the *Storting*.

Wergeland also wrote a book about what he perceived as Denmark's political and cultural crimes against Norway and forcefully defended the work of his son, the poet **Henrik Wergeland**, who had been attacked by the rival poet **Johan Sebastian Welhaven**. The elder Wergeland in turn attacked Welhaven's cycle of sonnets, *Norges Dæmring* (1834; Norway's Dawn), which argued in favor of maintaining Norway's cultural ties with Denmark.

**WHALING.** Whales have been caught and eaten along the cost of Norway at least since the beginning of historic time, providing both protein and fat. There is evidence that harpoons were used as early as around 1200 CE. Commercial whaling, however, is an invention of the early modern period, when whales were caught at sea but processed at land-based whaling stations. In the late 1860s, **Svend Foyn**'s invention and commercialization of the whale harpoon cannon increased the efficiency with which whales could be caught and killed. A harpoon, outfitted with a grenade and connected to a line, was fired by the cannon, and the grenade was timed to explode after the harpoon had entered the body of the whale. Foyn and his later competitors whaled with steam-driven vessels along the coast of Finnmark, in the Arctic Ocean, and in the area close to Iceland, and their rendering plants were located along the coast of Finnmark. In 1904, the Norwegian government set a 10-year moratorium on whaling in northern Norway.

Norwegian whaling in the Antarctic Ocean began in the 1890s, and the first whaling station on South Georgia Island was established in 1904. Whaling with floating processing plants began in the Antarctic in 1905, but the processing ships did not yet have the tools to bring large whales onboard, so they had to operate close to land. That changed in the 1930s with the invention of the equipment that allowed them to hoist large whale carcasses onboard. The processors were then able to operate in the open sea, which enabled a huge expansion of the **industry** during the years after **World War II**. Whale oil was used in a large number of products, for example, margarine, soap, and explosives, and whaling created tremendous wealth in the two Norwegian cities where it was concentrated, Sandefjord and Tønsberg. It gradually became apparent, however, that several species of whale were facing extinction.

As the Norwegian **fishing** fleet was motorized in the 1920s, small-scale whaling became an increasingly important part of life among the coastal population. While Foyn had hunted large whales, Norwegian fishermen took mostly the smaller minke whales, which were comparatively plentiful. When the International Whaling Commission in 1982 introduced a moratorium on whaling, effective as of 1986, the Norwegian government placed an objection to it but temporarily stopped whaling in 1987, wanting to learn more about the size of the stocks. Small-scale Norwegian whaling was begun again in 1993, with quotas based on scientific estimates of the whale population in the areas where the whaling is carried out, the northeast and central Atlantic Ocean. Based on a 2004 estimate of 107,000 minke whales, the 2005 total quota for Norwegian whalers was set at 670, of which 639 were taken. The 2006 quota was set at 1,052, and the total catch was 546. The hunting methods used by Norwegian whalers are comparable with those used in other forms of big-game hunting. It is estimated that 80 percent of the whales die or lose consciousness immediately, 10 percent die soon after being shot, while 10 percent survive the first shot and have to be shot a second time. The crew members on Norwegian whaling vessels receive mandatory training in the use of both harpoon cannon and rifle.

**WILLOCH, KÅRE (1928– ).** Norwegian politician. Perhaps the most brilliantly articulate conservative in recent Norwegian political life, Willoch was born in **Oslo** on 3 October 1928 and is credited with moving Norwegian society markedly toward the right end of the political spectrum in the late 1970s and the 1980s. Trained as an **economist** at the University of Oslo, he was both personally and professionally opposed to the Keynesian policies promoted by the **Labor Party** during the early decades of the postwar era. Willoch's first significant political experience was gained as a member of the Oslo City Council from 1952 to 1959. He was elected to the *Storting* (**Parliament**) in 1957 and remained a member until 1989. He served as minister of trade in **John Lyng**'s brief government in 1963 and in **Per Borten**'s government in 1965–70. He was then the leader of the **Conservative Party** until 1974, when Erling Norvik took over.

Willoch led the Conservative Party's parliamentary caucus from 1970 to 1981, when he became the prime minister in a Conservative minority government. Norway's nonsocialist parties gained a parliamentary majority in the 1981 elections, and the Conservative government was supported by the **Christian Democrats** and the **Center Party**, which joined the government in 1983, thus creating a majority coalition government. In the parliamentary elections held in 1985, however, Willoch's government was again relegated to minority status and had to seek the support of the two representatives of the **Progress Party**, whose views were generally to the right of the Conservatives. When the Progress Party supported a vote of no confidence advanced by the Labor Party and the **Socialist Left Party** in 1986, Willoch was forced to resign, after which **Gro Harlem Brundtland** took over as prime minister and formed a minority government.

Willoch's neoliberal economic views had great influence on Norwegian society, and one of Labor's core values, government control of many aspects of social and economic life, was largely abandoned. The monopoly of the Norwegian Broadcasting Corporation was ended. Stores stayed open much later in the evening than what had been legal, and private medical clinics were allowed. Government control of credit markets were relaxed, which led to a significant increase in private consumption.

The strident nature of Willoch's public rhetoric undoubtedly galvanized his supporters, but it also led to a less civil political culture in Norway. His debates with Gro Harlem Brundtland are legendary for their acrimony. This aspect of Willoch's public involvement has not lessened since his retirement from national politics. Especially after his service as county governor of Oslo and Akershus (1989–98), he has been very outspoken in his criticism of the state of Israel and supportive of the Palestinians, as well as publicly opposed to greed, selfishness, and the exploitation of natural resources.

**WOMEN.** Women played an important role in traditional Norwegian society, where their labor was urgently needed. For example, in medieval times the woman was in charge of the household and supervised servants who worked in the family and with the farm animals. The menfolk were absent sometimes for long periods at a time because of business, **fishing** expeditions, or hunting, and the wife had to manage largely on her own. A woman's position in traditional society was therefore one of respect and authority. This relative equality between men and women was reflected in the **religious** beliefs and practices of pre-Christian Norway. The ancient Nordic pantheon had room for several female deities, and women appear to have been central to the cults of home and hearth. Their legal status was also superior to that of women in other contemporary European societies.

The position of women changed significantly with the arrival of Christianity. The inferiority of women was attested to by ancient philosophy, Roman law, biblical teachings, and the doctrines and practices of the medieval church. At the time of the Enlightenment, hardly anybody doubted that the sex roles that were in place were the proper ones. During the revolutionary ferment in France in the late 1700s and early 1800s, though, the idea arose that just like all men were created equal, so were all human beings, including women. A classic statement of this kind of thinking is Mary Wollstonecraft's *A Vindication of the Rights of Woman* (1792).

These ideas gradually migrated to Norway and influenced thinking men and women, including the novelist **Camilla Collett**, who soon after being widowed in 1851 published *Amtmandens Døttre* (1854–55; tr. *The District Governor's Daughters*, 1992), a novel that, based on her personal experience, depicted the familial and social oppression suffered by women at the time. Collett portrays oppression that was a matter of custom rather than law, but there was plenty of the latter, too, for women lacked the right to vote, the right to higher **education**, and equality before the law (e.g., inheritance rights equal to those of men). The rights to work and education were therefore the principal issues when the *Norsk Kvindesagsforening* (NKF; Norwegian Women's Rights Association) was established by Gina Krog (1847–1916) and Hagbard Emanuel Berner (1839–1920) in 1884. This association gave birth to the *Kvindestemmeretsforeningen* (Norwegian Women's Voting Rights Association) the following year; it was to work specifically for women's voting rights.

Krog and Berner had different views of what kind of strategy would take them to that goal, however, as Berner was cautious and perhaps overly so. After Krog's proposal for general voting rights for women had been rejected by the *Storting* (**Parliament**) in 1890 and the *Kvindestemmeretsforeningen* had decided to try Berner's proposal instead, which was to try to get voting rights for women only in local elections, Krog formed a splinter organization named the *Landskvindestemmeretsforeningen* (Norwegian Women's National Voting Rights Association) in 1898. Krog, the editor of the NKF's journal *Nylænde* (New Land), had become acquainted with the suffragettes while visiting England in 1880 and did not believe that half a loaf is better than none, or at least not when it was a matter of the franchise. The *Norske Kvinders Nationalraad* (National Council of Women) was established by Krog in 1904; it was to coordinate the work of 17 local and 9 national women's organizations that had been established by then.

In the early years of the struggle for equal rights for women, only the **Liberal Party** was supportive, and mostly the support came from its left wing. Gradually, however, the NKF received broader support from the Liberals as well as some support from moderate members of the **Conservative Party**. After all men had been given voting rights in 1898, women received the franchise in 1913.

In 1884, very few women received higher education in Norway. A law that gave women the right to take the *examen artium* (the degree conferred on students passing the university entrance examination) and the *examen philosophicum* (a preliminary general education degree offered at the university) had been passed overwhelmingly by the *Storting* and had taken effect on 15 June 1882. The first woman to sit for the *examen artium*, Ida Cecilie Thoresen, had done so the same year and matriculated at the university on 8 September 1882. She had had to prepare for her *examen artium* on her own, however, for there was still no college preparatory school that admitted women as students. The first such coeducational school was opened by Ragna Nielsen in 1885, and female university students gradually joined the ranks of their male colleagues.

The women who joined the associations coordinated through the *Norske Kvinders Nationalraad* largely had their background in the middle class. Women from the working class found them unresponsive to their concerns, so they were organized according to the pattern of male factory workers and gave their political allegiance to the **Labor Party**. A spontaneous strike at two match factories in Christiania (now **Oslo**) in 1889 had the effect of making the public increasingly aware of both the unsanitary and dangerous conditions in this particular **industry** and of the conditions under which women in general worked. The most important result of the strike, however, was that it led to the organization of a trade union, and soon other female workers in other industries—brewery workers, tobacco products workers, and seamstresses—organized their own unions as well. These unions cooperated with unions formed by male workers and saw the Labor Party as the natural home of their members.

As Norwegian society was gradually modernized during the closing decades of the 1800s and on into the 20th century, legal discrimination against women was gradually reduced. Women in Norway have had the same inheritance rights as men since 1854, and the right to own and control property gradually became the same as well. (Two exceptions are that women had no allodial rights to farmland until 1974, and a woman could not inherit the throne of Norway until 1990.) Except for the work that was being done by the women's organizations that had been formed between 1884 and 1904, there was little feminist activity during **World War I**. The personal freedom of women had increased significantly by the 1920s, so the need for further reforms did not appear to be as great as before. During the depression years and **World War II**, most people were focused on the crises at hand, and during the years of reconstruction that followed the war, everybody was simply very busy helping the country get back to normal again.

When the women's liberation movement arrived in Norway in the late 1960s and early 1970s, many of the impulses came from the **United States**. Women wanted to control their own bodies. As more reliable means of contraception made the sexual revolution possible, women could be sexually active without the constant threat of an unwanted pregnancy. Abortions were made legal in 1978, but a woman only has the right to choose to have one until the end of the 12th week of the pregnancy; later abortions must be approved by a medical commission. The *Storting* just barely passed the abortion law of 1978, but the most protracted battle has had to do with what Norwegians refer to as *likestilling*, equality of position in the home and society. Norwegian sex roles long kept women in the kitchen and certain women's occupations and excluded them from boardrooms and high government positions.

The *Likestillingsloven* (the Equality Act), passed in 1978 and most recently revised in 2005, has as its purpose to bring about real equality between men and women on all levels of society. Neither direct nor indirect discrimination is allowed. For example, a woman can in no way be disadvantaged at work because of pregnancy or childbirth. Employers must actively promote equality in the workplace; it is not enough simply to avoid discrimination. Compensation levels must be established according to the principle of comparable worth. It is not sufficient to adhere to the principle of equal pay for equal work within the same employment category, but the level of compensation for one type of employment must be in line with the wage level in jobs that are of similar social value. Governing boards must have at least 40 percent women and 40 percent men among its members.

Norway was the first country in the world to pass an equality act, and the government has followed through by applying its principles to itself. When **Gro Harlem Brundtland**, as Norway's first female prime minister, formed her government in 1981, 8 of its 18 members were women. Women occupy positions of responsibility and trust on all levels of the state administration, and private industry is gradually conforming to an increasingly progressive set of expectations. However, in other fields, women have long made a mark on Norwegian culture, especially in **literature** and the **arts** (e.g., the writer Cora Sandel and the painter Kitty Kielland) and social affairs (e.g., the psychologist Åse Gruda Skard and the educator Margrethe Vullum). *See also* JENSEN, SIV (1969– ); UNDSET, SIGRID (1882–1949).

**WORKER-DEMOCRATS.** The *Arbeiderdemokratene* was a regional party that had its center of gravity among small farmers and rural laborers in Oppland and Hedmark. While at times officially known by other names, among them *De forenede norske Arbeidersamfund* (The United Societies of Norwegian Workers) and *Det radikale Folkeparti* (The Radical People's Party), the *Arbeiderdemokratene* was their common appellation. While not a social-democratic party, the Worker-Democrats belonged to the left of the **Liberal Party**, with whom they often collaborated. Their most important leader was **Johan Castberg**, the central figure in the natural resource legislation, including its doctrine of reversion, which was passed in 1909. Some members of the party leaned toward the ideas of the American political **economist** Henry George, who argued that it should not be possible to profit solely from the ownership of land, and this kind of thinking resonated with the poorer classes in the countryside. The Worker-Democrats played a minor role in Norwegian politics in the 1920s and 1930s, and the party was formally dissolved in 1940.

**WORKERS' COMMUNIST PARTY.** The *Arbeidernes kommunistparti* (AKP) was formed in 1973 under the name AKP *(marxist-leninistene)* (AKP [m-l]; the Workers' Communist Party [Marxist-Leninist]). It participated in elections in cooperation with the *Rød Valgallianse* (**Red Electoral Alliance**), with which it was combined in 2007 under the name *Rødt* (**Red**). It had dropped the contents of the parenthesis from its name already in 1990.

**WORLD WAR I.** Serbian nationalism, expressed through the murder of Archduke Franz Ferdinand of Austria and his wife in Sarajevo, Bosnia, on 28 June 1914, led to a protracted war that pitted the Central Powers — Austria-Hungary, Germany, and the Ottoman Empire — against an alliance consisting of France, Great Britain, and Russia. In 1917, the **United States** declared war against Germany for having violated its neutrality, thus effectively joining the Allies. Even though officially neutral, Norway was deeply affected by this conflict.

Since the **dissolution of the union with Sweden**, Norway had followed a policy of strict neutrality. There had been significant international tension in the years between 1905 and 1914, but in 1907, Great Britain, Germany, France, and Russia had signed an agreement with Norway that guaranteed the integrity of Norwegian territory. Because its long coastline gives Norway a strategic position in any European war, the Norwegian government had also prepared militarily to defend Norway's neutrality. The warships acquired in the run-up to 1905 were still in good repair, and significant additional improvements had been made to both the navy and the army.

Although the war did come as a surprise to the Norwegian authorities, both the navy and the coastal artillery were mobilized on 2 August 1914, the day after Germany's declaration of war against Russia. Most Norwegians were friendly toward the Allies, and only three years before (1911), there had been an incident in which the German fleet had come into Norwegian fjords, which showed that Germany's guarantee of Norwegian territorial integrity might not offer much protection. Norway was also concerned about the Swedish foreign policy, for some leading Swedes wanted to join the Central Powers with the hope of reclaiming Finland from Russia (Sweden had ruled Finland until 1809, and there was a significant Swedish linguistic minority in Finland). Any such Swedish adventure would bring the war to the **Scandinavian** Peninsula, and the Norwegian attempt to maintain its neutrality would become precarious at best.

Norway's most difficult issues during the early part of the war had to do with international **trade**, which Norway insisted had to remain unfettered by both sides in the war. The Norwegian merchant fleet was very large and of tremendous **economic** significance. Britain's most effective weapon against Germany was its naval blockade, however, and the question was how to deal with Norwegian ships that carried fish and other supplies, particularly copper ore, to Germany. Britain could not prevent Norwegian ships from entering international waters, but they claimed the right to search them in British ports if their cargo was bound for the enemy, confiscating the cargo if it was deemed significant to Germany's war effort. This was not necessarily bad for Norwegian shipowners, however, for the delays and other troubles caused the **shipping** rates to increase astronomically. Britain also wanted Norway to stop German vessels from buying fish directly from Norwegian fishermen and attempted to accomplish this by buying up the fish themselves, which caused the price of fish to rise dramatically. When this policy proved too difficult and expensive, Britain threatened to withhold from Norway the **oil** and coal that the Norwegian **fishing** fleet needed. Norway had to walk a fine line between giving in to British demands, thus increasing the risk of a German invasion, and offending the British to the point that the Norwegian economy would become paralyzed through their sanctions. So, Norway promised to allow Germany to buy only a very small quantity of fish, which deeply angered the Germans.

The trade in copper ore was another sore spot. Germany depended on Norwegian copper ore for its armaments industry, but Norway needed to buy electrolytic copper from Great Britain. Not surprisingly, Britain resented having to sell Norway highly refined copper only to see Norway turn around and sell its own copper ore to the enemy. Britain therefore committed to both buy Norwegian copper ore and supply its need for electrolytic copper in exchange for a ban on the export of copper ore from Norway to Germany. This arrangement, too, angered the Germans.

As the war progressed, Norway was growing increasingly friendly toward the Allies because of Germany's submarine warfare, which was Germany's answer to the British blockade. At first, Germany sunk neutral merchant ships only after searching them for contraband, warning the crew of their intentions and allowing the seamen time to get into the lifeboats and away from the scene. The torpedoes were fired from a surface position. This procedure was according to international law and comparatively humane, as the purpose was to prevent the cargo from getting to the enemy, not to needlessly waste lives. As Germany's situation grew increasingly desperate, however, this policy changed to one of sinking without warning. Submarines fired their torpedoes while submerged, and lives were lost and injuries sustained when they hit their targets and exploded. Other sailors drowned in the icy sea or froze to death on the lifeboats. The conditions of the war were such that it was difficult to distinguish neutral ships from enemy ships, and Norwegian ships were often treated the same as identified enemy ships. In response to this cruel and illegal strategy, the Norwegian government issued a statement in which foreign submarines were barred from Norwegian territorial waters, which greatly upset the German government.

Norway experienced considerable freedom of choice during the first two years of the war. Later, and especially after the entrance of the United States into the conflict in 1917, the situation became more difficult both at home and abroad. Germany was sinking Norwegian merchant ships in an increasingly brutal manner, even firing on the crew members when they were trying to get into the lifeboats. It appeared that the purpose was to frighten Norwegian seamen into refusing to man the ships, but this strategy did not work; the Norwegians were not easily intimidated. Supplies on which Norway was dependent and were furnished by the Allies were more difficult both to obtain and to transport home than before. The result was rationing of some essential commodities.

During the war, the primary burden of leadership in Norway rested on the shoulders of two men, Prime Minister **Gunnar Knudsen** and the minister of foreign affairs, **Nils Claus Ihlen**. Both represented the **Liberal Party**, and no significant effort to form a unity government was made, but the crisis of the war meant that partisan political bickering declined. The government was blamed, though, for not having had the wisdom to stockpile food and other commodities in anticipation of the war, but most people had expected any war to be short lived and not lead to long-term disruptions of the supply of such necessary commodities as flour, sugar, and coffee. Knudsen wanted to keep the government from interfering with the economy as much as possible, but the shortage of commodities and the rise in prices hit wage earners and the poor particularly hard, so some price supports were instituted. But the tax receipts did not keep up with the expenditures, and after the end of the war, it became apparent that the national debt had increased substantially. On the other hand, shipowners and other businessmen and investors lived through a golden age that made it possible to quickly accumulate great fortunes but also led to a display of consumption and luxury that had been quite uncommon in Norway. The war profiteers and the common people experienced the war very differently, and those hardest hit were the 2,000 seamen who lost their lives in war-related incidents.

The Norwegian people for the most part kept their heads cool throughout the war years. Initially, there was some panic that manifested itself in hoarding of food and distrust in paper money, but that soon passed. While carrying out a campaign of intimidation against Norwegian sailors and, to some extent, against the government itself, Germany never managed to break Norway's determination to keep its neutrality reasonably intact. Facing the Atlantic Ocean, Norway is a natural ally of Great Britain, and one of the main reasons Norway managed to keep its neutrality is surely that this was in Britain's interests. The Norwegians were undoubtedly just as relieved as everybody else when the peace accord between Germany and the Allies was signed on 11 November 1918.

**WORLD WAR II.** The greatest military conflict in world history, World War II is usually considered to have begun on 1 September 1939, when Germany invaded Poland, after which Great Britain and France declared war. The two sides in the war are known as the Axis, comprised primarily of Germany, Italy, and Japan, and the Allies, consisting mainly of Great Britain, Canada, the **United States**, the Soviet Union, France, and China. The roots of the war are generally thought to lie in the conditions Germany was forced to accept at the end of **World War I** and that rankled German nationalists, helping to set the stage for Germany's territorial expansionism, typified by the annexation of Austria on 12 March 1938.

The German attack on Norway on the morning of 9 April 1940 came as a surprise to the Norwegian government. Norway had seen no hostile action for 125 years, Norwegian neutrality had proven effective during **World War I**, and it was simply unimaginable to the Norwegian authorities that Germany would attack. Both the government and the *Storting* (**Parliament**) were, in fact, more concerned about recent news that Great Britain had placed mines in Norwegian territorial waters.

The Norwegian lack of vigilance was in part the fault of the minister of foreign affairs, **Halvdan Koht**, who in hindsight did not take the threat of German invasion as seriously as he should have. There were a number of warning signs. Warships were observed leaving the Baltic, and the survivors from a German ship sunk off the coast of southern Norway reported that they were headed to the city of **Bergen**.

The attack hit all of the most important coastal cities at the same time: **Oslo**, Kristiansand, Egersund, **Stavanger**, Bergen, **Trondheim**, and Narvik. The only significant resistance offered was in Oslo, where the coastal fort at Oscarsborg near Drøbak had sufficient warning to prepare for resistance. When the German heavy cruiser *Blücher* approached, it was first hit with grenades from the land-based batteries and then with torpedoes. The engine room took a direct hit. As *Blücher* was sinking, German men were heard screaming while they were swimming through the burning oil that covered the sea.

The sinking of the *Blücher* was probably the most significant event during the German campaign in Norway in 1940. It gave the *Storting* and the government sufficient time to flee the capital and frustrated the German plan to take Norway's royal family and political leaders captive. Meeting at Elverum north of Oslo, the *Storting* charged the government with taking control and carrying out the *Storting*'s normal duties. This act made it possible to establish a legitimate Norwegian government in exile in London during the next five years; it also made it impossible for the German occupants to claim that they were in Norway simply for its protection against the British and that they were acting in concert with duly constituted Norwegian civil authorities. Although the Norwegian forces in Norway capitulated in the face of overwhelming German numbers, the capitulation only concerned action on Norwegian soil. Norwegian troops could later be organized in Sweden and Britain, and the Norwegian merchant marine, which was one of the largest such fleets in the world, as well as the most modern, could be enlisted in the Allied war effort.

Norway's King **Haakon VII** took a strong stance against the invaders during the early days of the war. As representatives of the German government attempted to bully the Norwegians into negotiating a peace settlement with them, the king stated in no uncertain terms that he would immediately abdicate if any negotiations were begun. After that, the Germans bombed the place where the king was located.

The seriously undersupplied and poorly trained Norwegian forces acted with great courage during the 1940 campaign. Lacking well-trained officers and decent equipment, the Norwegian troops fought to absolute exhaustion. There were some treasonous acts as well, for some of the officers were friendly toward the Nazi ideology. For example, during the initial attack on the northern Norwegian town Narvik, through which **Swedish** iron ore vital to the German war effort was shipped to Germany, a local commander with Nazi sympathies turned the city over to the Germans after but limited resistance. Allied forces came to assist the Norwegian troops, and Narvik was retaken, but the British government determined that its forces should be withdrawn. On 7 June 1940, the Norwegian king and government fled to Great Britain onboard the British cruiser *Devonshire*.

Norway spent the next five years, until the formal capitulation in Norway on 8 May 1945, under German occupation. At times, there were as many as 400,000 German troops in the country. These soldiers were well trained and mostly behaved well. The Norwegian population, however, endured many heavy burdens, as resources and labor power were commandeered to help with the German war effort. Some Norwegians saw an opportunity for financial prosperity by working for the enemy. Norway's indigenous Nazi Party, the *Nasjonal Samling* (NS; National Socialist Party), under the leadership of **Vidkun Quisling**, saw its membership increase dramatically. At the time of the invasion, Quisling had declared himself Norway's new prime minister; he had secretly conspired with the Germans prior to the invasion and expected to receive his reward. The German government appointed **Josef Terboven** *Reichskommisar* (commissioner) of Norway on 24 April 1940, however, and he set up his headquarters in the parliament building in Oslo, ruling Norway virtually as a dictator, although he did not have authority over all the German troops in the country. Quisling eventually headed a puppet government, but Terboven had little confidence in him.

The first weeks after the end of the military campaign were characterized by confusion and fear, as well as an **economic** crisis. The *Storting* had turned its power over to the government, which had fled the country. Under the authority of the Norwegian Supreme Court, an administrative council was appointed and charged with keeping the Norwegian economy going. Their main tasks were to keep Norwegian society functioning with as much normalcy as possible, to facilitate employment, to procure necessary supplies, and to secure markets for Norwegian exports. The Norwegian economy became increasingly tied to that of Germany.

The general Nazi policy in Norway is usually referred to as "Nazification." The occupiers wanted to replace Norwegian democratic institutions with a corporate state and also gain control over the various institutions and organizations that comprised civil society. After they had unsuccessfully pressured the Supreme Court, whose leader was **Paal Berg**, and the members of the *Storting* to declare that King Haakon VII was no longer the Norwegian king and that the exile government in London was illegitimate, all political parties except Quisling's NS were dissolved. NSs were appointed to every public position of significance, excepting a few cabinet posts where there was need for capable leadership if the economy were to keep functioning. The newspapers became tools of Nazi propaganda. Firearms were confiscated, as were radios so that people could not listen to the Norwegian broadcasts from London. Teachers and other public employees were asked to sign loyalty oaths. Elected local officials were replaced by Nazi appointees. The leadership of private organizations, for example, trade unions, was also placed in Nazi hands.

There was a strong and broadly based resistance to both the occupiers and their Norwegian fellow travelers, however. Members of the Nazi Party were shunned. Schoolteachers mounted massive resistance to the Nazification of the curriculum, and large numbers of them were arrested, out of which hundreds were severely mistreated. The State Church, under the leadership of Bishop **Eivind Berggrav**, took a strong position in defense of the freedom of conscience. Its statement "Kirkens grunn" (Foundation of the Church) was read from pulpits across the country, after which the ministers resigned the portion of their duties that pertained to their positions as government appointees while expressing their desires to continue serving as pastors. When Quisling introduced occupational associations according to the patterns of the Fascist corporate state, people canceled their memberships by the tens of thousands. Such symbols as a paperclip worn on a lapel or a comb stuck in a breast pocket signaled passive resistance.

As time passed, a network of active civil resistance was established and coordinated in concert with the Norwegian government in

London. Information from Allied radio broadcasts was communicated through various illegal newspapers. Workers did their best to lessen the value of what was produced for the benefit of the occupiers. In addition to the public attempts at resistance, however, there was a hidden military organization that in part dated to the days of the invasion and military campaign in 1940. Some of the soldiers who had managed to hide their weapons formed groups that became the nucleus of Milorg, a secret military organization that gradually came under the leadership of a common council. At first, the thinking was that these groups of potential partisans would rise up and assist the Allies during a hoped-for invasion, but later it was understood that they could also be used to keep order in the country subsequent to a German capitulation that seemed increasingly likely. As the Gestapo, the German secret police, increased its size and investigative power in Norway, some Milorg members were discovered and arrested, imprisoned, tortured, and executed. For example, when a group of commandoes were sent from Britain to organize and outfit a resistance group at Majavatn near Mo i Rana, 24 individuals were shot as the network was uncovered by the Germans. Similar incidents took place in other parts of the country as well, including the killing of Norwegians as reprisals and in order to frighten the population into complying with Nazi demands.

Many resistance workers had to escape to Sweden to evade arrest, and others fled to Shetland onboard **fishing** boats. Some of these returned to Norway as commandos and saboteurs. One celebrated incident involved an assault on a plant that produced heavy water at Vemork near the town of Rjukan. Heavy water was essential to the production of atomic bombs, and it was thought that the German nuclear research program depended on the heavy water produced at Vemork. Attempts were made to sabotage the plant, and a ferry that contained barrels of heavy water was sunk in Lake Tinn. Other highly dangerous work in Norway involved operating radio transmitters along the coast by which information guiding attacks on warships and cargo vessels was sent to England. One such location was a cave at Onøy, just barely south of where the Arctic Circle crosses the coastline of northern Norway, from which the resistance worker John Kristoffersen transmitted messages. His location was eventually discovered by the Germans. An example of the significance of this kind of resistance work is an incident that took place on 4 October 1943, when aircraft from the USS *Ranger* attacked German war and cargo ships along the coast of northern Norway under the codename "Operation Leader." One of the ships hit was *La Plata*, attacked when crossing the Rødøy fjord just barely north of the location of Kristoffersen's radio transmitter.

As the tide of war gradually turned against Germany, planning for its inevitable capitulation increasingly became a priority. Training of underground forces in Norway was intensified, and a force of 14,000 police troops was established among the Norwegian refugees in Sweden. The goal was to have sufficient forces to keep order in the country and to deal with Nazi Party members with a minimum of assistance from Allied troops. When Finland, which had been fighting on Germany's side, capitulated in September 1944, the German troops stationed there withdrew through Finnmark, making the area as uninhabitable as they could. With Russian troops close behind them, however, their destruction of homes and infrastructure in the eastern part of the county was not complete, but the damage was still substantial. When the Russian pursuit stopped, there was almost total destruction in western Finnmark, and the civilian population was forced to flee before the retreating and marauding Germans. The suffering of the population was terrible. The German forces, which were intended for further action on the continent, however, were unable to completely retreat from northern Norway before the German capitulation.

Another concern was what to do about the many thousands of Norwegians who were being held prisoner in German concentration camps. Through skilled diplomacy, the Swede Folke Bernadotte received permission to gather Danish and Norwegian prisoners in a special camp near Hamburg. The sickest among them were taken directly to Sweden, and later, Bernadotte received permission to bring the others as well to Sweden onboard his white buses.

When the German forces in Norway capitulated, in reality on 7 May 1945 but formally the following day, the Norwegian home front forces and police took control and did an exemplary job keeping order in the country. The German troops withdrew from the cities and towns, organizing their own disarmament, and were gradually provided with transportation back home. The Norwegian government returned from exile on 13 May, and on 7 June, King Haakon VII returned. *See also* RINNAN, HENRY OLIVER (1915–45).

# Appendix A: Norwegian Rulers

When dates overlap, it indicates that the kingship was shared between two individuals during the period in question. Usually, the co-regents were father and son or brothers.

| | |
|---|---|
| Harald (I) Fairhair | c. 872–c. 933 |
| Eirik Bloodaxe | c. 931–c. 933 |
| Haakon (I) the Good | 933–c. 960 |
| Harald (II) Gråfell | c. 960–c. 970 |
| Haakon Sigurdsson, Earl of Lade | c. 970–995 |
| Olaf (I) Tryggvason | 995–1000 |
| Eirik and Svein Haakonsson, Earls of Lade | 1000–1012 |
| Haakon Eiriksson and Svein Haakonsson, Earls of Lade | 1012–15 |
| Olaf (II) Haraldsson | 1015–28 |
| Haakon Eiriksson, Earl of Lade | 1028–30 |
| Svein Knutsson | 1030–35 |
| Magnus (I) the Good | 1035–47 |
| Harald (III) Hardrada | 1045–66 |
| Magnus (II) Haraldsson | 1066–69 |
| Olaf (III) Kyrre | 1067–93 |
| Haakon Magnusson | 1093–95 |
| Magnus (III) Berrføtt | 1093–1103 |
| Olaf Magnusson | 1103–15 |
| Øystein (I) Magnusson | 1103–23 |
| Sigurd (I) Jorsalfar | 1103–30 |
| Magnus (IV) Blinde | 1130–35 |
| Harald (IV) Gille | 1130–36 |
| Sigurd (II) Munn | 1136–55 |
| Inge Krokrygg | 1136–61 |
| Øystein (II) Haraldsson | 1142–57 |

| | |
|---|---|
| Haakon (II) Herdebrei | 1159–62 |
| Magnus (V) Erlingsson | 1161–84 |
| Sverre Sigurdsson | 1177–1202 |
| Haakon (III) Sverresson | 1202–4 |
| Guttorm Sigurdsson | 1204 |
| Inge (II) Baardsson | 1204–17 |
| Haakon (IV) Haakonsson | 1217–63 |
| Magnus (VI) Haakonsson Lagabøte | 1263–80 |
| Eirik (II) Magnusson | 1280–99 |
| Haakon (V) Magnusson | 1299–1319 |
| Magnus (VII) Eiriksson | 1319–55 |
| Haakon (V) Magnusson | 1343–80 |
| Olaf (IV) Haakonsson | 1380–87 |
| Queen Margareta Valdemarsdaughter | 1388–1412 |
| Erik of Pomerania | 1389–1442 |
| Christoffer of Bavaria | 1442–48 |
| Karl (I) Knutsson Bonde | 1449–50 |
| Christian I | 1450–81 |
| Hans | 1483–1513 |
| Christian II | 1513–23 |
| Frederik I | 1524–33 |
| Christian III | 1537–59 |
| Frederik II | 1559–88 |
| Christian IV | 1588–1648 |
| Frederik III | 1648–70 |
| Christian V | 1670–99 |
| Frederik IV | 1699–1730 |
| Christian VI | 1730–46 |
| Frederik V | 1746–66 |
| Christian VII | 1766–1808 |
| Frederik VI | 1808–14 |
| Christian Frederik | 1814 |
| Karl II | 1814–18 |
| Karl III Johan | 1818–44 |
| Oscar I | 1844–59 |
| Karl IV | 1859–72 |
| Oscar II | 1872–1905 |
| Haakon VII | 1905–57 |
| Olav V | 1957–91 |
| Harald V | 1991– |

# Appendix B: Norwegian Prime Ministers

| 1873 | Stang, Fredrik |
| 1880 | Selmer, Christian August |
| 1884 | Schweigaard, Christian Homann |
| 1884 | Sverdrup, Johan (Liberal) |
| 1889 | Stang, Emil (Conservative) |
| 1891 | Steen, Johannes (Liberal) |
| 1893 | Stang, Emil (Conservative) |
| 1895 | Hagerup, Francis (Conservative) |
| 1898 | Steen, Johannes (Liberal) |
| 1902 | Blehr, Otto Albert (Liberal) |
| 1903 | Hagerup, Francis (United) |
| 1905 | Michelsen, Christian (Liberal) |
| 1907 | Løvland, Jørgen (Liberal) |
| 1908 | Knudsen, Gunnar (Liberal) |
| 1910 | Konow, Wollert (Conservative) |
| 1912 | Bratlie, Jens (Conservative) |
| 1913 | Knudsen, Gunnar (Liberal) |
| 1920 | Halvorsen, Otto Bahr (Conservative) |
| 1921 | Blehr, Otto Alberg (Liberal) |
| 1923 | Halvorsen, Otto Bahr (Conservative) |
| 1923 | Berge, Abraham (Liberal Left) |
| 1924 | Mowinckel, Johan Ludvig (Liberal) |
| 1926 | Lykke, Ivar (Conservative) |
| 1928 | Hornsrud, Christopher (Labor) |
| 1928 | Mowinckel, Johan Ludvig (Liberal) |
| 1931 | Kolstad, Peder (Agrarian) |
| 1932 | Hundseid, Jens (Agrarian) |
| 1933 | Mowinckel, Johan Ludvig (Liberal) |
| 1935 | Nygaardsvold, Johan (Labor) |

| 1945 | Gerhardsen, Einar (Unity Government) |
| 1945 | Gerhardsen, Einar (Labor) |
| 1951 | Torp, Oscar (Labor) |
| 1955 | Gerhardsen, Einar (Labor) |
| 1963 | Lyng, John (Conservative) |
| 1963 | Gerhardsen, Einar (Labor) |
| 1965 | Borten, Per (Center) |
| 1971 | Bratteli, Trygve (Labor) |
| 1972 | Korvald, Lars (Christian Democratic) |
| 1973 | Bratteli, Trygve (Labor) |
| 1976 | Nordli, Odvar (Labor) |
| 1981 | Brundtland, Gro Harlem (Labor) |
| 1981 | Willoch, Kåre (Conservative) |
| 1986 | Brundtland, Gro Harlem (Labor) |
| 1989 | Syse, Jan Peder (Conservative) |
| 1990 | Brundtland, Gro Harlem (Labor) |
| 1996 | Jagland, Thorbjørn (Labor) |
| 1997 | Bondevik, Kjell Magne (Christian Democratic) |
| 2000 | Stoltenberg, Jens (Labor) |
| 2001 | Bondevik, Kjell Magne (Christian Democratic) |
| 2005 | Stoltenberg, Jens (Labor) |

# Bibliography

## INTRODUCTION

This bibliography is designed both to serve the needs of readers who have little or no command of the Norwegian language and to be helpful to those who do. While the overwhelming majority of the books and articles mentioned are in English, there is also a generous sampling of works in Norwegian. Most of the works mentioned are of relatively recent date, although some are older, including classics in the field; for example, works by Carl Joachim Hambro and Halvdan Koht.

Norwegian history, politics, and society, along with literature and the arts, are studied most intensively in Norway by scholars who are either native Norwegians or who have come there to work because of their intellectual and professional interests. Much of this work is published in Norwegian, but some of it appears in English. In U.S. colleges and universities, the study of Norwegian language and literature has a long tradition, and both immigrant and Norwegian history have been studied as well, especially in colleges that were founded by Norwegian immigrants and in strong departments of Scandinavian studies found at some of the larger research universities, for example, the University of Minnesota, the University of Wisconsin, the University of Washington, and the University of California, Berkeley. In Great Britain, the study of Norwegian history, culture, and literature has a long and illustrious tradition, with much excellent work coming out of Oxford and Cambridge, but in recent years full-fledged departments of Scandinavian studies have been in place only at University College London and the University of East Anglia.

Historians, political scientists, sociologists, and literary critics associated with the larger research universities throughout Europe and the world have written on Norwegian themes as well, but seldom will a scholar be able to devote all of his or her professional attention to Norwegian subjects. For some, it has become a research specialty, while for others it is a cherished professional sideline. Academics whose work is not exclusively focused on Norway, however, are often able to place their observations of Norwegian history, society, and culture in illuminating contexts.

International professional organizations also play a major role in the creation and dissemination of scholarly work related to Norway. For example, the Society for the Advancement of Scandinavian Study publishes the journal *Scandinavian Studies*, which regularly publishes work on Scandinavian, including Norwegian, history, society, and literature. The International Comparative Literature Association is sponsoring a three-volume *History of Nordic Literary Cultures*, with publication anticipated in 2010.

Because most of the scholarship devoted to Norway is done there and published in Norwegian, what appears in English tends to deal with questions or issues that are of theoretical or principal interest to the field or that are or have been matters of significant attention on the part of the general public. For example, Norway's resistance to joining the European Union will be of general interest to specialists in international studies, while the oil and gas policies of the Norwegian government will have some degree of impact on a large number of people (Norway is one of the world's largest exporters of oil and natural gas). Some more traditional topics (e.g., Norway's response to the Nazis during World War II and its security policy decisions during the cold war) still attract a good deal of interest. Many studies that appear in English are simply reflections of the scholar's own intellectual concerns; however, in the aggregate, the work done in response to such concerns offers very good coverage of the field, as this bibliography demonstrates.

The most recent multivolume work on Norwegian history to appear in Norway is Karsten Alnæs's five-volume *Historien om Norge* (the Story/History about/of Norway; the pun in Alnæs's title is difficult to render in English), published from 1996 to 2000. Distinguished by its lively narrative, it offers numerous concrete examples as illustrations of general historical trends. Since Alnæs is the author of all five volumes, totaling approximately 2,500 pages, there is a uniformity of tone and perspective throughout that makes for an engaging reading experience.

Fortunately, Alnæs has also provided a single-volume overview of Norway's history, written in English and titled *A History of Norway in Words and Pictures* (2001), which is highly recommended to those who do not read Norwegian. Another very good one-volume history is *Norway: A History from the Vikings to Our Own Times* (1995), written by some of Norway's most respected historians, Rolf Danielsen, Ståle Dyrvik, Tore Grønlie, Knut Helle, and Edgar Hovland. They have managed to pack a large amount of information into a single volume and divide their attention between political, social, and economic history.

Those who know or are able to learn Norwegian should consult the 15-volume *Norges historie* (History of Norway), edited by Knut Mykland and published from 1976 to 1980. With contributions from the most highly respected scholars of the generation then at the height of its intellectual and professional power, this series is informative and copiously illustrated. In many ways, it stands in a similar relationship to *Norway: A History from the Vikings to Our Own Times* as Alnæs's five-volume work stands to *A History of Norway in Words and Pictures*.

The defining moment in Norway's modern history came in 1814, when Europe's political situation at the end of the Napoleonic wars created an opportunity for Norway's leading citizens to frame a national constitution and declare independence. This event divides Norway's history into an older and a newer part, and it has a similar function in the way the topical studies in this bibliography are organized. Three of the scholars listed in the earlier part of the bibliography merit special mention. Jenny Jochens offers a fascinating discussion of the role of women in ancient Scandinavia in her book *Women in Old Norse Society* (1995). Her command of the sources is such as a lifetime of scholarship and study will bring, and her presentation is judicious and balanced throughout. Arnold Barton, who has written on the 50 years or so preceding 1814, offers a thoroughly researched and very informative presentation of Scandinavia as a whole during that period of time, particularly in *Scandinavia in the Revolutionary Era, 1760–1815* (1986). Byron Nordstrom, whose book is titled *Scandinavia since 1500* (2000), has provided a highly readable overview of Scandinavian, including Norwegian, history from 1500 until the present time. Nordstrom comes across as a master teacher as he addresses himself to students and general readers, and his book is generally acknowledged as the best available introduction to modern Scandinavian history in English.

Norway's darkest moment in recent times arrived on 9 April 1940, when Nazi Germany attacked. Great scholarly work can result from the study of a nation's trials, however, and a very good example of that is Oddvar Hoidal's magisterial *Quisling: A Study in Treason* (1989), the supreme significance of which is recognized both in Norway, where it has appeared in translation, and throughout the English-speaking world. Another engaging account related to Norway's World War II experience is Gunnar Sønsteby's autobiographical narrative *Report from #24* (1999), a firsthand narrative of what it was like to work in the resistance movement.

In this bibliography, the sections dealing with Norway's history are followed by sections on politics, economy, society, culture, and science. Special mention should be made of three works from these sections. Christine Ingebritsen's *Scandinavia in World Politics* (2006) offers a clear and engaging discussion of the role of the Scandinavian countries, including Norway, on which the author is a specialist, in world politics and economic life since the end of the cold war. Two literary studies, Ellen Rees's *On the Margins: Nordic Women Modernists of the 1930s* (2005) and Tanya Thresher's *Cecilie Løveid:*

*Engendering a Dramatic Tradition* (2005) place Norwegian 20th-century fiction and drama, respectively, in a European context.

The world's best collection of library materials related to Norway is found at the *Nasjonalbiblioteket* (National Library) in Oslo, which also has an excellent website, www.nb.no, that provides access to their numerous databases and other electronic resources. The best library collections related to Norway in the United States are found at the Library of Congress and the research universities with large departments of Scandinavian Studies, first and foremost the University of California, Berkeley; the University of California, Los Angeles; the University of Minnesota, Twin Cities; the University of Washington, Seattle; the University of Wisconsin, Madison; and the University of Texas, Austin. *Statistisk Sentralbyrå* (Statistics Norway) offers a wealth of numerical and statistical information found at www.ssb.no, and *Arkivverket* (the Archive Service) offers access to materials held at the Norwegian National Archives (*Riksarkivet*) as well as the regional state archives (*statsarkivene*) and the digital archives (*Digitalarkivet*), including electronic versions of the various Norwegian censuses and images of the actual pages of almost all Norwegian parish registers. Their website is www.riksarkivet.no and has both a Norwegian and an English interface.

## CONTENTS

## I. GENERAL

## 1. Bibliographies

Grønland, Erling. *Norway in English*. Oslo: Norwegian Universities Press, 1961.

Haukaas, Kaare, comp. *Norwegian Legal Publications in English, French and German*. Oslo: Universitetsforlaget, 1966.

Hoberman, John. "Bibliographical Spectrum." *Review of National Literatures* 12 (1983): 185–207.

Johansson, Eve, ed. *Official Publications of Western Europe*. London: Mansell, 1984.

Nordstrom, Byron J., ed. *Dictionary of Scandinavian History*. Westport, Conn.: Greenwood Press, 1986.

Sather, Leland B., and Hans H. Wellisch. *Norway*. World Bibliographical series, no. 67. Oxford: Clio Press, 1986.

## 2. Guidebooks

*Baedeker Scandinavia: Norway, Sweden, Finland.* New York: Macmillan Travel, 1996.

Berezin, Henrik. *Adventure Guide to Scandinavia.* Hunter Travel Guides. Edison, N.J.: Hunter, 2006.

Castberg, Frede. *The Norwegian Way of Life.* London: William Heinemann, 1954.

Collins, Andrew, ed. *Fodor's Norway.* Fodor's Travel Guides. New York: Fodor's Travel, 2000.

Evensberget, Snorre. *Norway.* Eyewitness Travel Guides. London: Dorling Kindersley, 2006.

Kiel, Anne Cohen, ed. *Continuity and Change: Aspects of Contemporary Norway.* Oslo: Scandinavian University Press, 1993.

Maagerø, Eva, and Birte Simonsen, eds. *Norway: Society and Culture.* Kristiansand, Norway: Portal Books, 2005.

*Norway and Sweden: Handbook for Travellers.* Leipzig, Germany: K. Baedeker, 1889.

Seaton, George W. *What to See and Do in Scandinavia: How to Get the Most Out of Your Trip to Norway, Sweden, Denmark, Iceland, Finland, and the North Cape.* New York: Prentice-Hall, 1939.

Selbyg, Arne. *Norway Today: An Introduction to Modern Norwegian Society.* Oslo: Norwegian University Press, 1986.

## 3. Map Collections and Statistical Abstracts

*Statistical Yearbook of Norway.* Oslo: Statistisk sentralbyrå, 2006.

Time-Life Books. *Scandinavia.* Library of Nations. Alexandria, Va.: Time-Life Books, 1987.

United States Board on Geographic Names. *Gazetteer of Norway Names Approved by the United States Board on Geographic Names.* Washington, D.C.: National Imagery and Mapping Agency, 1997.

## II. HISTORY

## 1. Surveys of Norwegian History

Alnæs, Karsten. *Historien om Norge.* 5 vols. Oslo: Gyldendal, 1996–2000.

———. *A History of Norway in Words and Pictures.* Oslo: Gyldendal, 2001.

Blom, Ida, and Sølvi Sogner, eds. *Med kjønnsperspektiv på norsk historie: Fra vikingtid til 2000-årsskiftet*. Oslo: Cappelen akademisk forlag, 1999.

Danielsen, Rolf, Ståle Dyrvik, Tore Grønlie, Knut Helle, and Edgar Hovland. *Grunntrekk i norsk historie: Fra vikingtid til våre dager*. Oslo: Universitetsforlaget, 1991.

———. *Norway: A History from the Vikings to Our Own Times*. Oslo: Universitetsforlaget, 1995.

Derry, Thomas Kingston. *A History of Scandinavia: Norway, Sweden, Denmark, Finland, and Iceland*. Minneapolis: University of Minnesota Press, 1979.

———. *A Short History of Norway*. London: Allen and Unwin, 1968.

Eriksen, Trond Berg, and Øystein Sørensen, eds. *Norsk idéhistorie*. 6 vols. Oslo: Aschehoug, 2001.

Gathorne-Hardy, Geoffrey Malcolm. *Norway*. London: Ernest Benn, 1925.

Gjerset, Knut. *A History of the Norwegian People*. New York: Macmillan, 1932.

Helle, Knut. *Norsk byhistorie: Urbanisering gjennom 1300 år*. Oslo: Pax, 2006.

Helle, Knut, Ottar Grepstad, Arnvid Lillehammer, and Anna Elisa Tryti. *Vestlandets historie*. 3 vols. Bergen, Norway: Vigmostad and Bjørke, 2006.

Larsen, Karen. *A History of Norway*. Princeton, N.J.: Princeton University Press, 1948.

Midgaard, John. *A Brief History of Norway*. Oslo: Tano, 1963.

Mykland, Knut, ed. *Norges historie*. 15 vols. Oslo: Cappelen, 1976–80.

*Norsk utenrikspolitikks historie*. 6 vols. Oslo: Universitetsforlaget, 1995–97.

Popperwell, Ronald. *Norway*. New York: Praeger, 1972.

Riste, Olav. *Norway's Foreign Relations: A History*. Oslo: Universitetsforlaget, 2001.

Sogner, Sølvi, ed. *I gode og vonde dagar: Familieliv i Noreg frå reformasjonen til vår tid*. Oslo: Samlaget, 2003.

Stenersen, Øivind, and Ivar Libæk. *The History of Norway: From the Ice Age to Today*. Lysaker, Norway: Dinamo Forlag, 2003.

## 2. From the Beginning to the Constitution (1814)

Andersen, P. Sveaas. *Samlingen av Norge og kristningen av landet 800–1130*. Handbok i Norges historie, vol. 2. Bergen, Norway: Universitetsforlaget, 1977.

———. *Vikings of the West: The Expansion of Norway in the Middle Ages*. Oslo: Tanum, 1971.

Bagge, Sverre. *Den kongelige kapellgeistlighet 1150–1319*. Bergen, Norway: Universitetsforlaget, 1976.

———. *Mennesket i middelalderens Norge: Tanker, tro og holdninger 1000–1300*. Oslo: Aschehoug, 1998.

Bagge, Sverre, and Knut Mykland. *Norge i dansketiden*. Politikens Danmarkshistorie. Copenhagen, Denmark: Politiken, 1987.

Barrett, James H., ed. *Contact, Continuity, and Collapse: The Norse Colonization of the North Atlantic*. Studies in the Early Middle Ages, no. 5. Turnhout, Belgium: Brepols, 2003.

Barton, H. Arnold. "*Iter Scandinavicum*: Foreign Travelers' Views of the Late Eighteenth-Century North." *Scandinavian Studies* 68 (1996): 1–18.

———. *Northern Arcadia: Foreign Travelers in Scandinavia, 1765–1815*. Carbondale: Southern Illinois University Press, 1998.

———. *Scandinavia in the Revolutionary Era, 1760–1815*. Minneapolis: University of Minnesota Press, 1986.

Bellamy, Martin. *Christian IV and His Navy: A Political and Administrative History of the Danish Navy 1596–1648*. The Northern World, vol. 25. Leiden, The Netherlands: Brill, 2006.

Bigelow, Gerald F., ed. *The Norse of the North Atlantic*. Copenhagen, Denmark: Munksgaard, 1991.

Brøgger, Anton Wilhelm, and H. Shetelig. *The Viking Ships*. Oslo: Dreyers, 1971.

Brøndsted, Johannes. *The Vikings*. Baltimore: Penguin, 1965.

DeVries, Kelly. *The Norwegian Invasion of England in 1066*. Warfare in History. Woodbridge, Suffolk, U.K.: Boydell Press, 1999.

Drake, Michael. *Population and Society in Norway 1735–1865*. Cambridge: Cambridge University Press, 1969.

Dyrvik, Ståle. *Året 1814*. Oslo: Samlaget, 2005.

———. *Norsk historie 1625–1814: Vegar til sjølvstende*. Norsk historie 800–2000, vol. 3. Oslo: Samlaget, 1999.

Ersland, Geir Atle, and Hilde Sandvik. *Norsk historie 1300–1625: Eit rike tek form*. Norsk historie 800–2000, vol. 2. Oslo: Samlaget, 1999.

Etting, Vivian. *Queen Margrete I, 1353–1412, and the Founding of the Nordic Union*. The Northern World, vol. 9. Leiden, The Netherlands: Brill, 2004.

Fladby, Rolf. *Fra lensmannstjener til Kongelig Majestets foged*. Oslo: Universitetsforlaget, 1963.

———. *Hvordan Nord-Norge ble styrt: Nordnorsk administrasjonshistorie fra 1530-åra til 1660*. Tromsø, Norway: Universitetsforlaget, 1978.

———. *Samfunn i vekst: Under fremmed styre, 1536–1660*. Handbok i Norges historie, vol. 5. Bergen, Norway: Universitetsforlaget, 1986.

Fladby, Rolf, and Jørn Sandnes. *På leiting etter den eldste garden*. Skrifter fra Norsk lokalhistorisk institutt, no. 6. Oslo: Universitetsforlaget, 1979.

Fladby, Rolf, Steinar Imsen, and Harald Winge. *Norsk historisk leksikon: Næringsliv, rettsvesen, administrasjon, mynt, mål og vekt, militære forhold, byggeskikk m.m. 1500–1850*. Oslo: Cappelen, 1974.

Foote, Peter, and David Wilson. *The Viking Achievement: The Society and Culture of Early Medieval Scandinavia*. London: Sidgwick and Jackson, 1989.

Gissel, Svend, et al. *Desertion and Land Colonization in the Nordic Countries, ca. 1300–1600*. Stockholm: Almqvist and Wiksell International, 1981.

Graham-Campbell, James. *The Viking World*. New Haven, Conn.: Ticknor and Fields, 1980.

Gustafsson, Harald. *Political Interaction in the Old Regime: Central Power and Local Society in the Eighteenth-Century Nordic States*. Lund, Sweden: Studentlitteratur, 1994.

Helle, Knut. *Konge og gode menn i norsk riksstyring ca. 1150–1319*. Bergen, Norway: Universitetsforlaget, 1972.

———. *Norge blir en stat 1130–1319*. Handbok i Norges historie, vol. 1. Bergen, Norway: Universitetsforlaget, 1964.

Holman, Katherine. *Historical Dictionary of the Vikings*. Lanham, Md.: Scarecrow Press, 2003.

Jochens, Jenny. *Women in Old Norse Society*. Ithaca, N.Y.: Cornell University Press, 1995.

Mágnusson, Mágnus. *Vikings!* New York: E. P. Dutton, 1980.

Marren, Peter. *1066: The Battles of York, Stamford Bridge, and Hastings*. Battleground Britain. Barnsley, U.K.: Leo Cooper, 2004.

Mawer, Allen. *The Vikings*. Cambridge: The University Press, 1930.

Nordstrom, Byron J. *Scandinavia since 1500*. Minneapolis: University of Minnesota Press, 2000.

Øye, Ingvild, ed. *Bergen and the German Hansa*. Bergen, Norway: Bryggens Museum, 1994.

Pulsiano, Phillip, ed. *Medieval Scandinavia: An Encyclopedia*. New York: Garland Press, 1993.

Rian, Øystein. *Embetsstanden i dansketida*. Oslo: Samlaget, 2003.

Sandvik, Hilde. *Kvinners rettslige handleevne på 1600- og 1700-tallet, med linjer fram til gifte kvinners myndighet i 1888*. Oslo: Unipub, 2002.

Sawyer, Birgit, and Peter Sawyer. *Medieval Scandinaia: From Conversion to Reformation circa 800–1500*. Minneapolis: University of Minnesota Press, 1993.

Sawyer, Peter. *Kings and Vikings: Scandinavia and Europe AD 700–1100*. London: Methuen, 1982.

Sogner, Sølvi, and Hilde Sandvik. "Minors in Law, Partners in Work, Equals in Worth? Women in the Norwegian Economy in the 16th to the 18th Centuries." In *La donna nell'economia secc. XIII–XVIII*, ed. Simonetta Cavaciocchi. Florence, Italy: Le Monnier, 1989.

Stummann Hansen, Steffen, and Klavs Randsborg, eds. *Vikings in the West*. Copenhagen, Denmark: Munksgaard, 2000.

Tønnesson, Kåre. "Tenancy, Freehold and Enclosure in Scandinavia from the Seventeenth to the Nineteenth Century." *Scandinavian Journal of History* 6 (1981): 191–206.

Urbánczyk, Przemysław. *Medieval Arctic Norway*. Warsaw: Semper, 1992.

Wilson, David M., ed. *The Northern World*. London: Thames and Hudson, 1980.

## 3. From the Constitution to the Present

Allen, Hilary. *Norway and Europe in the 1970s*. Oslo: Universitetsforlaget, 1979.

Amundsen, Kirsten. *Norway, NATO, and the Forgotten Soviet Challenge*. Berkeley, Calif.: Institute of International Studies, 1981.

Andenæs, Johannes, Olav Riste, and Magne Skodvin. *Norway and the Second World War*. Oslo: Tanum, 1966.

Barton, H. Arnold. *Sweden and Visions of Norway: Politics and Culture, 1814–1905*. Carbondale: Southern Illinois University Press, 2003.

Berg, Trond. *Growth and Development: The Norwegian Experience 1830–1980*. Oslo: NUPI, 1981.

Blegen, Theodore C. *The Norwegian Migration to America*. 2 vols. Northfield, Minn.: The Norwegian-American Historical Association, 1931–40.

Blom, Ida. "Women's Politics and Women in Politics in Norway since the End of the Nineteenth Century." In *Retrieving Women's History: Changing Perceptions of the Role of Women in Politics and Society*, ed. S. J. Kleinberg. Paris: UNESCO Press, 1988.

Cohen, Maynard M. *A Stand against Tyranny: Norway's Physicians and the Nazis*. Detroit, Mich.: Wayne State University Press, 1997.

Derry, Thomas Kingston. *A History of Modern Norway 1814–1972*. Oxford: Clarendon Press, 1983.

Eitrheim, Øyvind, Jan Tore Klovland, and Jan Fredrik Qvigstad, eds. *Historical Monetary Statistics for Norway, 1819–2003*. Norges banks skriftserie, no. 35. Oslo: Norges Bank, 2004.

Falnes, Oscar. *National Romanticism in Norway*. New York: Columbia University Press, 1933.

Fjaagesund, Peter, and Ruth A. Symes. *The Northern Utopia: British Perceptions of Norway in the Nineteenth Century*. Amsterdam: Rodopi, 2003.

Fladby, Rolf, and Tore Pryser. *Bygd og by under okkupasjonen*. Skrifter fra Norsk lokalhistorisk institutt, no. 12. Oslo: Norsk lokalhistorisk institutt, 1982.

Fuegner, Richard Stephen. *Beneath the Tyrant's Yoke: Norwegian Resistance to the German Occupation of Norway, 1940–1945*. Edina, Minn.: Beaver's Pond Press, 2003.

Furre, Berge. *Norsk historie. 1905–1940*. Oslo: Norske Samlaget, 1971.

Gjelsvik, T. *Norwegian Resistance 1940–1945*. Montreal: McGill-Queen's University Press, 1979

Greve, T. *Haakon VII of Norway*. London: Hippocrene Books, 1983.

Hagemann, Gro, and Hege Roll-Hansen, eds. *Twentieth-Century Housewives: Meanings and Implications of Unpaid Work*. Issues in Contemporary History. Oslo: Oslo Academic Press, 2005.

Hambro, Carl Joachim. *I Saw It Happen in Norway*. New York: D. Appleton-Century, 1940.

Hauge, Jens Christian. *The Liberation of Norway*. Oslo: Gyldendal, 1995.

Hellerud, Synnøve Veinan, and Jan Messel. *Oslo, a Thousand-Year History*. Oslo: Aschehoug, 2000.

Hodne, Fritz. *The Norwegian Economy 1920–1980*. New York: St. Martin's Press, 1983.

Hoidal, Oddvar K. *Quisling: A Study in Treason*. Oslo: Norwegian University Press, 1989.

Hubbard, William H., ed. *Making a Historical Culture: Historiography in Norway*. Oslo: Scandinavian University Press, 1995.

Kersaudy, François. *Norway 1940*. New York: St. Martin's Press, 1991.

Koht, Halvdan. *Norway: Neutral and Invaded*. New York: Macmillan, 1941.

Koht, Halvdan, and Sigmund Skard. *The Voice of Norway*. New York: Columbia University Press, 1944.

Lange, Even, and Helge Ø. Pharo. "Planning and Economic Policy in Norway 1945–1960." *Scandinavian Journal of History* 16 (1991): 215–28.

Leiren, Terje I. "Norwegian Independence and British Opinion: January to August 1814." *Scandinavian Studies* 47 (1975): 364–82.

Lieberman, Sima. *The Industrialisation of Norway, 1800–1920*. Oslo: Universitetsforlaget, 1970.

Lovoll, Odd S. *The Promise of America: A History of the Norwegian-American People*. Minneapolis: University of Minnesota Press, 1984.

Lucas, Colin. "Great Britain and the Union of Norway and Sweden." *Scandinavian Journal of History* 15 (1990): 269–78.

Lundestad, Geir. "The Evolution of Norwegian Security Policy: Alliance with the West and Reassurance in the East." *Scandinavian Journal of History* 17 (1992): 227–56.

Mann, Chris, and Christer Jörgensen. *Hitler's Arctic War: The German Campaigns in Norway, Finland, and the USSR, 1940–1945*. London: Brown Partworks, 2002.

Mendelsohn, Oskar. *The Persecution of the Norwegian Jews in WW II*. Oslo: Norges Hjemmefrontmuseum, 1991.

Milward, Alan. *The Fascist Economy in Norway*. Oxford: Clarendon Press, 1972.

Nerbøvik, Jostein. *Antiparlamentariske straumdrag i Noreg 1905–1914. Ei studie i motvilje*. Oslo: Universitetsforlaget, 1969.

———. *Bondevener og andre uvener: Ein studie frå Telemark*. Oslo: Samlaget, 1979.

——. *Norsk historie 1870–1905: frå jordbrukssamfunn mot organisasjon-ssamfunn*. Oslo: Samlaget, 1986.

Nissen, H. S., ed. *Scandinavia during the Second World War*. Minneapolis: University of Minnesota Press, 1983.

Olsen, Johan P. *Organized Democracy: Political Institutions in a Welfare State—The Case of Norway*. Oslo: Universitetsforlaget, 1980.

Petersen, Kaare. *The Saga of Norwegian Shipping: An Outline of the History, Growth and Development of a Modern Merchant Marine*. Oslo: Dreyer, 1955.

Pryser, Tore. *Hitlers hemmelige agenter: tysk etterretning i Norge 1939–1945*. Oslo: Universitetsforlaget, 2001.

——. *Norsk historie 1800–1870: frå standssamfunn mot klassesamfunn*. Oslo: Samlaget, 1985.

Riste, Olav. *The Neutral Ally: Norway's Relations with Belligerent Powers in the First World War*. Oslo: Universitetsforlaget, 1965.

——. *The Norwegian Intelligence Service: 1945–1970*. Cass series, Studies in Intelligence. London: Frank Cass, 1999.

Riste, Olav, and Berit Nøkleby. *Norway 1940–1945: The Resistance Movement*. Oslo: Aschehoug, 1973.

Robertson, Edwin Hanton. *Bishop of the Resistance: A Life of Eivind Berggrav, Bishop of Oslo, Norway*. St. Louis, Mo.: Concordia, 2000.

Sandnes, Jørn, ed. *Trondheim: One Thousand Years in the City of St. Olav*. Trondheim, Norway: Committee of City History, 1992.

Semmingsen, Ingrid. *Norway to America: A History of the Emigration*. Minneapolis: University of Minnesota Press, 1978.

Sønsteby, Gunnar. *Report from #24*. Fort Lee, N.J.: Barricade Books, 1999.

Thompson, David. *The Norwegian Armed Forces and Defense Policy, 1905–1955*. Lewiston, N.Y.: Edwin Mellen Press, 2004.

Udgaard, Nils Morten. *Great Power Politics and Norwegian Foreign Policy: A Study of Norway's Foreign Relations November 1940–February 1948*. Oslo: Universitetsforlaget, 1973.

Worm-Müller, Jacob S. *Norway Revolts against the Nazis*. London: L. Drummond, 1941.

## III. POLITICS

### 1. Government

Archer, Clive. *Norway outside the European Union: Norway and European Integration from 1994 to 2004*. Europe and the Nation State, no. 5. London: Routledge, 2005.

Archer, Clive, and Ingrid Sogner. *Norway, European Integration and Atlantic Security*. London: Sage, 1998.

Baldersheim, Harald, and Jean-Pascal Daloz. *Political Leadership in a Global Age: The Experience of France and Norway*. Aldershot, Hants, U.K.: Ashgate, 2003.

Brundtland, Gro Harlem. *The Politics of Oil: A View from Norway*. A. J. Meyer Memorial Lecture series. Cambridge, Mass.: Energy and Environmental Policy Center, John F. Kennedy School of Government, Harvard University, 1987.

Christensen, Tom, and B. Guy Peters. *Structure, Culture, and Governance: A Comparison of Norway and the United States*. Lanham, Md.: Rowman and Littlefield, 1999.

Council of Europe. *Structure and Operation of Local and Regional Democracy: Norway: Situation in 1997*. Strasbourg, France: Council of Europe, 1998.

Fossen, Erling. *Ni skritt mot en moderne stat*. Oslo: Pax, 1994.

Furre, Berge, and Ingolf Håkon Teigene. *Forsvar for fred*. Oslo: Pax, 1983.

Grønlie, Tore, ed. *Forvaltning for politikk: Norsk forvaltningspolitikk etter 1945*. Bergen, Norway: Fagbokforlaget, 1999.

Heidar, Knut. *Norway: Elites on Trial*. Nations of the Modern World. Boulder, Colo.: Westview Press, 2001.

Henriksen, Joan. *Norwegian Politics: A Primer for Non-Norwegians*. Oslo: Aschehoug, 1991.

Ingebritsen, Christine. *Scandinavia in World Politics*. Lanham, Md.: Rowman and Littlefield, 2006.

Jenssen, Anders Todal, Pertti Pesonen, and Mikael Gilljam, eds. *To Join or Not to Join: Three Nordic Referendums on Membership in the European Union*. Oslo: Scandinavian University Press, 1998.

Mathisen, Gunnar. *Stat, kjære stat: Om forholdet mellom politikk og administrasjon i den norske statsforvaltningen*. Oslo: Tano, 1988.

Neumann, Iver B., and Ole Jacob Sending, eds. *Regjering i Norge*. Oslo: Pax, 2003.

Nordby, Trond, ed. *Storting og regjering 1945–1985: Institusjoner, rekruttering*. Oslo: Kunnskapsforlaget, 1985.

Olsen, Johan P. *Organized Democracy: Political Institutions in a Welfare State, the Case of Norway*. Bergen, Norway: Universitetsforlaget, 1983.

Østerud, Øyvind, ed. *Norway in Transition: Transforming a Stable Democracy*. The West European Politics series. London: Routledge, 2007.

Rommetvedt, Hilmar. *The Rise of the Norwegian Parliament*. Library of legislative studies. London: F. Cass, 2003.

Waage, Hilde Henriksen. *Norwegians? Who Needs Norwegians?: Explaining the Oslo Back Channel: Norway's Political Past in the Middle East*. Oslo: Royal Norwegian Ministry of Foreign Affairs, 2000.

Wolf, Maria. *Youth Policy in Norway: Report by the International Team of Experts Appointed by the Council of Europe.* Strasbourg, France: Council of Europe, 2004.

## 2. Law

Andenæs, Mads Tønnesson, and Ingeborg Wilberg. *The Constitution of Norway: A Commentary.* Oslo: Universitetsforlaget, 1987.

Bø, Bente Puntervold. *Immigration Control, Law, and Morality: Visa Policies towards Visitors and Asylum Seekers. An Evaluation of the Norwegian Visa Policies within a Legal and Moral Frame of Reference.* Oslo: Unipub, 2002.

Borvik, Bjørnar. *The Norwegian Approach to Protection of Personality Rights: With a Special Emphasis on the Protection of Honour and Reputation.* Bergen, Norway: Fagbokforlaget, 2004.

Falkanger, Thor, Hans Jacob Bull, and Lasse Brautaset. *Introduction to Norwegian Maritime Law.* Oslo: Sjørettsfondet, 1987.

Gisle, Jon, ed. *Aschehoug og Gyldendals store norske leksikon. Lov og rett.* Oslo: Kunnskapsforlaget, 1995.

Gundersen, Fridtjof Frank, and Sverre Faafeng Langfeldt. *Lov og rett for næringslivet.* Oslo: Focus, 1990.

Holder, Harold D. *European Integration and Nordic Alcohol Policies: Changes in Alcohol Controls and Consequences in Finland, Norway and Sweden, 1980–1997.* Aldershot, Hants, U.K.: Ashgate, 1998.

Johnsen, Jon T. *Juss-Buss and Clinical Legal Education.* Publications from Institute for Sociology of Law. Oslo: University of Oslo, 1991.

Kjønstad, Asbjørn. *Norwegian Social Law.* Oslo: Norwegian University Press, 1987.

Krohn, Mads. *Norwegian Petroleum Law.* Oslo: Sjørettsfondet, 1978.

Mykland, Knut, Torkel Opsahl, and Guttorm Hansen. *Norges grunnlov i 175 år.* Oslo: Gyldendal, 1989.

Smith, Lucy, and Peter Lødrup. *Children and Parents: The Relationship between Children and Parents According to Norwegian Law.* Oslo: Ad Notam, 1991.

## 3. Political Parties

Brundtland, Gro Harlem. *Madam Prime Minister: A Life in Power and Politics.* New York: Farrar, Straus and Giroux, 2002.

Dagre, Tor. *Norway's Political Parties.* Oslo: Norwegian Ministry of Foreign Affairs, 1990.

Grepstad, Ottar, and Jostein Nerbøvik, eds. *Venstres hundre år*. Oslo: Gyldendal, 1984.

Grofman, Bernard, and Arend Lijphart, eds. *The Evolution of Electoral and Party Systems in the Nordic Countries*. New York: Agathon Press, 2002.

Halvorsen, Terje. *Partiets salt: AUFs historie*. Oslo: Pax, 2003.

Heidar, Knut. *Partidemokrati på prøve: Norske partieliter i demokratisk perspektiv*. Oslo: Universitetsforlaget, 1988.

Isaksen, Guttorm. *Ryddesjau: Arbeiderpartiet i maktens ruiner*. Oslo: Aschehoug, 2001.

Listhaug, Ola. *Citizens, Parties, and Norwegian Electoral Politics, 1957–1985: An Empirical Study*. Trondheim, Norway: Tapir, 1989.

Matthews, Donald R., and Henry Valen. *Parliamentary Representation: The Case of the Norwegian Storting*. Parliaments and Legislatures series. Columbus: Ohio State University Press, 1999.

Saeter, Martin. *Socialist Parties in Norway: Their European and Atlantic Profiles*. Oslo: Norsk Utenrikspolitisk Institutt, 1976.

Saglie, Jo. *Standpunkter og strategi: EU-saken i norsk partipolitikk 1989–1994*. Oslo: Unipax, 2002.

Shaffer, William R. *Politics, Parties, and Parliaments: Political Change in Norway*. Parliaments and Legislatures series. Columbus: Ohio State University Press, 1998.

Sjøli, Hans Petter. *Mao, min Mao: Historien om AKPs vekst og fall*. Oslo: Cappelen, 2005.

Strom, Kaare, and Lars Svåsand, eds. *Challenges to Political Parties: The Case of Norway*. Ann Arbor: University of Michigan Press, 1997.

Valen, Henry, and Daniel Katz. *Political Parties in Norway: A Community Study*. Oslo: Universitetsforlaget, 1964.

## IV. ECONOMY

### 1. Agriculture

Almås, Reidar, and Brynjulv Gjerdåker, eds. *Norwegian Agricultural History*. Trondheim, Norway: Tapir Academic, 2004.

Edland, Åsulv, ed. *Norsk landbruk og EF:Åtte artiklar om landbrukspolitikk, EF, EØS og GATT*. Oslo: Landbruksforlaget, 1993.

Furre, Berge. *Mjølk, bønder, og tingmenn: Studiar i organisasjon og politikk kring omsetninga av visse landbruksvarer 1929–30*. Oslo: Det Norske Samlaget, 1971.

Hammond, Jerome W. *Targeting Agricultural Policies in Norway for Income Maintenance and Rural Development*. St. Paul: Department of Agricultural and Applied Economics, University of Minnesota, 1990.

Nerbøvik, Jostein. *Bønder i kamp: Bygdefolkets krisehjelp 1925–35*. Oslo: Samlaget, 1991.

Organizsation for Economic Co-operation and Development. *National Policies and Agricultural Trade: Country Study, Norway*. Paris: Organiszation for Economic Co-operation and Development, 1990.

Tranberg, Anna, and Knut Sprauten, eds. *Norsk bondeøkonomi 1650–1850*. Oslo: Samlaget, 1996.

## 2. Industry

Børmer, Øystein. *Fjerning av tekniske handelshindre i EØS: Virkninger for norsk industri*. Oslo: Norsk utenrikspolitisk institutt, 1994.

Bruland, Kristine, ed. *Technology Transfer and Scandinavian Industralisation*. New York: Berg, 1992.

Hansen, Thorvald Buch, and Leif Berge. *Offshore Adventure: A Pictorial History of the Norwegian Petroleum Industry*. Oslo: Universitetsforlaget, 1982.

Kvinge, Torunn. *Utenlandske oppkjøp og etableringer i norsk industri: motiver, omfang og utvikling*. Oslo: Forskningsstiftelsen FAFO, 1994.

Møen, Jarle. *Produktivitetsutviklingen i norsk industri 1980–1990: En analyse av dynamikken basert på mikrodata*. Oslo: Statistisk sentralbyrå, 1998.

Noreng, Øystein. *The Oil Industry and Government Strategy in the North Sea*. London: Croom Helm, 1980.

*Norway's Industry: A Short Review of Its Development and Present Position*. Oslo: Federation of Norwegian Industries and the Norwegian Ministry of Foreign Affairs, 1958.

Shaffer, Ron E., and David W. Fischer. *Local and National Impacts from Landing North Sea Gas in Western Norway*. Bergen, Norway: Industriøkonomisk institutt, 1982.

Solheim, Anders, ed. *Ormen Lange: An Integrated Study for Safe Field Development in the Storegga Submarine Slide Area*. Amsterdam: Elsevier, 2005.

## 3. Finance

Akram, Qaisar Farooq. *When Does the Oil Price Affect the Norwegian Exchange Rate?* Oxford: Department of Economics, Oxford University, 2000.

*Banking in the EU, Switzerland and Norway 1996: Structures of the Financial Markets*. London: FT Financial, 1996.

Gerdrup, Karsten R. *Three Episodes of Financial Fragility in Norway since the 1890s.* BIS Working Papers, no. 142. Basel, Switzerland: Bank for International Settlements, Monetary and Economic Department, 2003.

International Monetary Fund. *Norway: Financial System Stability Assessment, Including Reports on the Observance of Standards and Codes on the Following Topics: Banking Supervision, Insurance Regulation, and Payment Systems.* IMF Country Report, no. 05/200. Washington, D.C.: International Monetary Fund, 2005.

Moe, Thorvald, Jon A. Solheim, and Bent Vale. *Norwegian Banking Crisis.* Norges banks skriftserie, no. 33. Oslo: Norges Bank, 2004.

Ongena, Steven, David C. Smith, and Dag Michalsen. *Firms and Their Distressed Banks: Lessons from the Norwegian Banking Crisis (1988–1991).* International Finance Discussion Papers, no. 686. Washington, D.C.: Board of Governors of the Federal Reserve System, 2000.

Roland, Kjell, Victor D. Norman, and Torger Reve, eds. *Rikdommens problem: Oljeformue, eierskap og fremtidens pensjoner.* Oslo: Universitetsforlaget, 2001.

Soikkeli, Jarkko. *Norway, Selected Issues.* IMF Country Report, no. 02/45. Washington, D.C.: International Monetary Fund, 2002.

## 4. Trade

Al-Kasim, Farouk. *Managing Petroleum Resources: The "Norwegian Model" in a Broad Perspective.* Oxford: Oxford Institute for Energy Studies, 2006.

Bergesen, Helge Ole, and Anne Kristin Sydnes, eds. *Naive Newcomer or Shrewd Salesman? Norway: A Major Oil and Gas Exporter.* Lysaker, Norway: Fridtjof Nansen Institute, 1990.

Bjerkholt, Olav, Øystein Olsen, and Jon Vislie, eds. *Recent Modelling Approaches in Applied Energy Economics.* International Studies in Economic Modelling. London: Chapman and Hall, 1990.

Fagerberg, Jan, and Lars Lundberg, eds. *European Economic Integration: A Nordic Perspective.* Aldershot, Hants, U.K.: Avebury, 1993.

Frengen, Geir, Frank Foyn, and Richard Ragnarsøn. *Innovation in Norwegian Manufacturing and Oil Extraction in 1992.* Oslo: Statistisk sentralbyrå, 1995.

Kindingstad, Torbjørn, and Fredrik Hagemann, eds. *Norwegian Oil History.* Stavanger, Norway: Wigestrand, 2002.

Matlary, Janne Haaland. *Norway's New Interdependence with the European Community: The Political and Economic Implications of Gas Trade.* NUPI rapport, no. 141. Oslo: Norsk Utenrikspolitisk Institutt, 1990.

Melchior, Arne. *Intra-Industry Trade, a Matter of Scale or Skills? Evidence from Norwegian Data, 1976–1991*. Oslo: Norwegian Institute of International Affairs, 1994.

Müller-Graff, Peter-Christian, and Erling Selvig, eds. *The European Economic Area: Norway's Basic Status in the Legal Construction of Europe*. Deutschnorwegisches Forum des Rechts, Bd. 1. Berlin: Berlin Verlag Arno Spitz, 1997.

Valvåg, Ola R. *Technology Transfer through Networks: Experiences from the Norwegian Seafood Industry*. FAO Fisheries Circular, no.1004. Rome: Food and Agriculture Organization of the United Nations, 2005.

## 5. Development

Aase, Tor Halfdan. *Oil and Decentralization: Offshore Petroleum Commuting and Local Spin-Offs in Rural Norway*. St. John's, Newfoundland: Institute of Social and Economic Research, Memorial University of Newfoundland, 1990.

El Mallakh, Ragaei, Øystein Noreng, and Barry Warren Poulson. *Petroleum and Economic Development: The Cases of Mexico and Norway*. Lexington, Mass.: Lexington Books, 1984.

*Environment and Development: Norwegian Policy Regarding Global Sustainable Development*. Oslo: Royal Norwegian Ministry of Foreign Affairs, 1988.

Greenwood, Robert Marshall. *The Local State and Economic Development in Peripheral Regions: A Comparative Study of Newfoundland and Northern Norway*. Coventry, U.K.: University of Warwick, 1991.

*National Strategy for Sustainable Development*. Oslo: Royal Norwegian Ministry of Foreign Affairs, 2002.

Norbye, Ole David Koht, and Arve Ofstad, eds. *Norwegian Development Aid Experiences: A Review of Evaluation Studies 1986–92*. Oslo: Royal Ministry of Foreign Affairs, 1996.

Persson, Karl Gunnar, ed. *The Economic Development of Denmark and Norway since 1870*. An Elgar Reference Collection, no. 2. Aldershot, Hants, U.K.: E. Elgar, 1993.

Wood, Kenneth Scott. *The North Norway Plan: A Study in Regional Economic Development*. Development Research Monographs, no. 3. Bergen, Norway: The Chr. Michelsen Institute, 1965.

## 6. Labor

Colbjørnsen, Tom. *Dividers in the Labor Market*. Oslo: Norwegian University Press, 1986.

De Coninck-Smith, Ning, Bengt Sandin, and Ellen Schrumpf, eds. *Industrious Children: Work and Childhood in the Nordic Countries, 1850–1990.* Odense, Denmark: Odense University Press, 1997.

Dølvik, Jon Erik, and Arild H. Steen, eds. *Making Solidarity Work: The Norwegian Labour Market in Transition.* Oslo: Scandinavian University Press, 1997.

Hagemann, Gro. *Kjønn og industrialisering.* Oslo: Universitetsforlaget, 1994.

Hippe, Jon Mathias. *Bargaining, Politics, and Solidarity: A Different Story? A Study of Employment Relations and Occupational Welfare in Norway.* Oslo: Fafo, Institute for Applied Social Science, 1997.

Hunnes, Arngrim, Jarle Møen, and Kjell G. Salvanes. *Wage Structure and Labor Mobility in Norway, 1980–1997.* Cambridge, Mass.: National Bureau of Economic Research, 2007.

Melkas, Helinä, and Richard Anker. *Gender Equality and Occupational Segregation in Nordic Labour Markets.* Geneva: International Labour Office, 1998.

Olstad, Finn. *Arbeiderklassens vekst og fall: Hovedlinjer i 100 års norsk historie.* Oslo: Universitetsforlaget, 1991.

Ringdal, Kristen. *Labour Market Structures and Social Mobility in Norway: A Study in Homogeneity and Segmentation.* Trondheim, Norway: Department of Sociology, University of Trondheim, 1990.

Stølen, Nils Martin. *Wage Formation and the Macroeconomic Function of the Norwegian Labour Market.* Oslo: Statistisk sentralbyrå, 1995.

## 7. Transport and Communications

Dalen, Dag Morten, and Andrés Gómez-Lobo. *Regulation and Incentive Contracts: An Empirical Investigation of the Norwegian Bus Transport Industry.* IFS Working Paper series, no. W96/8. London: Institute for Fiscal Studies, 1996.

Hetland, Per. *Exploring Hybrid Communities: Telecommunications on Trial.* Oslo: Department of Media and Communication, University of Oslo, 1996.

Hompland, Andreas, ed. *Byens veier: Lokal transport- og arealpolitikk.* Bergen, Norway: Fagbokforlaget, 2001.

Jean-Hansen, Viggo, and Odd Skarstad. *Impacts of European Integration on the Norwegian Road Transport Industry: The Sector Study Norway.* Oslo: Transportøkonomisk institutt, 1994.

Odeck, James. *Measuring Productivity Growth and Efficiency with Data Envelopment Analysis: An Application on the Norwegian Road Sector.* Göteborg, Sweden: Göteborgs universitet, 1993.

*Sector Report: Norway: Telecommunications.* London: Foreign and Commonwealth Office and Department of Trade and Industry, 1994.

# V. SOCIETY

## 1. Anthropology

Anderson, Myrdene. *Preliminary Remarks in Saami Ethnoecology: Resource Management in Norwegian Lapland*. West Lafayette, Ind.: Institute for the Study of Social Change, Department of Sociology and Anthropology, Purdue University, 1978.

Barth, Fredrik. *Ethnic Groups and Boundaries: The Social Organization of Culture Difference*. Oslo: Pensumtjenesten, 1994.

Braarvig, Jens, and Thomas Krogh, eds. *In Search of Symbols: An Explorative Study*. Oslo: Novus forlag, 1997.

Eidheim, Harald. *Aspects of the Lappish Minority Situation*. Oslo: Department of Social Anthropology, University of Oslo, 1987.

Krupnik, Igor, Rachel Mason, and Tonia W. Horton, eds. *Northern Ethnographic Landscapes: Perspectives from Circumpolar Nations*. Washington, D.C.: Arctic Studies Center, National Museum of Natural History, Smithsonian Institution in collaboration with the National Park Service, 2004.

Kyllingstad, Jon Røyne. *Kortskaller og langskaller: Fysisk antropologi i Norge og striden om det nordiske herremennesket*. Oslo: SAP, 2004.

Odner, Knut. *The Varanger Saami: Habitation and Economy, AD 1200–1900*. Oslo: Institute of Social Anthropology, Oslo University, 1989.

Rugkåsa, Marianne, and Kari Trædal Thorsen, eds. *Nære steder, nye rom: Utfordringer i antropologiske studier i Norge*. Oslo: Gyldendal akademisk, 2003.

Vorren, Ørnulv, and Ernst Manker. *Lapp Life and Customs: A Survey*. London: Oxford University Press, 1975.

## 2. Sociology

Almås, Reidar, K. Vik, and J. Ødegaard. *Women in Rural Norway: Recent Tendencies in the Development of the Division of Labour in Agriculture and the Participation of Rural Women on the Labour Market*. Trondheim, Norway: University of Trondheim, 1983.

Andersson, Mette. *Urban Multi-Culture in Norway: Identity Formation among Immigrant Youth*. Mellen Studies in Sociology, vol. 51. Lewiston, N.Y.: Edwin Mellen Press, 2005.

Eriksen, John. *Sociology of the Family in Norway in the 1970's: Expansion and Applicability*. Oslo: Institutt for anvendt sosialvitenskapelig forskning, 1980.

Holdsworth, C. M., and D. H. J. Morgan. *The Transition Out of the Parental Home in Britain, Spain and Norway*. Swindon, U.K.: Economic and Social Research Council, 2003.

Mjøset, Lars. *Kontroverser i norsk sosiologi*. Oslo: Universitetsforlaget, 1991.

Selid, Betty. *Women in Norway: Their Position in Family Life, Employment and Society*. Oslo: The Norwegian Joint Committee on International Social Policy in Association with the Department of Cultural Relations, Royal Ministry of Foreign Affairs, 1970.

Sweetser, Dorrian Apple. *Urban Norwegians: Kinship Networks, and Sibling Mobility*. Oslo: Institute of Applied Social Research, 1973.

Wikan, Unni. *Mot en ny norsk underklasse: Innvandrere, kultur og integrasjon*. Oslo: Gyldendal, 1995.

## 3. Education

Bleiklie, Ivar, Roar Høstaker, and Agnete Vabø. *Policy and Practice in Higher Education: Reforming Norwegian Universities*. Higher Education Policy series, no. 49. London: J. Kingsley, 2000.

Eide, Kjell. *Problems in Education and Employment in Norway*. Paris: UNESCO, 1976.

Einarsdottir, Johanna, and Judith T. Wagner, eds. *Nordic Childhoods and Early Education: Philosophy, Research, Policy, and Practice in Denmark, Finland, Iceland, Norway, and Sweden*. International Perspectives on Educational Policy, Research, and Practice. Greenwich, Conn.: Information Age, 2006.

Fetveit, Anne Marie. *Alternatives to Universities in Higher Education: Country Study, Norway*. Paris: Organisation for Economic Co-operation and Development, 1988.

Fredriksen, Birger. *Main Trends in Norwegian Higher Education since 1960*. Oslo: Norsk Utenrikspolitisk Institutt, 1984.

Organisation for Economic Co-operation and Development. *Lifelong Learning in Norway*. Reviews of National Policies for Education. Paris: OECD, 2002.

Tønnessen, Liv Kari. *Norsk utdanningshistorie: En innføring*. Oslo: Universitetsforlaget, 1995.

## 4. Religion

Amundsen, Arne Bugge, ed. *Norges religionshistorie*. Oslo: Universitetsforlaget, 2005.

Aukrust, Knut, and Berge Furre, eds. *Diakoni og samfunn*. Oslo: Norges forskningsråd, 1998.

Bloch-Hoell, Nils E. *Religion in Norway*. Oslo: International Summer School, 1987.

Furre, Berge. *Soga om Lars Oftedal*. Oslo: Norske samlaget, 1990.

Furseth, Inger. *A Comparative Study of Social and Religious Movements in Norway, 1780s–1905.* Lewiston, N.Y.: Edwin Mellen Press, 2002.

Hale, Frederick. *Norwegian Religious Pluralism: A Trans-Atlantic Comparison.* Texts and Studies in Religion, vol. 59. Lewiston, N.Y.: Edwin Mellen Press, 1992.

Haslam, Gerald M. *Clash of Cultures: The Norwegian Experience with Mormonism, 1842–1920.* American University Studies, vol. 7. New York: Peter Lang, 1984.

Hassing, Arne. *Religion and Power: The Case of Methodism in Norway.* Lake Junaluska, N.C.: General Commission on Archives and History, the United Methodist Church, 1980.

Jacobsen, Knut A, ed. *Verdensreligioner i Norge.* Oslo: Universitetsforlaget, 2001.

Molland, Einar. *Church Life in Norway 1800–1850.* Minneapolis: Augsburg Publishing House, 1957.

## VI. CULTURE

## 1. Archeology

Blindheim, Charlotte, Birgit Heyerdahl-Larsen, and Roar L. Tollnes. *Kaupangfunnene.* Norske oldfunn, no. 11. Oslo: Universitets oldsaksamling, 1981.

Boaz, Joel. *Hunter-Gatherer Site Variability: Changing Patterns of Site Utilization in the Interior of Eastern Norway between 8000 and 2500 B.P.* Universitetets oldsaksamlings skrifter, new series, no. 20. Oslo: Universitetets oldsaksamling, 1998.

———. *The Mesolithic of Central Scandinavia.* Universitetets oldsaksamlings skrifter, new series, no. 22. Oslo: Universitetets Oldsaksamling, 1999.

Christensen, Arne Emil, Anne Stine Ingstad, and Bjørn Myhre. *Osebergdronningens grav: Vår arkeologiske nasjonalskatt i nytt lys.* Oslo: Schibsted, 1992.

Hansen, Gitte. *Bergen c. 800–c. 1170: The Emergence of a Town.* The Bryggen Papers, no. 6. Bergen, Norway: Fagbokforlaget, 2005.

Larsen, Arne J. *Footwear from the Gullskoen Area of Bryggen.* Bryggen Papers, vol. 4. Bergen, Norway: University of Bergen, 1992.

Munch, Gerd Stamsø, Olav Sverre Johansen, and Else Roesdahl, eds. *Borg in Lofoten: A Chieftain's Farm in North Norway.* Arkeologisk skriftserie, no. 1. Trondheim, Norway: Tapir Academic Press, 2003.

Myhre, Lise Nordenborg. *Trialectic Archaeology: Monuments and Space in Southwest Norway, 1700–500 BC.* Stavanger, Norway: Arkeologisk museum i Stavanger, 2004.

Næroy, Arne Johan. *Stone Age Living Spaces in Western Norway*. BAR International series, no. 857. Oxford: Archaeopress, 2000.

Øye, Ingvild, ed. *Medieval Fishing Tackle from Bergen and Borgland*. The Bryggen Papers, vol. 5. Bergen, Norway: Fagbokforlaget, 2004.

Selsing, Lotte, ed. *Norwegian Quaternary Botany 2000*. Stavanger, Norway: Arkeologisk museum i Stavanger, 2000.

Simonsen, Povl. *Steinalderbosetningen i sandbukt på Sørøya, Vest-Finnmark: Rapport og tolkning*. Tromsø, Norway: Tromsø Museum, 1996.

Simpson, David N. *Archaeological Investigations at Krossnes, Flatøy, 1988–1991*. Bergen, Norway: Historisk Museum, Universitetet i Bergen, 1992.

Skre, Dagfinn, and Frans-Arne Stylegar. *Kaupang: The Viking Town, the Kaupang Exhibition at UKM, Oslo, 2004–2005*. Oslo: University of Oslo, University Museum of Cultural History, 2004.

Sognnes, Kalle, ed. *Rock Art in Landscapes—Landscapes in Rock Art*. Trondheim, Norway: Tapir akademisk forlag, 2003.

Solberg, Bergljot. *Jernalderen i Norge: ca. 500 f. Kr.–1030 e. Kr*. Oslo: Cappelen akademisk forlag, 2000.

Solli, Brit. *Narratives of Veøy: An Investigation into the Poetics and Scientifics of Archaeology*. Universitetets oldsaksamlings skrifter, no. 19. Oslo: Universitetet i Oslo, 1996.

Vinsrygg, Synnøve. *Merovingartid i Nord-Noreg: Studie i utvalt materiale frå gravfunn*. Arkeologiske avhandlinger fra Historisk museum, Universitetet i Bergen, no. 2. Bergen, Norway: Historisk museum, Universitetet i Bergen, 1979.

## 2. Architecture

Almaas, Ingerid Helsing. *Norway: A Guide to Recent Architecture*. London: Batsford, 2002.

Bergan, Gunvor Øverland, and Trinelise Dysthe. *Hjemme i Norge: Tradisjon og fornyelse*. Oslo: Cappelen, 1994.

Brekke, Nils Georg, Per Jonas Nordhagen, and Siri Skjold Lexau. *Norsk arkitekturhistorie: Frå steinalder og bronsealder til det 21. hundreåret*. Oslo: Samlaget, 2003.

Elton, Lars, and Petter T. Moshus, eds. *Norsk olympisk design: Design og arkitektur til de XVII olympiske vinterleker Lillehammer 1994*. Oslo: Norsk forum, 1995.

Grønvold, Ulf, ed. *Architecture from Norway: Buildings, Architects, History*. Oslo: Nasjonalmuseet for Kunst, Arkitektur og Design, 2005.

Holan, Jerri. *Norwegian Wood: A Tradition of Building*. New York: Rizzoli, 1990.

Liepe, Lena. *Medieval Stone Churches of Northern Norway: The Interpretation of Architecture as a Historical Process*. Tromsø, Norway: Universitetsbiblioteket, 2001.

Martens, Johan-Ditlef. *Norwegian Housing*. Oslo: Norsk Arkitekturforlag, 1993.

Norberg-Schulz, Christian. *Modern Norwegian Architecture*. Oslo: Norwegian University Press, 1986.

Stigum, Hilmar, and Torill Sand. *Building Customs*. Oslo: Institute for Folkelivsgransking, 1972.

Thiis-Evensen, Thomas, Sissi Solem Winge, and Svein Aamold. *The Norwegian Parliament: Its Art and Architecture*. Oslo: Stortinget, 2000.

Tostrup, Elisabeth. *Architecture and Rhetoric: Text and Design in Architectural Competitions, Oslo, 1939–97*. London: Andreas Papdakis, 1999.

———. *Norwegian Wood: The Thoughtful Architecture of Wenche Selmer*. Princeton, N.J.: Princeton Architectural Press, 2006.

## 3. Arts

Bay Sjøvold, Aase. *Norwegian Tapestries*. Oslo: C. Huitfeldt Forlag, 1982.

Bringaker, Arve, and Louise E. Shaw. *Between Space and Time: Contemporary Norwegian Sculpture and Installation*. Oslo: Association of Norwegian Sculptors, 2000.

Bryne, Arvid. *They Painted Norway: Glimpses of Norwegian Nature and Norwegian Artists*. Oslo: Andresen and Butenschøn, 2004.

Danbolt, Gunnar. *Norsk kunsthistorie: Bilde og skulptur frå vikingtida til i dag*. Oslo: Samlaget, 1997.

Goertzen, Chris. *Fiddling for Norway: Revival and Identity*. Chicago Studies in Ethnomusicology. Chicago: University of Chicago Press, 1997.

Grimley, Daniel M. *Grieg: Music, Landscape and Norwegian Identity*. Woodbridge, U.K.: Boydell Press, 2006.

Grinde, Nils. *A History of Norwegian Music*. Lincoln: University of Nebraska Press, 1991.

Hale, Nathan Cabot, and David Finn. *Embrace of Life: The Sculpture of Gustav Vigeland*. New York: H. N. Abrams, 1969.

Hauglid, Roar. *Native Art of Norway*. New York: Praeger, 1967.

Heller, Reinhold. *Edvard Munch: The Scream*. New York: Viking Press, 1973.

Hohler, Erla Bergendahl, Nigel J. Morgan, Anne Wichstrøm, Unn Plahter, and Bjørn Kaland. *Painted Altar Frontals of Norway, 1250–1350*. London: Archetype, 2004.

Jerman, Gunnar, ed. *A Cultural Odyssey: Focus on Norwegian Art*. Oslo: Index, 1997.

Kleivi, Bjørg Oseid. *Rosemaling: Decorative Painting from Norway*. Norway: Boksenteret Forlag, 1995.

Lange, Kristian, and Arne Østvedt. *Norwegian Music: A Brief Survey*. London: D. Dobson, 1958.

Lincoln, Louise, ed. *The Art of Norway: 1750–1914*. Minneapolis, Minn.: Minneapolis Institute of Arts, 1978.

Pahlke, Rosemarie E., ed. *Munch Revisited: Edvard Munch and the Art of Today*. Dortmund, Germany: Museum am Ostwall, 2005.

Parmann, Øistein. *Norwegian Sculpture: With 131 Plates*. Oslo: Dreyer, 1969.

Prelinger, Elizabeth. *After the Scream: The Late Paintings of Edvard Munch*. New Haven, Conn.: Yale University Press, 2002.

Prideaux, Sue. *Edvard Munch: Behind the Scream*. New Haven, Conn.: Yale University Press, 2005.

Wikborg, Tone. *Guide to the Vigeland Park in Oslo*. Oslo: Normanns kunstforlag, 1991.

## 4. Literature

Andersen, Per Thomas. *Norsk litteraturhistorie*. Oslo: Universitetsforlaget, 2001.

Garton, Janet. *Norwegian Woman Writers, 1850–1990*. London: Athlone Press, 1992.

Haugen, Einar. *Ibsen's Drama: Author to Audience*. Minneapolis: University of Minnesota Press, 1979.

Kittang, Atle. *Ibsens heroisme: Frå Brand til Når vi døde vågner*. Oslo: Gyldendal, 2002.

Koht, Halvdan. *Life of Ibsen*. New York: Blom, 1971.

Lyngstad, Sverre. *Sigurd Hoel's Fiction: Cultural Criticism and Tragic Vision*. Westport, Conn.: Greenwood Press, 1984.

Meyer, Michael. *Ibsen: A Biography*. Harmondsworth, U.K.: Penguin, 1974.

Naess, Harald S., ed. *A History of Norwegian Literature*. Lincoln: University of Nebraska Press, 1993.

Rasmussen, Janet. "Dreams and Discontent: The Female Voice in Norwegian Literature." *Review of National Literatures* 12 (1983): 123–40.

Rees, Ellen. *On the Margins: Nordic Women Modernists of the 1930s*. Norwich, U.K.: Norvik Press, 2005.

Sjåvik, Jan. *Historical Dictionary of Scandinavian Literature and Theater*. Lanham, Md.: Scarecrow Press, 2006.

———. *Reading for the Truth: Rhetorical Constructions in Norwegian Fiction*. Christchurch, New Zealand: Cybereditions, 2004.

Templeton, Joan. *Ibsen's Women*. Cambridge: Cambridge University Press, 1997.

Thresher, Tanya. *Cecilie Løveid: Engendering a Dramatic Tradition*. Scandinavian Women Writers, vol. 2. Laksevåg, Norway: Alvheim and Eide, 2005.

Zagar, Monika. *Ideological Clowns: Dag Solstad—From Modernism to Politics*. Vienna, Austria: Praesens, 2002.

## 5. Linguistics

Åfarli, Tor A. *The Syntax of Norwegian Passive Constructions*. Amsterdam: J. Benjamins, 1992.

Andvik, Eric E. *A Pragmatic Analysis of Norwegian Modal Particles*. Dallas, Texas: Summer Institute of Linguistics, 1992.

Borthen, Kaja. *Bare Singulars in Norwegian*. Trondheim, Norway: Department of Linguistics, NTNU, 1991.

Fiva, Toril. *Possessor Chains in Norwegian*. Tromsø-studier i språkvitenskap, vol. 9. Oslo: Novus Forlag, 1987.

Haugen, Einar. *Language Conflict and Language Planning: The Case of Modern Norwegian*. Cambridge, Mass.: Harvard University Press, 1966.

Haugland, Kjell. *Striden om skulespråket: Frå 1860-åra til 1902*. Oslo: Samlaget, 1985.

Hellan, Lars. *Anaphora in Norwegian and the Theory of Grammar*. Studies in Generative Grammar, no. 32. Dordrecht: Foris, 1988.

Jahr, Ernst Håkon, ed. *Sociolinguistics in Norway*. International Journal of the Sociology of Language, no. 115. Berlin: Mouton de Gruyter, 1995.

Jahr, Ernst Håkon, and Olav Skare, eds. *Nordnorske dialektar*. Oslo: Novus, 1996.

Kleiven, Jo, ed. *Språk og samfunn: Bidrag til en norsk sosiolingvistikk*. Oslo: Pax, 1979.

Kristoffersen, Gjert. *The Phonology of Norwegian*. New York: Oxford University Press, 2000.

Larson, Karen A. *Learning without Lessons: Socialization and Language Change in Norway*. Lanham, Md.: University Press of America, 1985.

Linn, Andrew Robert. *Constructing the Grammars of a Language: Ivar Aasen and Nineteenth Century Norwegian Linguistics*. The Henry Sweet Society Studies in the History of Linguistics, vol. 4. Münster, Germany: Nodus, 1997.

Nilsen, Øystein. *The Syntax of Circumstantial Adverbials*. Oslo: Novus, 2000.

Nilsen, Randi Alice. *On Prosodically Marked Information Structure in Spoken Norwegian*. Working Papers in Linguistics, no. 7. Trondheim, Norway: Department of Linguistics, University of Trondheim, 1989.

Strahan, Tania E. *Long-Distance Reflexives in Norwegian: A Quantitative Study*. LINCOM Studies in Germanic Linguistics, No. 20. Munich, Germany: Lincom Europa, 2003.

Vikør, Lars S. *The New Norse Language Movement*. Oslo: Novus, 1975.

## 6. Media and Publishing

Bastiansen, Henrik G., and Hans Fredrik Dahl. *Norsk mediehistorie*. Oslo: Universitetsforlaget, 2003.

Bastiansen, Henrik G., and Øystein Meland, eds. *Fra Eidsvoll til Marienlyst: Studier i norske mediers historie fra Grunnloven til TV-alderen*. Kristiansand, Norway: Høyskoleforlaget, 2001.

Gaski, Harald. *Sami Culture in a New Era: The Norwegian Sami Experience*. Kárásjohka, Norway: Davvi Girji, 1997.

Gripsrud, Jostein, and Suzanne de Cheveigné, eds. *Media and Knowledge: The Role of Television: Papers from a Seminar at The University of Bergen, September 30–October 1, 1995*. Working Papers, no. 2, 1996. Bergen, Norway: University of Bergen, 1996.

Harrie, Eva, comp. *Media Trends 2006: In Denmark, Finland, Iceland, Norway and Sweden: Radio, TV and Internet: Descriptive Analyses and Statistics*. Nordic Media Trends, no. 8. Göteborg, Sweden: Nordicom, 2006.

Murschetz, Paul. *State Support for the Press: Theory and Practice: A Survey of Austria, France, Norway, and Sweden*. Düsseldorf, Germany: European Institute for the Media, 1997.

Nilsen, Bjørn, and Finn Sjue. *Skjult dagsorden: Mediene og de hemmelige tjenestene*. Oslo: Universitetsforlaget, 1998.

Østbye, Helge. *Massemediene*. Oslo: Tiden, 1984.

Puijk, Roel, ed. *Global Spotlights on Lillehammer: How the World Viewed Norway during the 1994 Winter Olympics*. Luton, Bedfordshire, U.K.: University of Luton Press, 1997.

Skogerbø, Eli. *Privatising the Public Interest: Conflicts and Compromises in Norwegian Media Politics 1980–1993*. IMK Report, no. 20. Oslo: University of Oslo, Department of Media and Communication, 1996.

## VII. SCIENCE

### 1. Geography and Geology

Andersen, Bjørn G. *Glacial Geology of Western Troms, North Norway*. Oslo: Universitetsforlaget, 1968.

Berg, Kåre, et al. *Norwegian Maritime Explorers and Expeditions over the Past Thousand Years*. Oslo: Index, 1999.

Broughton, Peter. *Challenges of Subsidence at the Norwegian Ekofisk Oil Field*. London: Royal Academy of Engineering, 1998.

Christensen, Arne Lie. *Det norske landskapet: Om landskap og landskapsforståelse i kulturhistorisk perspektiv*. Oslo: Pax, 2002.

Elders, W. A., and Scott B. Smithson. *On the Form and Mode of Emplacement of the Herefoss Granite.* Oslo: Universitetsforlaget, 1963.

Helvig, Magne, and Viggo Johannessen. *Norway: Land—People—Industries: A Brief Geography.* Oslo: Johan Grundt Tanum Forlag, 1966.

Holtedahl, Hans. *Marine Geology of the Norwegian Continental Margin.* Trondheim, Norway: Norges geologiske undersøkelse, 1993.

Holtedahl, Olaf, ed. *Geology of Norway.* Norges Geologiske Undersøkelse, no. 208. Oslo: H. Aschehoug, 1960.

Kimble, G. T., and D. Good, eds. *Geography of the Northlands.* New York: J. Wiley, 1955.

Michelsen, Olaf. *Stratigraphy and Distribution of Jurassic Deposits of the Norwegian-Danish Basin.* Copenhagen: C. A. Reitzel, 1978.

Sømme, Axel, ed. *A Geography of Norden.* Oslo: Cappelen, 1960.

Spencer, A. M., ed. *Geology of the Norwegian Oil and Gas Fields: An Atlas of Hydrocarbon Discoveries, Containing Full Descriptions of 37 of Norway's Major Oil and Gas Fields and Finds.* London: Graham and Trotman, 1987.

## 2. Public Health and Medicine

Baggott, Rob. *Health v. Wealth: The Politics of Smoking in Norway and the UK.* Strathclyde Papers on Government and Politics, no. 57. Glasgow, U.K.: Department of Politics, University of Strathclyde, 1988.

Broberg, Gunnar, and Nils Roll-Hansen, eds. *Eugenics and the Welfare State: Sterilization Policy in Denmark, Sweden, Norway, and Finland.* East Lansing: Michigan State University Press, 1996.

Chambers, Graham R., ed. *The Health Care Systems in the European Union: A Comparative Analysis: Austria, Finland, Sweden, and Norway.* Luxembourg: European Parliament, 1995.

Elstad, Jon Ivar. *Distribution of Welfare Services in the Decentralized Welfare State: The Case of Primary Health Services in Norway.* Oslo: INAS, 1989.

Larsen, Øivind, and Bent Olav Olsen, eds. *The Shaping of a Profession: Physicians in Norway, Past and Present.* Canton, Mass.: Science History/USA, 1996.

Noord, Paul van den, Terje Hagen, and Tor Iversen. *The Norwegian Health Care System.* Paris: OECD, 1998.

Olson, R. Paul, ed. *Mental Health Systems Compared: Great Britain, Norway, Canada, and the United States.* Springfield, Ill.: Charles C. Thomas, 2006.

Siem, Harald. *Choices for Health: An Introduction to the Health Services in Norway.* Oslo: Universitetsforlaget, 1986.

## 3. Science and Technology

Bing, Jon, and Knut S. Selmer, eds. *A Decade of Computers and Law*. Publications of Norwegian Research Center for Computers and Law, no. 7. Oslo: Universitetsforlaget, 1980.

Egeland, Alv, and William J. Burke. *Kristian Birkeland: The First Space Scientist*. Astrophysics and Space Science Library, vol. 325. Dordrecht, The Netherlands: Springer, 2005.

Friedman, Robert Marc. *Appropriating the Weather: Vilhelm Bjerknes and the Construction of a Modern Meteorology*. Ithaca, N.Y.: Cornell University Press, 1989.

Organisation for Economic Co-operation and Development. *Reviews of National Science Policy. Norway*. Paris: Organisation for Economic Co-operation and Development, 1985.

Sørensen, Knut H, ed. *The Spectre of Participation: Technology and Work in a Welfare State*. Oslo: Scandinavian University Press, 1998.

## VIII. NEWSPAPERS, JOURNALS, AND WEBSITES

### 1. Norwegian Newspapers with Websites

*Adresseavisen* (Trondheim), www.adressa.no
*Aftenposten* (Oslo), www.aftenposten.no
*Bergens Tidende* (Bergen), www.bt.no
*Dag og Tid* (Oslo), www.dagogtid.no
*Dagbladet* (Oslo), www.dagbladet.no
*Dagens Næringsliv* (Oslo), www.dn.no
*Dagsavisen* (Oslo), www.dagsavisen.no
*Morgenbladet* (Oslo), www.morgenbladet.no
*Nationen* (Oslo), www.nationen.no
*Nordlys* (Tromsø), www.nordlys.no
*Rogalands Avis* (Stavanger), www.rogalandsavis.no
*Stavanger Aftenblad* (Stavanger), www.stavanger-aftenblad.no
*Verdens Gang* (Oslo), www.vg.no

### 2. Scholarly Journals

*Historisk tidsskrift* (Journal of History), started in 1871, is published four times each year by Den norske historiske forening (The Norwegian Historical Society).

*Scandinavian Economic History Review*, started in 1953, is published three times each year by the Scandinavian Society for Economic and Social History and Historical Geography.

*Scandinavian Journal of History*, started in 1976, is published four times each year for the Historical Associations of Denmark, Finland, Norway, Sweden, and the Scandinavian subcommittees of the International Committee of Historical Sciences.

*Scandinavian Studies*, started in 1911, is the journal of the Society for the Advancement of Scandinavian Study and publishes articles in English on Scandinavian literature, history, and other topics.

## 3. Other Useful Websites

Antiquarian Booksellers, www.antikvariat.net
Aschehoug Publishers, www.aschehoug.no
Bergen, City of, www.bergen.kommune.no
Gyldendal Publishers, www.gyldendal.no
The Ibsen Center, www.hf.uio.no/ibsensenteret
Ibsen website, www.ibsen.net
Ibsen's dramas online, people.opera.com/howcome/2006/ibsen
The National Museum, www.nasjonalmuseet.no
Norwegian encyclopedia, www.caplex.no
Norwegian Folk Museum, www.norskfolke.museum.no
Oslo, City of, www.oslo.kommune.no
Stavanger, City of, www.stavanger.kommune.no
Tromsø, City of, www.tromso.kommune.no
Trondheim, City of, www.trondheim.com
University of Bergen, www.uib.no
University of Oslo, www.uio.no
University of Tromsø, www.uit.no

# About the Author

**Jan Sjåvik** (B.A. Brigham Young University; Ph.D. Harvard University) is a professor of Scandinavian Studies at the University of Washington, Seattle, where he has been a faculty member since 1978. He has published *Arne Garborgs Kristiania-romaner: En beretterteknisk studie* (1985; Arne Garborg's Kristiania Novels: A Study in Narrative Technique), *Reading for the Truth: Rhetorical Constructions in Norwegian Fiction* (2004), and *Historical Dictionary of Scandinavian Literature and Theater* (Scarecrow Press, 2006) and has recently completed the manuscript of *Reading Knut Faldbakken: Growth, Intersubjectivity, Truth*. He is also the author of a large number of articles on Norwegian and other Scandinavian writers, including Knut Hamsun, Ole E. Rølvaag, Alfred Hauge, Dag Solstad, and Johan Sebastian Welhaven. He has written entries on Scandinavian writers for many references and regularly reviews books for *Scandinavian Studies*, *Skandinavistik*, and *World Literature Today*.

A native Norwegian, Sjåvik received his primary and secondary education in Norway, followed by a semester at the Norwegian Technological and Scientific University (NTNU) in Trondheim before immigrating to the United States in December 1972. Regularly visiting Norway for both personal and professional reasons, he has presented his work in guest lectures at the Universities of Oslo, Bergen, Tromsø, and Agder, as well as at the NTNU in Trondheim. He also does research at the manuscript collection of the National Library, Oslo, most recently in 2004 and 2006.

Printed in Great Britain
by Amazon

15653752R00173